HIGH BEGINNING
Workbook

OXFORD
PICTURE
DICTIONARY

CANADIAN EDITION

Marjorie Fuchs

OXFORD
UNIVERSITY PRESS

8 Sampson Mews, Suite 204, Don Mills, Ontario M3C 0H5
www.oupcanada.com

Oxford University Press is a department of the University of Oxford.

It furthers the University's objective of excellence in research, scholarship, and education by publishing worldwide in

Oxford   New York

Auckland   Cape Town   Dar es Salaam   Hong Kong   Karachi
Kuala Lumpur   Madrid   Melbourne   Mexico City   Nairobi
New Delhi   Shanghai   Taipei   Toronto

With offices in

Argentina   Austria   Brazil   Chile   Czech Republic   France   Greece
Guatemala   Hungary   Italy   Japan   Poland   Portugal   Singapore
South Korea   Switzerland   Thailand   Turkey   Ukraine   Vietnam

Oxford is a trade mark of Oxford University Press
in the UK and in certain other countries

Published in Canada
by Oxford University Press

Copyright © Oxford University Press Canada 2010

The moral rights of the author have been asserted

Database right Oxford University Press (maker)

First Published 2010

Originally published by Oxford University Press, 198 Madison Avenue,
New York, NY 10016, USA. Copyright © Oxford University Press 2008

Oxford Picture Dictionary High Beginning Workbook was originally published
in 2008. This edition is published by arrangement with Oxford University Press.

Disc 1 audio tracks 5, 6, 7, 9, 14, 15, 18, 23, 31, 32 and Disc 2 audio tracks 2, 4, 7, 8,
9, 13, 14 copyright © Oxford University Press Canada 2010.

All other tracks originally published in Oxford Picture Dictionary Lesson Plans in 2009.
This edition is published by arrangement with Oxford University Press.

Library and Archives Canada Cataloguing in Publication

Fuchs, Marjorie, 1949-
        The Oxford picture dictionary, second Canadian edition.
High beginning workbook / Marjorie Fuchs.

ISBN 978-0-19-543352-4

        1. Picture dictionaries, English--Problems, exercises, etc. 2. English
language—Textbooks for second language learners. I. Title.

PE1629.S49 2009 Suppl. 2   423'.17   C2009-901412-2

Oxford University Press is committed to our environment. This book is printed
on Forest Stewardship Council certified paper, harvested from a responsibly
managed forest.

Printed and bound in Canada.

4 5 6 – 16 15 14

Distributed By:
Grass Roots Press
Toll Free: 1-888-303-3213
Fax: (780) 413-6582
Web Site: www.grassrootsbooks.net

Chapter icons designed by Von Glitschka/Scott Hull Associates

Art

Vilma Ortiz-Dillon: 2 (top); 250 (female sewing and male working in flower shop);
277; Andrea Champlin: 6 (desk with school supplies); 55; 121; 182; Mike Gardner:
7; 10; 35; 137; 142; Janos Jantner/Beehive Illustration: 11; 111; 250 (waitress and
customer); Ben Shannon/Magnet Reps: 12; 26; 64; 96; 105; 148; 161; 174; 179; Gary
Antonetti/Ortelius Design: 13; 200; 210; Barb Bastian: 14; 40 (chart); 50; 54; 57; 67;
74; 92; 95; 98; 114; 144; 184; 209; 217 (chart); 220; 221; 250 (swimming pool); 262;
Jody Emery: 17 (books); 24; 47; 48; 78; 83; 84; 127; 142 (TV Guide); 152; 176; 236;
317; Argosy: 18; 46; 80; 91; 94;102; 104; 105; 108; 113; 119; 151; 157; 194; 250
(respirator); Karen Minot: 21; 32; 82 (Guest Check); 97; 133; Zina Saunders: 22; 33;
40; 59; 60; 81; 82; 86; 99; 100 (skirts); 107 (top); 125; 178 (adhesive); 206; Ken
Batelman: 23; 38; 53; 66 (bottom); 70 (meat and poultry); 100 (sewing box); 110;
136; 215; 224; 227; 240 (bottom); Glenn Gustafson: 27 (top); 75; 76; 79; 101; 117;
128; 155; 271; Mike Renwick/Creative Eye: 28; 56; 62; 66 (top); 73; 85; 89; 126; 138;
141; 146; Simon Williams/Illustration Ltd.: 38 (top right); 39; 44; 45; Bob Kaganich/
Deborah Wolfe: 41; Kev Hopgood: 42; Nina Wallace: 63; 268; Annie Bissett: 65; 77
(h. turn on oven); 90 (catalog and text); 129; 134; 150; 158; 167; Ken Joudrey/Munro
Campagna: 68; 69; 177; 218; 239; Scott MacNeill: 51; 61; 112; 208; 225; 238; Mary
Chandler: 71; 213; 246; 250; Stacey Schuett: 72; Jim Delapine: 77; 109; 214; 235;
Ralph Voltz/Deborah Wolfe: 90; 154; 162; 258; Garth Glazier: 107; Tony Randazzo:
156; 232; Mark Reidy/Scott Hull Associates: 163 (stamp); Kevin Brown: 242; 243; 253;
Rob Schuster: 166; 168; 183; 195; 214; 226; 228; 234; Mohammad Masoor: 178; 180;
Eileen Bergman: 202; Shelley Himmelstein: 204; Dennis Godfrey/Mike Wepplo: 204
(island); Sally Bansusen: 211; 310; Barbara Harmon: 212; Alan Male: 210; 212; Paul
Mirocha: 216; 217; Jeff Sanson: 240; Pamela Johnson: 244; 252; Chris Pavely: 245;
Uldis Klavins/Hankins & Tegenborg, Ltd.: 247; Anna Veltfort: 248; 249; Jeff Lindberg:
250 (nurse and patient); Adrian Mateescu/The Studio: 250 (female painting).

Cover Art: CUBE/Illustration Ltd. (hummingbird), 9 Surf Studios (lettering).

Pronk&Associates: 4; 5; 6 (Back to School and Spelling Test); 8; 9; 15: 16; 17 (pie chart);
19; 20; 25; 27 (Be a Smart Shopper); 29; 30; 33; 35 (note at bottom); 36; 37 (crossword);
38 (To Do List); 43; 47 (Home Preference Checklist); 49; 52; 60 (To Do List); 61 (To Buy);
63; 66 (shopping list); 68 (web browser); 68 (chart); 69 (chart); 70 (chart); 73 (Grocery
List); 81 (Food Order Form); 86 (Clothing Rules); 88; 89 (Hotel Stationary); 91 (receipt);
97; receipt); 100 (form); 102 (price stickers); 103; 105 (Patient Form); 108 (list); 109
(To Buy list); 110 (Patient Form); 111 (forms); 117 (check list); 118; 121 (Supply List);
123; 130 (Mall Directory); 131; 132; 138 (chart); 139; 140 (forms); 145 (newspaper
headlines); 146 (Emergency Plan and Disaster Checklist); 148 (Oak Street
Association); 149; 152; 156 (chart); 158 (list); 163 (postcard); 165; 170; 172 (form);
173; 174 (forms); 175; 176 (checklist); 177 (chart); 179 (checklist); 181 (chart); 183
(clipboard); 187; 189; 190; 192; 196; 197; 198; 203; 207; 210 (chart); 214 (chart); 218
(newspaper headlines); 221 (postcard); 223; 229; 230; 231 (chart); 237; 241; 243
(crossword); 244 (word search); 251; 252 (crossword puzzle); 254 (forms).

Photos

Shutterstock: 2 (bottom right); Photodisc/Age Fotostock: 3; Jack Hollingsworth/
Photodisc/Inmagine: 31 (African American male student); AsiaPix/Age Fotostock:
31 (Asian middle-aged male); istockphoto.com: 31 (elderly female); istockphoto.
com: 31 (10 year-old Caucasian girl);Shutterstock: (two year-old Hispanic boy);
bigstockphoto.com: 31 (2-month-old Caucasian baby); Image Source/Inmagine:
32 (Asian youngfemale); Photodisc/Inmagine: 32 (Caucasian male, 30's); Brand X/
Jupiter Unlimited:32 (African American female); Goodshoot/Jupiter Unlimited: 32
(young Caucasianmale in wheelchair); Corbis/Age Fotostock: elderly Caucasian
female); DennisKitchen; istock: 37; istock.com: 38 (PDA); istockphoto.com: (Hispanic
male); istockphoto.com: 58; Mixa/Inmagine: 66 (Asian female shopper);
istockphoto.com: 71 (sandwich);Photodisc/Age Fotostock: 113 (medicine cabinet);
Digital Vision/Punch Stock: 120; istockphoto: 130 (eyeglasses); Shutterstock: 130
(work boots); Keith Leighton/Alamy:130 (children's blocks); Shutterstock: 130
(MP3 Player); Ingram Publishing/AgeFotostock: 130 (dog bone); Shutterstock:
130 (earrings); Time & Life Pictures/GettyImages: dreamstime.com, 130 (CD);
Digitalvision/Inmagine: 130 (flowers);istockphoto.com: 130; Graeme Teague:
135; Shutterstock: 136; dreamstime.com: 140 (peaceful assembly); istockphoto.
com:140 (freedom of thought, belief, opinion, expression); istockphoto.com:140
(mosque); dreamstime: 141, (Supreme Court of Canada); dreamstime.com: 145
(tidal wave); istockphoto.com: 145 (firefighters); Alamy: Frances M. Roberts, 145
(streetexplosion); istockphoto.com: 145 (volcano); bigstockphoto.com: 145 (flood);
istockphoto.com: 145 (child and parent); istockphoto.com: 147; Imagesource/
Inmagine: 172; Istockphotos.com:179 (warning symbols); Istockphotos.com:
180 (can of yellow paint); Dennis Kitchen:180 (screws, nuts, bolts, washers, and
hooks); Istockphotos.com: 181; Istockphotos.com: 193; Istockphotos.com: 197
(bike); istockphoto.com: 199 (war) istockphoto.com: 199 (invention); istockphoto.
com: 199 (exploration); Collections Canada:199 (immigration); dreamstime.com:
100 (musical score); dreamstime. com: 199 (The Acropolis); dreamstime.com,199
(Hong Kong); Canadian Heritage: 199 (Queen Elizabeth); Istockphotos.com: 201;
Istockphotos.com: 211 (ground); ; Istockphotos.com: 231; Istockphotos.com: 244
(pan, pot, and fence); Istockphotos. com: 246 (tie, ring); Istockphotos.com:247
(nurse); Istockphotos.com: 250 (pipe and rake); Istockphoto.com: 254 (cellphone0;
istockphotos.com: 217.

Acknowledgements

The publisher and author would like to acknowledge the following individuals for their invaluable feedback during the development of this workbook:

Patricia S. Bell, Lake Technical County ESOL, Eustis, FL

Patricia Castro, Harvest English Institute, Newark, NJ

Druci Diaz, CARIBE Program and TBT, Tampa, FL

Jill Gluck, Hollywood Community Adult School, Los Angeles, CA.

Frances Hardenbergh, Southside Programs for Adult and Continuing Ed, Prince George, VA

Mercedes Hern, Tampa, FL

(Katie) Mary C. Hurter, North Harris College, Language and Communication, Houston, TX

Karen Kipke, Antioch Freshman Academy, Antioch, TN

Ivanna Mann-Thrower, Charlotte Mecklenburg Schools, Charlotte, NC

Holley Mayville, Charlotte Mecklenburg Schools, Charlotte, NC

Jonetta Myles, Salem High School, Conyers, GA

Kathleen Reynolds, Albany Park Community Center, Chicago, IL

Jan Salerno, Kennedy-San Fernando CAS, Grenada Hills, CA

Jenni Santamaria, ABC Adult School,Cerritos, CA

Geraldyne Scott, Truman College/ Lakeview Learning Center, Chicago, IL

Sharada Sekar, Antioch Freshman Academy, Antioch, TN

Terry Shearer, Region IV ESC, Houston, TX

Melissa Singler, Cape Fear Community College, Wilmington, NC

Cynthia Wiseman, Wiseman Language Consultants, New York, NY

Special thanks to:

Stephanie Karras and Sharon Sargent for their dedication and hard work in managing a very complex project; Jaclyn Smith, Robin Fadool, and Maj-Britt Hagsted for ensuring that the many graphic elements illustrated and enhanced the text; and Pronk&Associates for their commitment and skill.

Bruce Myint, who contributed to the early stages of the Workbook and made excellent suggestions for bringing this new edition into a new century;

Katie La Storia, who applied her sharp mind and eyes to the manuscript, always offering excellent advice. With her steadfast energy, enthusiasm, and encouragement, she was a pleasure to work with;

Vanessa Caceres, who worked hard and fast on the manuscript. The *Workbook* has benefited greatly from her classroom experience;

Alexis Vega-Singer, who carefully checked text, art, photos, and facts. Her suggestions were always thoughtful and intelligent, even at 3:00 in the morning;

Ellen Northcutt, who made insightful comments and queries.

Sarah Dentry, who made things flow smoothly, assuring that I always had what I needed wherever I was;

Jayme Adelson-Goldstein, who provided support and who, along with Norma Shapiro, created a rich trove of materials on which to base the exercises in the Workbook;

Rick Smith, as always, for his unswerving support and for his insightful comments on all aspects of the project. Once again, he proved himself to be equally at home in the world of numbers and the world of words.

The publisher would like to thank the following for their permission to reproduce copyrighted material:

pp. 199 (immigration): © Copyright 2009, Library and Archives Canada

To the Teacher

The *Low Beginning*, *High Beginning*, and *Low Intermediate Workbooks* that accompany the *Oxford Picture Dictionary* have been designed to provide meaningful and enjoyable practice of the vocabulary that students are learning. These workbooks supply high-interest contexts and real information for enrichment and self-expression.

Writing a second edition has given us the wonderful opportunity not only to update material, but also to respond to the requests of our first-edition users. As a result, this new edition of the *High Beginning Workbook* contains more graphs and charts, more writing and speaking activities, more occasions for critical thinking, opportunities to use the Internet, and a brand-new listening component. It still, of course, has the features that made the first edition so popular.

The Workbooks conveniently correspond page-for-page to the 163 topics of the Picture Dictionary. For example, if you are working on page 50 in the Dictionary, the activities for this topic, Apartments, will be found on page 50 in all three Picture Dictionary Workbooks.

All topics in the *High Beginning Workbook* follow the same easy-to-use format. Exercise 1 is always a "look in your dictionary" activity where students are asked to complete a task while looking in their Picture Dictionaries. The tasks include answering questions about the pictures, judging statements true or false, counting the number of illustrated occurrences of a vocabulary item, completing a timeline, or speculating about who said what.

Following this activity is at least one content-rich contextualized exercise, such as true or false questions, matching activities, categorizing activities, finding the odd-one-out, or completion of forms. These exercises often feature graphs and charts with real data for students to work with as they practise the new vocabulary. Many topics include a personalization exercise that asks "What about you?" where students can use the new vocabulary to give information about their own lives or to express their opinions.

Many topics also include a Challenge which can be assigned to students for additional work in class or as homework. Challenge activities provide higher-level speaking and writing practice, and for some topics will

require students to interview classmates, conduct surveys, or find information outside of class by looking in the newspaper, for example, or online.

At the end of the 12 units is a section called Another Look, a review which allows students to practise vocabulary from all the topics of a unit in a game or puzzle-like activity, such as picture crosswords, word searches, or C-searches, where students search in a picture for items which begin with the letter c. These activities are at the back of the *High Beginning Workbook* on pages 242–253.

A variety of listening activities are available on the Companion Website (http://www.oupcanada.com.OPDWorkbook). The audio files give students the opportunity to hear the language of each topic in natural, real-life contexts. The listening exercises are in the back of the Workbook beginning on page 257. In some cases, the target language is in the listening itself and students need to recognize it. In other cases, the target language is in the exercise text and students need to interpret the listening to choose the correct answer.

Throughout the Workbook, vocabulary is carefully controlled and recycled. Students should, however, be encouraged to use their Picture Dictionaries to look up words they do not recall, or, if they are doing topics out of sequence, may not yet have learned.

The *Oxford Picture Dictionary Workbooks* can be used in the classroom or at home for self-study.

I hope you and your students enjoy using this Workbook as much as I have enjoyed writing it.

Marjorie Fuchs

Marjorie Fuchs

To the Student

The *Oxford Picture Dictionary* has over 4,000 words. This workbook will help you use them in your everyday life.

It's easy to use! The Workbook pages match the pages in your Picture Dictionary. For example, to practise the words on page 23 in your Picture Dictionary, turn to page 23 in your Workbook.

This book has exercises you will enjoy. Some exercises show real information. A bar graph of people's favourite colours is on page 24 and a chart showing popular sports is on page 229. Other exercises, which ask "What about you?" give you a chance to use your own information. You will find stories, puzzles, and conversations, too.

At the end of many topics there is a Challenge: a chance to use your new vocabulary more independently. There are also listening exercises in which you will hear conversations, TV and radio ads, and store announcements. And finally, every unit has a game or puzzle activity called Another Look. This can be found at the back of the book.

Learning new words is both challenging and fun. I had a lot of fun writing this Workbook. I hope you enjoy using it!

Marjorie Fuchs

Marjorie Fuchs

Table of Contents

4. Food

5. Clothing

6. Health

Contents

10. Areas of Study

11. Plants and Animals

12. Recreation

1. Look in your dictionary. Label the pictures.

a. _____Shake hands._____

b. _____

c. _____

d. _____

e. _____

f. _____

2. Circle the answer.

a. **Say, "Hello."**

Good evening.   (Hi.)   Fine, thanks.

b. **Introduce a friend.**

Ana, this is Meng.   Hi, I'm Ana.   Nice to meet you, Ana.

c. **Greet people.**

Luis, this is Mia.   Hello, everyone.   Fine, thanks.

d. **Say, "Goodbye."**

Good evening.   Hello.   Good night.

3. What about you? Imagine Jessica is your friend. You see her in school. Check (✓) the things you do.

☐ Say, "Hello."   ☐ Ask, "How are you?"

☐ Introduce yourself.   ☐ Smile.

☐ Wave.   ☐ Hug.

☐ Kiss.   ☐ Bow.

☐ Shake hands.   ☐ Say, "Goodbye."

Jessica

4. Look in your dictionary. *True* or *False*?

    a. Picture A: He introduces himself.   *false*

    b. Picture C: She introduces a friend.   _____

    c. Picture D: He waves.   _____

    d. Picture E: They hug.   _____

    e. Picture F: She smiles.   _____

    f. Picture H: They bow.   _____

    g. Picture I: She introduces a friend.   _____

    h. Picture J: They shake hands.   _____

5. What about you? Complete the conversations. Use the instructions in parentheses ( ).

    a. You: _Hello, I'm_ _____

        (Introduce yourself to Rahib.)

    Rahib: Hi. I'm Rahib.

Rahib

    b. You: _____

        (Say, "Hello," to a friend.)

    Friend: Hi.

    c. You: _____

        (Ask your friend, "How are you?")

    Friend: Fine, thanks.

    d. You: _____

        (Introduce your friend to Rahib.)

    Rahib: Nice to meet you.

    Friend: Nice to meet you, Rahib.

    e. You: _____

        (Say, "Goodbye.")

    Rahib and Friend: Goodbye!

Challenge Introduce yourself to two classmates. Then, introduce the two classmates to each other.

1. **Look in your dictionary. What is Carlos Soto's . . .**

   a. postal code? ___T1J 0N0___   c. apartment number? _____

   b. area code? _____   d. social insurance number? _____

2. **Match.**

   _9_ a. middle initial   1. female

   ___ b. signature   2. Ontario

   ___ c. city   3. (416)

   ___ d. sex   4. 548-000-000

   ___ e. area code   5. Toronto

   ___ f. social insurance number   6. Miriam S. Shakter

   ___ g. name   7. M5J 3A1

   ___ h. postal code   8. *Miriam S. Shakter*

   ___ i. province   9. S.

3. **What about you? Fill out the form. Use your own information.**

   ## Toronto Adult Centre

   REGISTRATION FORM
   (Please print.)

   Last name _____ First name _____ Middle initial _____

   Sex: ☐ Male ☐ Female

   Place of birth _____ Date of birth _____

   Address _____ Apartment number _____

   _____ _____
   (City)   (Province)   (Postal code)

   Phone _____ Cellphone _____

   _____
   Signature

Challenge Interview a classmate. Find out his or her last name, first name, middle initial, address, and place of birth.

 See page 259 for listening practice.

1. **Look in your dictionary. Put the words in the correct columns.**

People	Places	
principal	_courtyard_	

2. **Look at the floor plan. Match the rooms on the directory with the letters.**

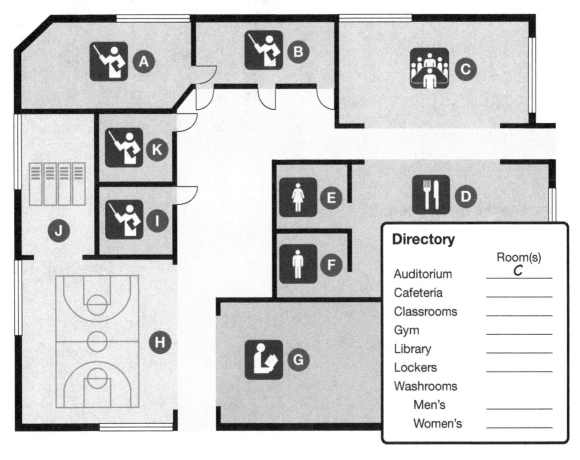

Directory	
	Room(s)
Auditorium	_C_
Cafeteria	
Classrooms	
Gym	
Library	
Lockers	
Washrooms	
Men's	
Women's	

3. **What about you? Check (✓) the places your school has.**

☐ auditorium   ☐ library   ☐ track   ☐ computer lab   ☐ cafeteria

Challenge Draw a floor plan or write a directory for your school.

A Classroom

1. **Look at the top picture in your dictionary. How many of the following things are in the classroom?**

    a. teachers _____1_____   c. students _____   e. bookcases _____

    b. computers _____   d. desks _____   f. chairs _____

2. **Look at the list of school supplies. Check (✓) the items you see in the picture.**

Back to School

☑ pencil sharpener

☐ pencils

☐ pens

☐ dry-erase marker

☐ pencil eraser

☐ spiral notebook

☐ 3-ring binder

☐ notebook paper

☐ picture dictionary

3. **Complete the spelling test.**

    Spelling Test

    1. s _c_ r _e_ e n

    2. o __ e __ h e a __   p __ o j e __ __ o r

    3. w h __ __ __ b o a __ __

    4. __ l o __ k

    5. c __ a l __

    6. __ r __ s __ r

    7. a __ p h a __ e __

    8. m __ __

    9. __ i c __ i o n a __ y

    10. b u __ __ e __ i n   b __ a r __

6

4. Label the pictures. Use the words in the box.

Listen to a CD.	~~Open your workbook.~~	Stand up.
Pick up your pencil.	Close your workbook.	Put down your pencil.
Take a seat.	Raise your hand.	Talk to the teacher.

a. _Open your workbook._

b. _____

c. _____

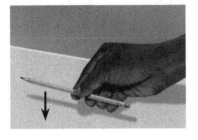

d. _____

e. _____

f. _____

g. _____

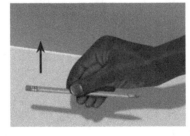

h. _____

i. _____

5. What about you? Check (✓) the items you use in your classroom.

- ☐ pencils
- ☐ spiral notebook
- ☐ pencil sharpener
- ☐ dictionary
- ☐ textbook
- ☐ Other: _____

- ☐ headphones
- ☐ markers
- ☐ notebook paper
- ☐ picture dictionary
- ☐ computer

- ☐ pens
- ☐ 3-ring binder
- ☐ LCD projector
- ☐ workbook
- ☐ chalkboard

Challenge Write about the items in Exercise 5. **Example:** *I have one dictionary. I have two pens. I don't have any pencils.*

See page 260 for listening practice.

1. Look in your dictionary. *True* **or** *False*?

   a. Picture A: The student is copying a word.   _____false_____

   b. Picture C: The student is translating the word.   _____

   c. Picture J: The students are sharing a book.   _____

   d. Picture K: The woman is asking a question.   _____

   e. Picture M: The students are putting away their books.   _____

   f. Picture N: The man is dictating a sentence.   _____

2. Match.

   _3_ **a.** Ask a question.

   ___ **b.** Answer the question.

   ___ **c.** Look up the word.

   ___ **d.** Translate the word.

   ___ **e.** Check the pronunciation.

   ___ **f.** Copy the word.

   ___ **g.** Draw a picture of the word.

   ___ **h.** Circle the answer.

1.   pencil /ˈpensl/

2.   pencil
         pencil

3.   What's a pencil?

4.

5.   pence /pens/ n. (pl.) pennies.
         pencil /ˈpensl/ n. instrument for writing
         and drawing, made of a thin piece of wood
         with lead inside it.
         penetrate /ˈpenɪtreɪt/ v. go into or through
         something: A nail penetrated the car tire.

6.   A pencil is something
         you write with.

7.   This is a pen /(pencil.)

8.   pencil = えんぴつ

8

3. Complete this test.

Name: _____   Class: _____

1. Fill in the blanks. Use the words in the box.

away	~~in~~	out

a. I'm filling _____*in*_____ the blanks.

b. The students are taking _____ their picture dictionaries.

c. The teacher is putting _____ the books.

2. Cross out the word that doesn't belong.

a. help   share   ~~match~~   brainstorm

b. ask   underline   circle   fill in

c. brainstorm   copy   dictate   discuss

3. Underline the words that begin with *c*.
Circle the words that begin with *d*.

read   <u>copy</u>   (draw)   share   help

dictate   circle   check   discuss   choose

4. Match.

_3_ a. Look up   1. a picture.

____ b. Draw   2. a question.

____ c. Ask   3. a word.

5. Unscramble the words.

a. tedicta   _*dictate*_   c. scudiss   _____

b. wrad   _____   d. lastetran   _____

4. What about you? Look in your dictionary. Which classroom activities do you like to do? Which activities don't you like to do? Make two lists.

Challenge Look up the word *thimble* in your dictionary.
a. Translate the word.
b. Draw a picture of a thimble.
c. Label the picture.

1. **Look in your dictionary. *True* or *False*?**

   a. **Picture A:**   Sergio is taking notes.   _____false_____

   b. **Picture B:**   He is participating in class.   _____

   c. **Picture D:**   He is studying at home.   _____

   d. **Picture G:**   He is not making progress.   _____

   e. **Picture H:**   He is getting good grades.   _____

   f. **Picture J:**   He is asking for help.   _____

   g. **Picture K:**   He is taking a test.   _____

   h. **Picture L:**   He is not checking his work.   _____

   i. **Picture N:**   He is correcting the mistake.   _____

2. **Sergio is taking a test. Number the activities in the correct order.
   (1 = the first thing Sergio does)**

   ____ a. He checks his work.

   ____ b. He fills in the answer on the answer sheet.

   ____ c. He hands in his test.

   _1_ d. He clears off his desk.

   ____ e. He corrects the mistake.

   ____ f. He passes the test.

   ____ g. He erases the mistake.

3. **What about you? Check (✓) the things you do.**

   ☐ set goals   ☐ fill in answers

   ☐ participate in class   ☐ check my work

   ☐ take notes   ☐ ask my teacher for help

   ☐ study at home   ☐ ask my classmates for help

Challenge Write three study goals. **Example:** *Learn five words a day.*

   a. _____

   b. _____

   c. _____

1. Look in your dictionary. Circle the words to complete the sentences.

a. Five students ~~enter the room~~ / leave the room.

b. The teacher <u>runs to class</u> / <u>turns on the light</u>.

c. One student is carrying <u>books</u> / <u>trash</u>.

d. He's delivering them to room <u>102</u> / <u>202</u>.

e. Two teachers <u>have a conversation</u> / <u>buy a snack</u> during the break.

f. After the break, they <u>leave</u> / <u>go back to</u> class.

2. Look at the pictures. Match.

1.  **2.**  **3.**

4.  **5.**  **6.**

_____ **a.** The students leave the room.

_____ **b.** The students enter the room.

_____ **c.** The class takes a break.

_____ **d.** The teacher turns off the lights.

_1_ **e.** The students walk to school.

_____ **f.** The students go back to class.

3. What about you? Check (✓) the things you do at school.

☐ walk to class   ☐ run to class

☐ carry books   ☐ turn off the light

☐ take a break   ☐ buy a snack

☐ eat   ☐ drink

☐ throw away trash   ☐ lift books

Challenge Look in your dictionary. Write sentences about pictures H–L. What are people eating? What are they drinking? What are the teachers having a conversation about?

1. Look in your dictionary. Circle the correct words.

a. | Hi. I'm Danny. | make small talk / (start a conversation)

b. | Is that *Donny*? | check your understanding / explain something

c. | Nice day, isn't it? | compliment someone / make small talk

d. | That's a nice jacket. | agree / compliment someone

e. | I'm having a party tonight. Please come. | accept an invitation / invite someone

2. Complete the conversations from Amy's party. Use the sentences in the box.

| This food is great! | ~~Coats go in there.~~ | Oh! Sorry! | There? |
| No. It's very bad! | Here's a napkin. | Thanks! | That's OK. |

a. *Coats go in there.*

b.

c.

d.

3. Look at Exercise 2. In which picture is someone doing the following things?

1. accepting an apology   _c_
2. apologizing   ___
3. checking understanding   ___
4. disagreeing   ___
5. offering something   ___
6. thanking someone   ___

Challenge What are good topics for small talk? What are bad topics? Make a list.

1. Look in your dictionary. Describe the temperatures.

    a. Fahrenheit: 95°   ___*hot*___   35° _____   60° _____

    b. Celsius: 25° _____   –10° _____   40° _____

2. Look at the weather map. Circle the words to complete the sentences.

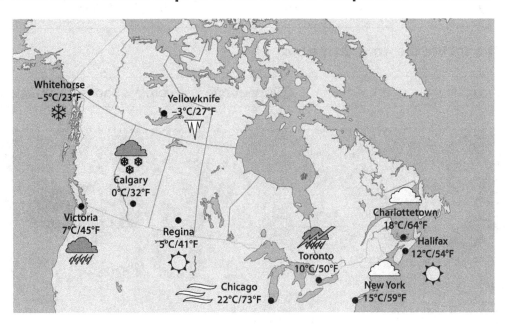

    a. It's <u>foggy</u> / <u>(windy)</u> in Chicago.

    b. There's a <u>heat wave / snowstorm</u> in Calgary.

    c. Toronto is having a <u>dust storm / thunderstorm</u>.

    d. It's <u>clear / cloudy</u> in Halifax.

    e. The temperature is <u>cold / warm</u> in Whitehorse.

    f. It's <u>raining / snowing</u> in Victoria.

    g. It's <u>icy / smoggy</u> in Yellowknife.

    h. It's <u>cloudy / raining</u> in New York.

    i. It's <u>cool / cold</u> and sunny in Regina.

    j. It's cloudy and <u>warm / hot</u> in Charlottetown.

3. What about you? What kinds of weather do you like? Check (✓) the columns.

	I like it.	It's OK.	I don't like it.
humid			
cool and foggy			
raining and lightning			
warm and sunny			
hailstorm			

Challenge Write a weather report for your city. **Example:** *Monday, January 25. Today it's sunny and warm in San Antonio. The temperature is . . . .*

See page 261 for listening practice. 13

1. Look in your dictionary. Check (✓) the things with numbers.

a. ✓ phone bill   e. ☐ cord   i. ☐ key pad

b. ☐ phone jack   f. ☐ star key   j. ☐ pound key

c. ☐ charger   g. ☐ calling card   k. ☐ pay phone

d. ☐ country code   h. ☐ receiver   l. ☐ antenna

2. Complete the ad. Use the words in the box.

answering machine   smart phone   ~~cellular phone~~   cordless phone   headset

The BUSY Signal

Save! Save! Save!

~~$79⁹⁵~~ $69⁹⁵

a. _cellular phone_

~~$29⁹⁵~~ $19⁹⁵

b. _____

~~$19⁹⁵~~ $14⁹⁵

c. _____

~~$209⁹⁵~~ $179⁹⁵

d. _____

~~$94⁹⁵~~ $84⁹⁵

e. _____

3. Circle the words to complete the sentences.

> Hi. It's me.
> I'll be home late.

a. This is a text /(voice) message.

> This call requires a coin deposit.
> Please hang up and dial again.

c. This is a smart / pay phone.

> Can you hear me now?
> Can you hear me now?

b. The cellular phone has a weak / strong signal.

> Please press 1 for customer service.

d. This is an automated phone system / Internet phone call.

4. Look in your dictionary. Match.

_2_ **a.** (905)   **1.** emergency call

___ **b.** 411   **2.** area code

___ **c.** 0   **3.** operator

___ **d.** 56-2-555-1394   **4.** directory assistance

___ **e.** 911   **5.** international call

5. Circle the words to complete the instructions.

Follow these instructions for an (emergency) / international call:
              a.

First, dial 411 / 911. Give your calling card / name to the operator. Then state / spell the
              b.   **c.**   **d.**

emergency. Is there a fire? Do you need a doctor? Tell the operator. Stay on the line.

Hang up / Don't hang up! The operator will ask you other questions.
              e.

6. What about you? Complete the chart.

Important Phone Numbers		
	Emergency	911
	Non-emergency	
	Directory assistance (local calls)	
	Doctor	
	School	
	Other: _____	

Challenge Find out the area codes for five cities. Look in a phone book, on the Internet, or ask your classmates. **Example:** *Winnipeg—204*

Numbers

1. Look in your dictionary. Write the types of numbers. What comes next?

a. <u>*Ordinal numbers*</u> : tenth, twentieth, thirtieth, <u>*fortieth*</u>

b. _____ : VI, VII, VIII, _____

c. _____ : 70, 80, 90, _____

2. Complete the chart.

Word	Number	Roman Numeral
ten	10	X
		III
	15	
		L
	20	
one hundred		
		D
one thousand		

3. Look at the bar graph. Ana is first (= best) in her class. What about the other students? Complete the sentences.

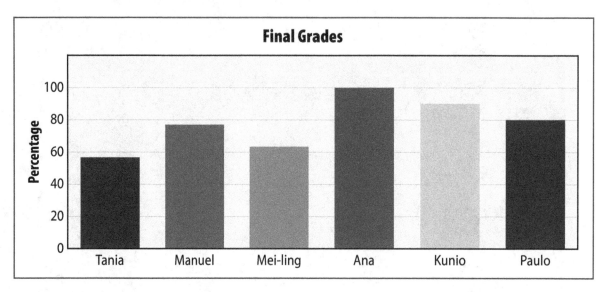

Final Grades

a. Ana is <u>*first*</u> in her class.
b. Manuel is _____.
c. Mei-ling is _____.
d. Kunio is _____.
e. Tania is _____.
f. Paulo is _____.

Challenge Work with a partner. Where can you see cardinal numbers? Ordinal numbers? Roman numerals? Write sentences. Compare your answers with a classmate's.
Example: *Telephone numbers have cardinal numbers.*

  See page 262 for listening practice.

1. **Look in your dictionary. What kind of numbers are these?**

   a. 1/5 ___fraction___   b. 20% _____   c. .20 _____

2. **Look at the chart. Complete the sentences.**

   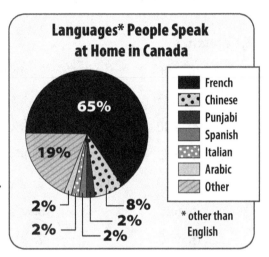

   Languages* People Speak at Home in Canada

   French — 65%
   Chinese
   Punjabi
   Spanish
   Italian
   Arabic
   Other — 19%
   2%   2%   8%   2%   2%
   * other than English

   a. ___Seventy percent___ speak French.

   b. _____ speak Punjabi.

   c. _____ speak Spanish.

   d. _____ speak Chinese.

   e. _____ speak Italian.

   f. _____ speak other languages.

3. **Look at the books. Complete the sentences.**

   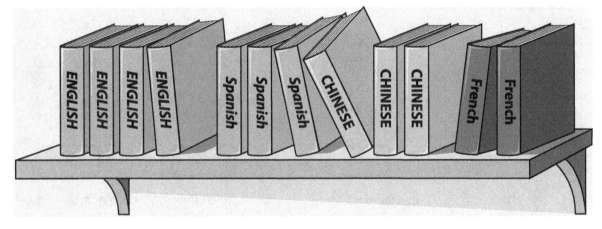

   ENGLISH ENGLISH ENGLISH ENGLISH Spanish Spanish Spanish CHINESE CHINESE CHINESE French French

   a. ___One fourth___ of the books are in Chinese.

   b. _____ are in English.

   c. _____ are in Spanish.

   d. _____ are in either English or French.

4. **What about you? Measure a bookcase in school or at home. Write the measurements.**

   width _____   height _____   depth _____

Challenge How many students in your class speak your language? How many students speak other languages? Calculate the percents. **Example:** *There are twenty students in my class. Ten students speak Punjabi. That's fifty percent.*

1. Look in your dictionary. What's another way to say the following?

   a. ten-thirty   _half past ten_   **c.** a quarter after three   _____

   b. two-forty-five   _____   **d.** twenty after six   _____

2. Match.

   _3_ **a.** 3:00   **1.** It's ten to nine.

   ___ **b.** 5:25   **2.** It's a quarter to seven.

   ___ **c.** 2:30   **3.** It's three o'clock.

   ___ **d.** 6:45   **4.** It's a quarter after six.

   ___ **e.** 8:50   **5.** It's a quarter to six.

   ___ **f.** 6:15   **6.** It's two-thirty.

   ___ **g.** 9:10   **7.** It's five-twenty-five.

   ___ **h.** 5:45   **8.** It's ten after nine.

3. Complete the clocks.

 4 : 10   :   :   :

   a. ten after four   **b.** half past six   **c.** eight o'clock   **d.** a quarter to twelve

4. What about you? Answer the questions. Use words and numbers.

   Example: What time is it? It's _____ _four–fifteen p.m. (4:15 p.m.)_ _____.

   a. What time is it? It's _____.

   b. What time is your class? It's from _____ to _____.

   c. Do you come to class early, on time, or late? _____

   If you come early or late, at what time? At _____

   d. What time do you leave class? At _____

   e. What time do you get home? At _____

5. Look at the map in your dictionary. In which time zones are the following cities?

a. Halifax _____Atlantic_____   **c.** Toronto _____

b. Winnipeg _____   **d.** Vancouver _____

6. Look at the chart. It's 12:00 noon in Montreal. What time is it in the following cities? Use numbers and the words in the box.

At 12:00 noon, Eastern Standard Time, the time in . . . is . . .			
Athens	7 P.M.	Mexico City	11 A.M.
Baghdad	8 P.M.	Montreal	12 noon
Bangkok	12 midnight*	New York City	12 noon
Barcelona	6 P.M.	Panama	12 noon
Buenos Aires	3 P.M.	Paris	6 P.M.
Frankfurt	6 P.M.	Rio de Janeiro	3 P.M.
Halifax	1 P.M.	Riyadh	8 P.M.
Hanoi	12 midnight*	Rome	6 P.M.
Havana	12 noon	St. Petersburg	8. P.M.
Hong Kong	1 A.M.*	San Juan	1 P.M.
Houston	11 A.M.	Seoul	2 A.M.*
Kolkata	10:30 P.M.	Sydney	4 A.M.*
London	5 P.M.	Tel Aviv	7 P.M.
Los Angeles	9 A.M.	Tokyo	2 A.M.*
Mecca	8 P.M.	Zurich	6 P.M.
* = the next day			

| in the morning | in the afternoon | in the evening | at night | noon | midnight |

a. Athens _____7:00 in the evening_____   **g.** St. Petersburg _____

b. London _____   **h.** Bangkok _____

c. Kolkata _____   **i.** Mexico City _____

d. Panama _____   **j.** Frankfurt _____

e. Halifax _____   **k.** Los Angeles _____

f. Tokyo _____   **l.** Hanoi _____

7. What about you? Does your native country have the following? Write *Yes* or *No*.

a. different time zones? _____   **b.** daylight saving time? _____

Challenge Find out the time for sunrise and sunset in your area. Look in a newspaper or online.

1. Look in your dictionary. In May, how many of the following are there?

a. days   <u>31</u>

b. Mondays   ___

c. Thursdays   ___

d. weekdays   ___

e. two-day weekends   ___

f. seven-day weeks   ___

2. Unscramble the months. Then number them in order. (1 = the first month)

a. r a J n y u a   <u>January</u>   <u>1</u>

b. y a M   _____   ___

c. m e D b r e c e   _____   ___

d. n u J e   _____   ___

e. c h a r M   _____   ___

f. b r e t o c O   _____   ___

g. l i p r A   _____   ___

h. l y J u   _____   ___

i. p r e S e t m e b   _____   ___

j. b r u F y e a r   _____   ___

k. s A t u g u   _____   ___

l. v e N o m b e r   _____   ___

3. Write the seasons.

Seasons in Canada			
December 21 – March 20	March 21 – June 20	June 21 – September 20	September 21 – December 20

a. <u>winter</u>   b. _____   c. _____   d. _____

4. Look at the dates. Write the seasons. Use the information from Exercise 3.

a. January 5   <u>winter</u>

b. November 28   _____

c. March 22   _____

d. May 6   _____

e. December 19   _____

f. June 25   _____

5. Look at Antonio's calendar. *True* or *False*?

March

SUN.	MON.	TUES.	WED.	THURS.	FRI.	SAT.
	1 Science Lab English	2 Computer Lab Math	3 English	4 Gym Math	5 Language Lab English	6 To Edmonton
7 Daylight Saving Time	8	9	10 NO CLASSES	11	12 To Quebec City	13 Ming 7:00 p.m.
14	15 Science Lab English	16 Auditorium 2:00 Math	17 English	18 Gym Math	19 Language Lab English	20 Track & Field
21 Mary 6:00 p.m.	22 Science Lab English	23 Counsellor's Office 3:15 Math	24 English	25 Gym Math	26 Language Lab English	27 Library with Frank
28	29 Science Lab English	30	31			

TODAY'S DATE → 19

a. Antonio has class every day this month.	*false*
b. He has Math twice a week.	_____
c. He has Math on Wednesday and Friday.	_____
d. He has English three times a week.	_____
e. He has Gym once a week.	_____
f. He was in Edmonton last weekend.	_____
g. Tomorrow he has Track & Field.	_____
h. Yesterday was Tuesday.	_____
i. He is going to see Mary on Saturday night.	_____
j. He sees Mary every weekend.	_____
k. There were no classes last week.	_____
l. Daylight saving time begins this week.	_____
m. Next week Antonio is going to see the school counsellor.	_____

Challenge Make a calendar of your monthly activities. Write ten sentences about your calendar.

**1. Look in your dictionary. Number the statutory holidays in order.
(1 = the first holiday in the year)**

____ **a.** Labour Day   ____ **f.** Victoria Day

____ **b.** Christmas Day   ____ **g.** Thanksgiving

____ **c.** Canada Day   ____ **h.** Good Friday

_1_ **d.** New Year's Day   ____ **i.** Boxing Day

____ **e.** Remembrance Day

2. Look at the pictures. Match.

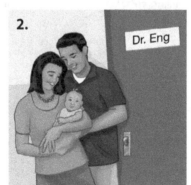

_2_ **a.** Melia's first doctor's appointment   ____ **d.** Our tenth anniversary

____ **b.** Our wedding   ____ **e.** Thanksgiving

____ **c.** Vacation, Summer 2007   ____ **f.** Melia's eighth birthday

Challenge Bring some photos to class. Write captions on your own paper.

1. **Look in your dictionary. Write the opposites.**

    a. big   _little_   **d.** cheap _____

    b. same _____   **e.** ugly _____

    c. heavy _____   **f.** slow _____

2. **Look at the classroom. _True_ or _False_? Change the <u>underlined</u> word in the false sentences. Make the sentences true.**

    a. The chairs are <u>soft</u>.   _False. The chairs are hard._

    b. There's a <u>big</u> clock in the room. _____

    c. Bob is a <u>good</u> student. _____

    d. His book is <u>thin</u>. _____

    e. The teacher's glass is <u>empty</u>. _____

    f. The words on the board are <u>easy</u>. _____

    g. The classroom is <u>noisy</u>. _____

3. **What about you? Check (✓) the words that describe your classroom.**

    ☐ beautiful   ☐ big   ☐ quiet

    ☐ noisy   ☐ ugly   ☐ Other: _____

Challenge Describe your classroom. Write six sentences.

1. Look at page 156 in your dictionary. What colours are the following vehicles?

    a. convertible   _____red_____   **c.** sedan   _____

    b. school bus   _____   **d.** pickup truck   _____

2. Look at the bar graph. Put the colours in order. (1 = favourite)

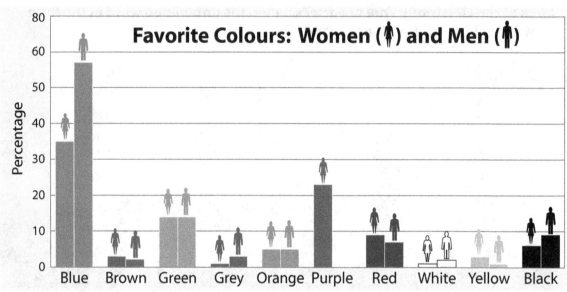

Based on information from: Hallock, Joe (2003) "Female Favorite Color Pie Chart" and "Male Favorite Color Pie Chart." http://www.joehallock.com/edu/com498/preferences.html

Women's Favourite Colours	Men's Favourite Colours
1. _____blue_____	1. _____
2. _____	2. _____
3. _____	3. _____
4. _____	4. _____
5. _____	5. _____
6. _____	6. _____
7. _____ and _____	7. _____ and _____
8. _____ and _____	8. _____

3. What about you? Put the colours in order. (1 = your favourite)

    ____ red   ____ turquoise   ____ yellow   ____ pink   ____ violet

    ____ brown   ____ light blue   ____ dark blue   ____ orange   ____ beige

Challenge Make a list of the colours in Exercise 2. Ask five women and five men their favourite colours. Do their answers agree with the information in Exercise 2?

1. **Look at page 24 in your dictionary. *True* or *False*?**

   a. The red sweaters are above the yellow sweaters.   _____true_____

   b. The purple sweaters are next to the orange sweaters.   _____

   c. The white sweaters are between the black and grey sweaters.   _____

   d. The brown sweaters are on the left.   _____

   e. The dark blue sweaters are below the turquoise sweaters.   _____

2. **Follow the instructions below.**

   a. Put the letter **W** in the first shaded box.

   b. Put a **Y** below it.

   c. Put an **E** in the last shaded box.

   d. Put an **I** above the **E**.

   e. Put a **P** next to the **E**, on the left.

   f. Put a **U** in the second shaded box.

   g. Put an **O** between the **Y** and the **U**.

   h. Put an **E** above the **U**.

   i. Put an **R** next to the **U**, on the right.

   j. Put an **H** between the **W** and the **E**.

   k. Put the letters **E**, **N**, **R**, and **S** in the correct boxes to complete the question.

3. **What about you? Look at Exercise 2. Answer the question.**

   _____

Challenge Draw a picture of your classroom. Write about the locations of the classroom items in your picture. **Example:** *The map is next to the board, on the right.*

1. **Look in your dictionary. How much money is there in the following?**

   a. coins   <u>$3.41</u>   b. bills <u>   </u>   c. coins and bills <u>   </u>

2. **Look at the money. How much is it? Use numbers.**

   a. <u> $5.10   </u>   b. <u>   </u> or <u>   </u>   c. <u>   </u> or <u>   </u>

   d. <u>   </u>   e. <u>   </u>   f. <u>   </u>

3. **Read the cartoon. Who is doing the following things? Check (✓) the correct column.**

	The Man	The Woman
a. wants to gets change	✓	☐
b. lends money	☐	☐
c. borrows money	☐	☐
d. pays back money	☐	☐

Challenge How many different ways can you get change for a dollar? **Example:** *four quarters*

1. Look in your dictionary. Match.

1.

2.

3.

4.

5.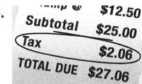

6.

_3_ **a.** SKU number

____ **b.** bar code

____ **c.** use a debit card

____ **d.** use a gift card

____ **e.** sales tax

____ **f.** regular price

2. Complete the shopping tips. Use the words in the box.

cash register	credit	debit	exchange	pay	total
price	price tag	receipt	return	sales	

Be a $mart $hopper

★ Watch the ___cash register___. Is the _____ the same as the price
    a.   **b.**
  on the _____?
           c.

★ Always get a _____ —and keep it.
              d.

★ Is the _____ tax correct?
        e.

★ Look at the last line. Is the _____ correct?
                        f.

★ Do you _____ cash? Count your change.
        g.

★ Do you use a _____ card or a _____ card? Check the
              h.   **i.**
  items on your receipt.

Ask: ★ Can I _____ this for something else?
                j.

     ★ Can I _____ this for cash?
                k.

3. What about you? What has sales tax in your province? How much is it?

Challenge Look at page 254 in this book. Complete the sales slip.

Go To Page 242 For Another Look (Unit 1). | See Page 265 For Listening Practice.

1. **Look in your dictionary. *True* or *False*?**

   a. Anya and Manda are twins. _____true_____

   b. Mrs. Kumar is shopping for matching sweaters. _____

   c. She buys two navy blue sweaters. _____

   d. Manda is happy with her sweater. _____

   e. Anya is happy with her sweater. _____

   f. Mrs. Kumar looks disappointed. _____

   g. Anya keeps her sweater. _____

2. **Put the sentences in order. (1 = the first event) Use your dictionary for help.**

   ___ a. The twins look at the sweaters.

   _1_ b. Mrs. Kumar shops for Manda and Anya.

   ___ c. Anya exchanges her sweater.

   ___ d. Manda is happy with the sweater, but Anya is a little disappointed.

   ___ e. Mrs. Kumar pays for the sweaters.

   ___ f. The twins are happy with their sweaters.

   ___ g. Mrs. Kumar chooses matching green sweaters.

3. **What about you? Imagine a friend gives you this sweater. Answer the questions.**

   a. Are you happy or disappointed with the sweater?

   _____ Why? _____

   b. Are you going to keep it? _____

   c. Are you going to exchange it? _____

   If *yes*, for what? _____

4. **Look in your dictionary. Circle the words to complete the sentences.**

   a. Mrs. Kumar thinks her twins are (the same)/ different.

   b. Mrs. Kumar buys the same / different sweaters for the twins.

   c. The regular / sale price of the sweater is $19.99.

   d. The total price / sales tax is $43.38.

   e. Mrs. Kumar pays cash / uses a credit card.

   f. Manda exchanges / keeps the sweater.

5. **Look in your dictionary. Complete the receipt. Write the total and the change.**

```
            A&G
    DATE: __10/20/11__
*****************************
ITEM
1 GREEN SWEATER    $_____
                   $_____
_____
SUBTOTAL           $ 39.98
SALES TAX          $  3.40
TOTAL              $_____
CASH               $ 45.00
CHANGE             $_____

*****************************
   THANK YOU FOR SHOPPING WITH US.
```

6. **Complete Manda's journal entry. Use the words in the box.**

disappointed	happy	keep	matching
navy blue	~~shop~~	sweaters	twins

October 22

Mom really likes to _____shop_____ for us! Yesterday, she gave us two beautiful
                      a.

_____ green _____. I'm very _____ with my sweater.
      b.   c.   d.

I love the colour, and it's thick and warm. Anya was a little _____.
                                                                    e.

She wants to be different. I'm going to _____ my sweater, but Anya
                                              f.

exchanged her sweater for a _____ sweater. Anya said to Mom,
                                   g.

"Our sweaters are now different colours, but they are still the same sweaters."

And Mom said, "You're different people, but you're still _____!"
                                                              h.

7. **What about you? Look in your dictionary. Which colour sweater do you like?**

Challenge Imagine you are Anya. Write a journal entry about the sweaters.

Adults and Children

1. **Look in your dictionary. How many of the following are there?**

    a. men   _3_   **d.** infants   ___

    b. women   ___   **e.** teenagers   ___

    c. senior citizens   ___   **f.** girls   ___

2. **Which words are for males? Which words are for females? Which words are for both?**
    Put the words in the box in the correct spaces in the circles.

~~baby~~	infant	teen
boy	man	toddler
girl	senior citizen	woman

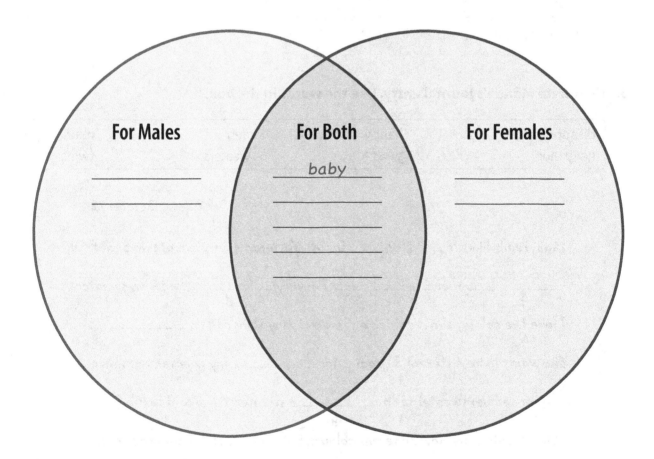

For Males   For Both   For Females

baby

3. **What about you? How many of the following people are in your class?**

men   ___

women   ___

senior citizens   ___

teenagers   ___

4. Look in your dictionary. *True* or *False*? Write a question mark (?) if you don't know.

    a. The senior citizen is a woman.   _____true_____

    b. The toddler is a girl.   _____

    c. The infant is a boy.   _____

    d. The teenager is sitting next to a 10-year-old boy.   _____

    e. The baby is sitting next to a woman.   _____

    f. A man is holding the infant.   _____

5. Match.

    __2__ **a.** man   **1.** 78 years old

    ____ **b.** toddler   **2.** 40 years old

    ____ **c.** teen   **3.** 10 years old

    ____ **d.** girl   **4.** 2 months old

    ____ **e.** infant   **5.** 2 years old

    ____ **f.** senior citizen   **6.** 18 years old

6. Label the pictures. Use the words from Exercise 5.

a. _____teen_____   **b.** _____   **c.** _____

d. _____   **e.** _____   **f.** _____

Challenge Look in your dictionary. How old are the people? Discuss your answers with a classmate.
          Example: *A: I think this man is 40. What about you? B: I think he's only 30.*

Describing People

1. Look in your dictionary. Write the opposites.

a. young   <u> *elderly* </u>

b. tall   <u>   </u>

c. thin   <u>   </u> or <u>   </u>

2. Look at the ads. Circle the words that describe age and appearance. Match the ads with the photos.

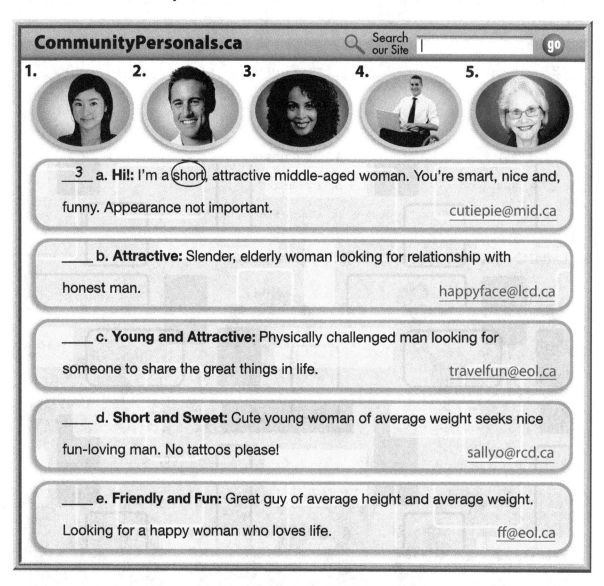

CommunityPersonals.ca   Search our Site [   ] **go**

1.   2.   3.   4.   5.

<u> 3 </u> **a. Hi!:** I'm a (short), attractive middle-aged woman. You're smart, nice and, funny. Appearance not important.   cutiepie@mid.ca

<u>   </u> **b. Attractive:** Slender, elderly woman looking for relationship with honest man.   happyface@lcd.ca

<u>   </u> **c. Young and Attractive:** Physically challenged man looking for someone to share the great things in life.   travelfun@eol.ca

<u>   </u> **d. Short and Sweet:** Cute young woman of average weight seeks nice fun-loving man. No tattoos please!   sallyo@rcd.ca

<u>   </u> **e. Friendly and Fun:** Great guy of average height and average weight. Looking for a happy woman who loves life.   ff@eol.ca

3. Look at the photos in Exercise 2. Do people have the following things? Check (✓) the boxes. For the boxes with checks, write the number of the picture.

☑ pierced ears <u> 1 </u>   ☐ a mole <u>   </u>   ☐ a tattoo <u>   </u>

Challenge Name a famous person who was or is . . . .
   a. physically challenged   **b.** visually impaired   **c.** hearing-impaired.

See page 266 for listening practice.

1. **Look at the top picture in your dictionary. How many of the following do you see?**

   a. combs <u> 5 </u>
   c. blow dryers ___
   e. people with grey hair ___

   b. rollers ___
   d. brushes ___
   f. scissors ___

2. **Look at the pictures of Cindi. Check (✓) the things The Hair Salon did to Cindi's hair.**

   Before

   Now

   THE HAIR
   SALON

   ✓ cut

   ☐ set

   ☐ colour

   ☐ perm

3. **Circle the words to complete the paragraph about Cindi.**

   Cindi is very happy with her new hairstyle. Before, she had <u>short / (long) curly / straight</u>,
    a.   b.

   <u>blond / brown</u> hair with <u>cornrows / bangs</u> and <u>a part / no part</u>. Now she has very
   c.   d.   e.

   <u>long / short</u>, <u>curly / straight</u>, <u>red / black</u> hair. Cindi looks great!
   f.   g.   h.

4. **What about you? Draw a picture of a friend's hair. Check (✓) the correct boxes.**
   My friend has . . . .

   ☐ short hair   ☐ shoulder-length hair   ☐ long hair

   ☐ no hair (bald)   ☐ straight hair   ☐ wavy hair

   ☐ curly hair   ☐ a part   ☐ bangs

   ☐ cornrows   ☐ a moustache   ☐ a beard

   ☐ sideburns   ☐ _____ hair
                         (list hair colour)

   Challenge Find three pictures of hairstyles in your dictionary, a newspaper or magazine, or online.
   Write descriptions.

1. Look in your dictionary. Put the words in the box in the correct category.

> ~~aunt~~   brother-in-law   cousin   daughter   grandmother
> husband   niece   parent   son   uncle

Male	Female	Male or Female
_____	_____ *aunt* _____	_____
_____	_____	_____
_____	_____	
_____	_____	

2. Look in your dictionary. *True* or *False*?

Tim Lee's family:

a. Tim has two sisters.   _____ *false* _____

b. Min is Lu's wife.   _____

c. Dan is Min and Lu's nephew.   _____

d. Tim and Emily have the same grandparents.   _____

e. Rose is Emily's aunt.   _____

Ana Garcia's family:

f. Ana is Carlos's sister-in-law.   _____

g. Sara is Eva and Sam's granddaughter.   _____

h. Felix is Alice's brother.   _____

i. Marta is Eddie's mother-in-law.   _____

j. Marta is Eva and Sam's daughter-in-law. _____

3. What about you? Answer the questions.

a. What is your name?   _____

b. What is your mother's name?   _____

c. What is your father's name?   _____

d. What is your marital status?   ☐ single   ☐ married   ☐ divorced

   If you are married, what is your husband's or wife's name?   _____

e. Do you have children?   ☐ yes   ☐ no

   If *yes*, what are their names?   _____

4. Look in your dictionary. Circle the answers.

a. Carol was Bruce's (wife) / sister.

b. Sue is Kim's stepmother / mother.

c. Rick is a single father / father.

d. David is Mary's brother / half brother.

e. Lisa is Bill's half sister / stepsister.

f. Bruce is Bill and Kim's father / stepfather.

5. Look at Megan's pictures. Put the sentences in order.

1. Megan and Chet—2004

2. Megan, Chet, and Nicole—2005

3. Megan   Chet

4. Megan and Nicole—2007

5. Megan, Brian, Nicole, and Jason—2009

6. Megan, Nicole, and Jason—2009

___ a. Megan is remarried.

___ b. Megan is a stepmother.

_1_ c. Megan is married.

___ d. Megan has a baby.

___ e. Megan is a single mother.

___ f. Megan is divorced.

6. Complete Nicole's story. Use the information in Exercise 5.

Name: Nicole Parker   October 10, 2012

My name is Nicole. My _____mother_____'s name is Megan.
                              a.

My _____'s name is Chet. I have a _____.
              b.   c.

His name is Brian. Brian has a _____.
                                            d.

His name is Jason. Jason is my _____.
                                            e.

Challenge Draw your family tree. Use the family trees in your dictionary as a model.

1. Look in your dictionary. Who is doing the following things to the child? Check (✓) the answers.

	Mother	Father	Grandmother
a. bathing	✓	☐	☐
b. reading to	☐	☐	☐
c. disciplining	☐	☐	☐
d. holding	☐	☐	☐
e. kissing	☐	☐	☐
f. undressing	☐	☐	☐
g. rocking	☐	☐	☐
h. buckling up	☐	☐	☐
i. feeding	☐	☐	☐
j. dressing	☐	☐	☐
k. praising	☐	☐	☐

2. Look at Gita's *To Do* list. What is Gita doing? Write sentences.

a. It's 10:00.   _She's bathing the baby._

b. It's 12:00.   _____

c. It's 11:30.   _____

d. It's 10:30.   _____

e. It's 1:15.   _____

> **TO DO**
>
> 10:00 a.m. bathe Lila
>
> 10:30 a.m. dress her
>
> 11:00–11:45 a.m. play with her
>
> 12:00 p.m. feed her
>
> 1:00–1:30 p.m. read to her

3. What about you? Check (✓) the things you can do.

	Yes	No
a. comfort a baby	☐	☐
b. read nursery rhymes to a child	☐	☐
c. feed baby food to a child	☐	☐
d. dress a child in training pants	☐	☐
e. change a cloth diaper	☐	☐
f. rock a baby to sleep	☐	☐

4. Cross out the word that doesn't belong.

a. Places to sit   high chair   ~~diaper pail~~   potty seat

b. Things a baby wears   pacifier   bib   disposable diaper

c. Things a baby eats   formula   baby food   baby lotion

d. Things with wheels   rocking chair   carriage   stroller

e. Things to put in a baby's mouth   teething ring   baby bag   nipple

f. Things for changing diapers   baby powder   training pants   wipes

g. Things a baby plays with   night light   rattle   teddy bear

h. Things that hold a baby   safety pins   baby carrier   car safety seat

5. There are eight child care and parenting words. They go across (→) and down (↓). Two are circled for you. Find and circle six more. Use the pictures as clues.

Challenge Make a list of things to put in a baby bag. What can you use them for?
Example: *bottle—to feed the baby*

See page 268 for listening practice.

1. Look in your dictionary. Complete Dan Lim's schedule.

6:00 A.M.	wake up
6:30 A.M.	get dressed
7:00 A.M.	_____
7:30 A.M.	_____
_____	drive to work
5:00 P.M.	_____
_____	exercise at the gym
	have dinner
8:00 P.M.	_____
8:30 P.M.	_____
_____	go to sleep

2. Look at the picture of the Lims' things. Match each item with the correct activity.

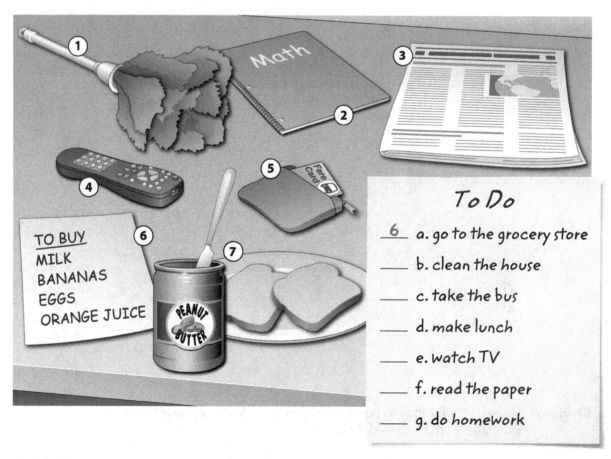

TO BUY
MILK
BANANAS
EGGS
ORANGE JUICE

To Do

_6_ a. go to the grocery store

____ b. clean the house

____ c. take the bus

____ d. make lunch

____ e. watch TV

____ f. read the paper

____ g. do homework

3. **Read about Nora Lim. Complete the story. Use the words in the boxes.**

checks	eats	gets up	~~relaxes~~	takes

Nora Lim has a busy week. Sundays are busy, too,

but she __*relaxes*__ a little more. She _____
a.   b.

at 8:00 and _____ a long, hot shower. Then,
                      c.

she _____ email and _____ breakfast
            d.   e.

with her family.

drives	goes	leaves	makes	picks up	works

After breakfast, she _____ her husband to the shoe store. (He _____ on
                              f.   g.

Sundays, too.) Then, she takes the children to visit their Aunt Ellen. Ellen _____ lunch
                                                                                          h.

for them. After lunch, Nora _____ Ellen's house and _____ to the library for
                                    i.   j.

two hours. At 4:00, she _____ the children from Ellen's house.
                                k.

cooks	gets	goes	has	takes	watches

Nora _____ home at 5:00 and _____ dinner for her family. Her daughter,
              l.   m.

Sara, helps her. Dan _____ the bus home. The family _____ dinner at 6:00.
                              n.   o.

They talk about their day. After dinner, Nora _____ TV with her family. At 10:00,
                                                          p.

Nora _____ to bed.
              q.

4. **What about you? Complete your weekday or weekend schedule. Use the schedule in Exercise 1 as an example.**

Challenge Interview someone you know (a friend, family member, or classmate). Write a schedule of his or her daily routine.

See page 269 for listening practice.

Life Events and Documents

1. Look in your dictionary. Complete the timeline for Martin Perez.

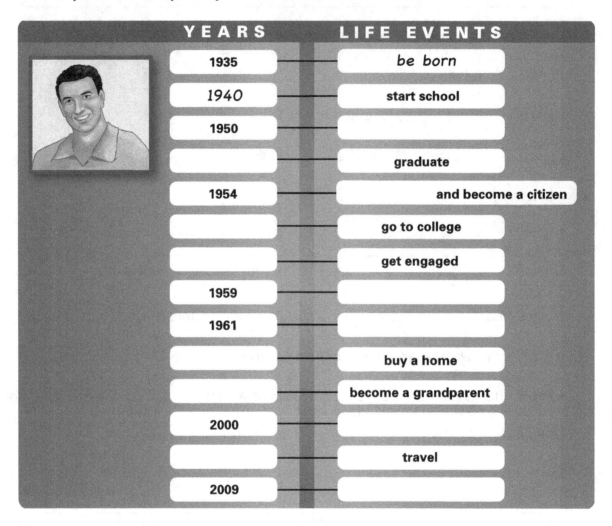

YEARS	LIFE EVENTS
1935	be born
1940	start school
1950	
	graduate
1954	and become a citizen
	go to college
	get engaged
1959	
1961	
	buy a home
	become a grandparent
2000	
	travel
2009	

2. Complete the story about Rosa Lopez. Use the words in the box.

~~was~~	died	fell	got	graduated	had	got	learned

Rosa Prodi _____was_____ born in Canada in 1938. She _____ from
      a.   **b.**

high school in 1955. In 1956, she _____ to drive and _____
                                           c.   **d.**

a job in Toronto. Then, she met Martin.

They _____ in love, _____ married, and
                e.   **f.**

_____ two children. They were very happy until Martin
    g.

_____ in 2009. Today Rosa lives in Montreal with her daughter and grandchildren.
    h.

40

3. Look at the documents. Answer the questions.

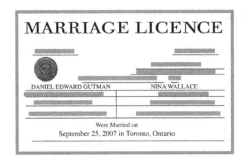

MARRIAGE LICENCE

DANIEL EDWARD GUTMAN   NINA WALLACE

Were Married on
September 25, 2007 in Toronto, Ontario

Driver's Licence
Permis de conduire   ON CANADA

GUTMAN
DANIEL EDWARD
341 MAPLE STREET
TORONTO, ON, M0M 0M0

00000 - 00000 - 00000

DATE OF BIRTH/DATE DE NAIS
1983/04/06

A07688-324   10/9/2007

LAND DEED

DANIEL EDWARD GUTMAN
and NINA WALLACE

CARLETON UNIVERSITY

Daniel Edward Gutman

Bachelor of Arts
High Honours in English

June 2005

Toronto General Hospital
BIRTH CERTIFICATE

DANIEL EDWARD GUTMAN
April-06-1983

a. When was Daniel born?   _____1983_____

b. Where did he get his driver's licence?   _____

c. When did he get married?   _____

d. Where did he travel to?   _____

e. When did he graduate from university?   _____

f. When did he buy a new home?   _____

4. What about you? Check (✓) the documents you have.

- ☐ birth certificate
- ☐ diploma
- ☐ university degree
- ☐ deed
- ☐ social insurance number card
- ☐ driver's licence
- ☐ passport
- ☐ marriage licence
- ☐ permanent resident card

Challenge Draw a timeline for important events in your life. Use the timeline in Exercise 1 for ideas.

See page 270 for listening practice.

Feelings

1. Look in your dictionary. Write all the words that end in *-y* and *-ed*.

-y	-ed	
thirsty	satisfied	_____
_____	_____	_____
_____	_____	_____
_____	_____	_____
_____	_____	_____
_____	_____	_____

2. How do these people feel? Use words from Exercise 1.

a. _____relieved_____

b. _____

c. _____

d. _____

e. _____

f. _____

g. _____

h. _____

i. _____

3. Put the words in the correct columns.

~~calm~~	full	~~homesick~~	full	in love	in pain
nervous	proud	sad	uncomfortable	sick	well

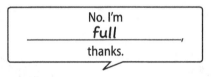

_____ *calm* _____   _____   *homesick* _____   _____

_____ _____   _____   _____

_____ _____   _____   _____

4. Complete the conversations. Use words from Exercise 3.

a. Are you still hungry?

No. I'm _____ *full* _____, thanks.

b. Do you like Sandy?

Like? I'm _____!

c. What's wrong?

Oh. I'm _____. I miss my family, my friends, my country . . . .

d. Wow! Your son got 100%!

Yes. I'm very _____ of him.

e. What's wrong?

I'm _____. Please call a doctor.

5. What about you? How do you feel when you do the following things? Circle as many words as possible. Add new words, too.

a. wake up	sleepy	happy	calm	_____
b. start a new class	nervous	confused	excited	_____
c. have problems in school	worried	upset	homesick	_____
d. exercise	happy	proud	uncomfortable	_____

Challenge What do you do when you feel nervous? Bored? Homesick? Confused? Angry? Discuss your answers with a classmate.

Go to page 243 for Another Look (Unit 2). | **See page 271 for listening practice.**

1. Look in your dictionary. How many of these things can you see?

a. banners   _1_

b. balloons   ___

c. children misbehaving   ___

d. relatives   ___

2. Look in your dictionary. Label Ben's relatives. Use the words in the box.

| ~~Ben~~ | aunt | grandfather | mother-in-law | son | cousin | wife |

a. _____Ben_____

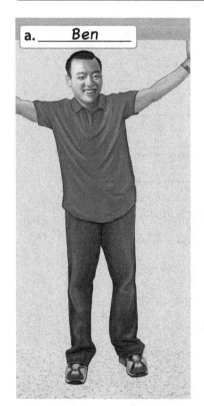

b. _____

c. _____

d. _____

e. _____

f. _____

g. _____

3. **Look in your dictionary. Who are Ben's other relatives? Guess. Complete the sentences. Then, discuss your answers with a classmate. Do you and your classmate agree?**

   a. The woman to the right of Ben is his <u>cousin (or aunt or sister)</u>.

   b. The physically-challenged man is his _____.

   c. The little girl near the food table is his _____.

   d. The boy watching TV is his _____.

4. **Look in your dictionary. What did people do at the reunion? Check (✓) the answers.**

✓ eat	☐ misbehave
☐ clean	☐ laugh
☐ go to sleep	☐ exercise
☐ cook	☐ check email
☐ talk	☐ read
☐ watch TV	☐ play baseball
☐ sing	

5. **Look in your dictionary. Circle the words to complete the sentences.**

   a. Ben Lu is single / (married).

   b. He has a family reunion every year / month.

   c. The reunion is at Ben's / his aunt's house.

   d. Ben is talking to relatives / watching TV.

   e. His grandfather and aunt have the same / different opinions about the baseball game.

   f. His grandfather has a beard / grey hair.

   g. His mother / son is misbehaving.

   h. Ben is glad / sad his family is all there.

6. **What about you? Imagine you are at Ben's family reunion. Who do you want to talk to? Why?**

   Example: *I want to talk to Ben's aunt and grandfather. I like baseball, too.*

Challenge Look in your dictionary. Choose three of Ben's relatives. Describe them to a partner. Your partner will point to the correct picture. **Example:** *She is elderly and has grey hair. She is near the food.*

The Home

1. Look in your dictionary. *True* or *False*?

a. This home has three bedrooms.   *true*

b. There's a door between the bedroom and the bathroom.   _____

c. The baby's room is next to the parents' bedroom.   _____

d. There's an attic under the roof.   _____

e. The kitchen is under the kids' bedroom.   _____

f. There's a window in the bathroom.   _____

g. There are books on the floor in the kids' bedroom.   _____

2. Look at the pictures. Which rooms do they go in? Match.

1.

2.

3.

4.

5.

6.

7.

8.

9.

____ **a.** living room   ____ **d.** garage   _1_ **g.** kitchen

____ **b.** bathroom   ____ **e.** baby's room   ____ **h.** kids' bedroom

____ **c.** dining area   ____ **f.** attic   ____ **i.** basement

3. What about you? Do you like the house in your dictionary? Why or why not? Talk about it with a partner.

4. Look in your dictionary. Complete the sentences.

   a. The mother is in the _____ *living room* _____.

   b. The father is in the _____.

   c. The teenage daughter is in the _____.

   d. The 10-year-old girl is in the _____.

   e. The baby is in the _____.

   f. The car is in the _____.

5. Look in your dictionary. Correct the mistakes in the ad.

FOR SALE

3
~~4~~ bedroom house with 2 bathrooms

Large kitchen and dining area. Attic and basement,

2-car garage. Good for a family. Call 555-3434.

6. What about you? What's important to you in a home? Complete the chart.

Home Preference Checklist — J&R REALTORS

Number of bedrooms _____ Number of bathrooms _____

	very important	important	not important
Kitchen with a dining area?	☐	☐	☐
Window in the kitchen?	☐	☐	☐
Window in the bathroom?	☐	☐	☐
A basement?	☐	☐	☐
An attic?	☐	☐	☐
A garage?	☐	☐	☐

Challenge Write an ad for a home. It can be for your home, the home of someone you know, or the home on page 53 of this workbook. Use the ad in Exercise 5 as an example.

1. Look at pictures 1 and 2 in your dictionary. *True* or *False*?

Internet Listing

a. The Internet listing is for a house.   _____false_____

b. It has one bedroom.   _____

c. The rent is $900 a week.   _____

Classified Ad

d. The classified ad is for a furnished apartment.   _____

e. Utilities are included.   _____

f. It has two bathrooms.   _____

2. Check (✓) the things people do when they rent an apartment and / or buy a house.

	Rent an Apartment	Buy a House
a. make an offer	☐	✓
b. sign a rental agreement	✓	☐
c. get a loan	☐	☐
d. ask about the features	☐	☐
e. take ownership	☐	☐
f. move in	☐	☐
g. pay the rent	☐	☐
h. make a mortgage payment	☐	☐
i. unpack	☐	☐
j. arrange the furniture	☐	☐
k. meet with a realtor	☐	☐
l. put the utilities in their name	☐	☐
m. meet the neighbours	☐	☐
n. submit an application	☐	☐

3. What about you? Look at the Internet listing and the classified ad in your dictionary. Which apartment do you like better? Why? Tell a partner.

4. Look in your dictionary. Circle the words to complete the sentences.

a. The woman in picture A wants to buy / (rent) an apartment.

b. She talks to the manager / realtor.

c. The rent is $850 / $1,700 a month.

d. The man and woman in picture H are looking at a new apartment / house.

e. The realtor makes / man and woman make an offer.

f. The rent / mortgage is $2,000 a month.

5. Look at the listings. *True* or *False*?

708 Apartments for rent	708 Apartments for rent
Westside Apartments	**Eastside Apartments**
3 bdrm 2 ba furn apt New kit $1000/mo Util incl Call mgr	2 bdrm 1 ba unfurn apt Large yd $850/mo Util incl Call mgr
555-1002 eves	**555-1002 eves**

a. The Westside apartment is furnished.   _____true_____

b. The Eastside apartment has a new kitchen.   _____

c. The Eastside apartment has more bedrooms.   _____

d. The Westside apartment has more bathrooms.   _____

e. The Eastside apartment's rent is more.   _____

f. Utilities are included for both apartments.   _____

g. Both apartments have the same manager.   _____

h. You can call the manager in the morning.   _____

6. What about you? Check (✓) the things you and your family did the last time you moved.

☐ rented an apartment   ☐ looked at houses

☐ submitted an application   ☐ signed a rental agreement

☐ paid rent   ☐ met with a realtor

☐ made an offer   ☐ got a loan

☐ made a mortgage payment   ☐ called a manager

☐ painted   ☐ met the neighbours

Challenge How did you find your home? Write a paragraph.

See page 272 for listening practice.

1. Look at page 50 in your dictionary. Circle the words to complete the sentences.

a. There's a fire escape on the first /(second) floor.

b. The building on the right has a playground / roof garden.

c. A tenant / The manager is hanging a vacancy sign.

d. A tenant / The manager is entering the building.

e. There's an intercom in the entrance / lobby.

f. The mailboxes are in the entrance / lobby.

g. A tenant is using the elevator / stairs.

h. There's a big-screen TV in the laundry room / recreation room.

i. There's a security camera in the garage / recreation room.

j. There's a pool table / washer in the recreation room.

2. Look at the sign. *True* or *False*?

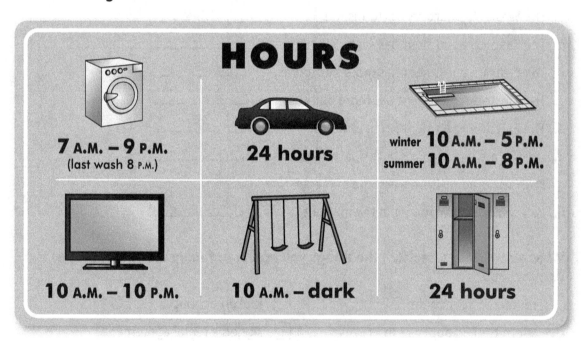

HOURS

7 A.M. – 9 P.M.
(last wash 8 P.M.)

24 hours

winter 10 A.M. – 5 P.M.
summer 10 A.M. – 8 P.M.

10 A.M. – 10 P.M.

10 A.M. – dark

24 hours

a. The swimming pool is always open until 8:00 p.m.   *false*

b. You can use the washer and dryer all night.   _____

c. The garage is always open.   _____

d. The playground closes at different times each day.   _____

e. You can use the storage lockers at midnight.   _____

f. The recreation room is open twenty-four hours.   _____

g. You can watch a movie on the big-screen TV at 9:00 p.m.   _____

3. **Look in your dictionary. *True* or *False*? Correct the underlined words in the false sentences.**

a. Each apartment has a ~~fire escape~~. *balcony*   _____false_____

b. The apartment complex has a <u>swimming pool and courtyard</u>.   _____

c. The <u>garbage chute</u> is in the alley.   _____

d. The emergency exit is in the <u>hallway</u>.   _____

e. The landlord is talking about a <u>lease</u>.   _____

f. A tenant is using her <u>peephole</u>.   _____

4. **Complete the signs. Use the words in the box.**

buzzer	elevator	~~emergency exit~~	intercom
mailbox	tenants	garbage bin	garbage chute

a.

IN CASE OF FIRE
use the
emergency exit
DO NOT
use the
_____

b.

NEW _____:
Please put your
name on your
_____ .

c.
NOTICE Do not throw...
...down the _____ .
Put them in the _____
in the alley.

d.

ATTENTION
ALL TENANTS:
Do not allow strangers
into the building.
Always use the _____
BEFORE you use the _____ !

5. **What about you? Check (✓) the items in your home.**

☐ fire escape   ☐ security camera   ☐ laundry room

☐ garage   ☐ balcony   ☐ smoke detector

☐ lobby   ☐ third floor   ☐ security gate

☐ door chain   ☐ dead bolt lock   ☐ peephole

Challenge Look at Exercise 5. Which three items are most important to you? Why? Tell a classmate.

See page 273 for listening practice.

1. Look in your dictionary. Where are they?

a. students   _college residence_

b. an elderly, physically-challenged woman   _____

c. a man with a newspaper   _____

2. Look at the chart. Circle the words to complete the sentences.

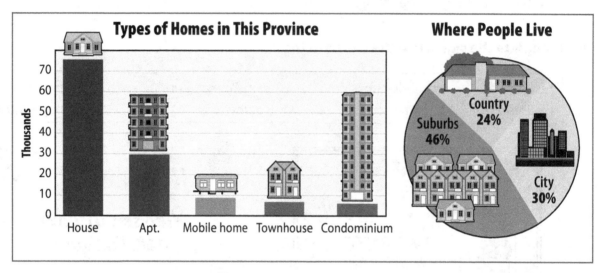

a. Most people live in the city / (suburbs)

b. Only 24% of people live in the city / country.

c. About 30% live in the city / suburbs.

d. Most people live in houses and apartments, but there are almost nine thousand
mobile homes / condominiums.

e. There are more townhouses than condominiums / mobile homes.

f. The chart does NOT have information about the number of nursing homes / townhouses.

3. What about you? Check (✓) the places you've lived.

☐ city   ☐ country   ☐ college dorm

☐ suburbs   ☐ farm   ☐ townhouse

☐ small town   ☐ ranch   ☐ mobile home

☐ senior housing   ☐ condo   ☐ Other: _____

Challenge Take a class survey. Where do your classmates live? Write the results.
Example: _Ten students live in the suburbs._

1. Look in your dictionary. Check (✓) the locations.

	On the Lawn	On the Patio
a. patio furniture	☐	✓
b. hose	☐	☐
c. hammock	☐	☐
d. barbecue	☐	☐
e. compost pile	☐	☐
f. garbage can	☐	☐
g. sliding glass door	☐	☐

2. Look at the house. *True* or *False*? Correct the <u>underlined</u> words in the false sentences.

a. There are three ~~mailboxes~~ _steps_ in front of the front door. _____false_____

b. The <u>doorbell</u> is to the right of the doorknob. _____

c. The <u>storm</u> door is open. _____

d. The <u>porch light</u> is on. _____

e. There's a <u>vegetable garden</u> in the front lawn. _____

f. The <u>chimney</u> is white. _____

g. The satellite dish is near the <u>driveway</u>. _____

h. The <u>front walk</u> stops at the steps. _____

3. What about you? Do you like this house? Check (✓) *Yes* or *No*.

☐ Yes　　☐ No　　Why? _____

Challenge Draw a picture of your "dream house." Describe it to a partner.

1. Look in your dictionary. Where can you find the following things? Use *on* or *under*.

a. paper towels   _under the cabinet_   d. pot   _____

b. dish rack   _____   e. broiler   _____

c. coffee maker   _____   f. garbage disposal _____

2. Look at the bar graph. How long do things last? Put the words in the correct columns.

How Long Things Last

Based on information from: *Consumer Reports Buying Guide* (2000).

1–5 Years	6–10 Years	11–15 Years	16–20 Years
_____	_blender_	_____	_____
	_____	_____	

3. What about you? Check (✓) the items you have.

		Where is it?	How long have you had it?
☐	blender	_on the counter_	_two years_
☐	electric can opener	_____	_____
☐	coffee maker	_____	_____
☐	electric mixer	_____	_____
☐	food processor	_____	_____
☐	microwave	_____	_____
☐	kettle	_____	_____
☐	toaster oven	_____	_____

Challenge Look at the kitchen appliances in your dictionary. List the five you think are the most important. Compare your list with a partner's list.

1. Look in your dictionary. _True_ or _False_?

a. There's a teacup on the tray. _____true_____

b. The fan has two light fixtures. _____

c. The tablecloth is blue. _____

d. There's a vase on the buffet. _____

e. The salt shaker is on the table. _____

f. There's a coffee mug on the dining room table. _____

g. The sugar bowl and creamer are in the hutch. _____

2. Look at the table setting. Complete the sentences.

a. The _____plate_____ is under the bowl.

b. It's on a dark _____.

c. A white _____ is on the plate.

d. There are two _____ to the left of the plate.

e. They're on the _____.

f. There are two _____. They're to the right of the plate.

g. There's also a _____ to the right of the plate.

h. There's a _____ above the spoons.

3. What about you? What does _your_ table setting look like? Draw a picture on your own paper. Then, complete the charts.

Item	How Many?	Where?
knife		
fork		
spoon		
plate		
bowl		

Item	How Many?	Where?
teacup		
placemat		
napkin		
Other: _____		

Challenge Describe your table setting to a partner. Your partner will draw it. Does it look the same as your picture in Exercise 3?

1. Look in your dictionary. How many of the following things can you see?

a. paintings __2__   c. throw pillows ___   e. windows ___

b. walls ___   d. fireplaces ___   f. end tables ___

2. Look at the Millers' new living room. Cross out the items they already have.

To Buy

~~throw pillows~~	DVD player	houseplant
loveseat	couch	basket
armchair	candle holder	drapes
entertainment centre	carpet	fire screen
TV	floor lamp	coffee table
stereo system	magazine holder	end table
		candles

3. What about you? Look at the list in Exercise 2. List the items you have.

Challenge Write six sentences about the Millers' living room.
Example: *They have a couch, but they don't have a loveseat.*

1. Look in your dictionary. Check (✓) the locations.

	Sink	Bathtub	Wall
a. hot and cold water	✓	✓	☐
b. towel racks	☐	☐	☐
c. shower curtain	☐	☐	☐
d. faucets	☐	☐	☐
e. tiles	☐	☐	☐
f. drains	☐	☐	☐
g. grab bar	☐	☐	☐
h. toilet paper	☐	☐	☐

2. Look at the ad. Circle the words to complete the sentences.

THE **BIG** SPLASH
The Place for Big Bath Buys

$18.99 $8.99 $9.99 $6.99

$44.99 $7.99 $5.99 $3.99 $4.99 $1.99

$.99 $4.99 $2.99 $37.99 $6.99

a. The (bath mat)/ rubber mat is $9.99.

b. The hamper / wastebasket is $6.99.

c. The bath towel / hand towel is $5.99.

d. The soap dish / soap is $2.99.

e. The toilet brush / toothbrush is $4.99.

f. The shower head / washcloth is $3.99.

g. The mirror / scale is $37.99.

h. The toothbrush holder / soap dish is $4.99.

Challenge What items do people put in a medicine cabinet? Make a list.

1. Look in your dictionary. What colour are the following things?

a. pillow ___white___   b. mattress _____   c. dust ruffle _____

2. Cross out the word that doesn't belong.

a. **They're electric.**	~~mirror~~	outlet	light switch	lamp
b. **They're soft.**	pillowcase	quilt	headboard	blanket
c. **They're part of a bed.**	mattress	alarm clock	box spring	bed frame
d. **They're on the wood floor.**	dresser	lampshade	rug	night table
e. **They make the room dark.**	light switch	curtains	mini-blinds	flat sheet
f. **You put things in them.**	closet	drawer	photos	picture frame

3. Complete the conversations. Use words from Exercise 2.

a. **Lee:** What time is it?

   Mom: I don't know. There's an ___alarm clock___ on the night table.

b. **Tom:** I'm cold.

   Ana: Here's an extra _____.

c. **Ray:** The bed's uncomfortable.

   Mia: The _____ is too soft.

d. **Amir:** There are no curtains.

   Marwa: No, but there are _____.

e. **Bill:** My sweater isn't in the drawer.

   Molly: Look in the _____.

4. What about you? Check (✓) the items that are on your bed.

☐ fitted sheet   Colour: _____

☐ flat sheet   Colour: _____

☐ quilt   Colour: _____

☐ pillow(s)   How many? _____   Hard or soft? _____

☐ mattress   Hard or soft? _____

☐ blankets   How many? _____

Challenge Write a paragraph describing your bedroom.

1. **Look in your dictionary. Which three items are for safety?**

   a. _____bumper pad_____

   b. _____

   c. _____

2. **Look at Olivia and Emma's room. There are ten dolls. Find and circle nine more.**

3. **Write the locations of the dolls. Use *on*, *under*, and *in*. Use your own paper.**

   Example: *on the chest of drawers*

4. **What about you? Check (✓) the things you had when you were a child.**

   ☐ dolls   ☐ mobile   ☐ crayons   ☐ Other: _____

   ☐ stuffed animals   ☐ balls   ☐ puzzles

Challenge Look at the toys you checked in Exercise 4. Write a paragraph about your favourite one.

1. Look in your dictionary. What are the people doing? Circle the words.

   a. "Can we do this with magazines, too?"   ~~recycling the newspapers~~ / taking out the garbage

   b. "Dad, does this truck go here?"   dusting the furniture / putting away the toys

   c. "I like this new blanket."   making the bed / sweeping the floor

   d. "Is this the last plate, Dad?"   cleaning the oven / drying the dishes

2. Look at the room. Check (✓) the completed jobs.

To Do

✓	wash the sheets
☐	change the sheets
☐	sweep the floor
☐	empty the trash
☐	polish the dresser
☐	scrub the sink
☐	mop the bathroom floor
☐	recycle the newspapers

3. What about you? How often do you do the following? Check (✓) the columns.

	Every Day	Every Week	Every Month	Never
dust the furniture				
polish the furniture				
recycle the newspapers				
wash the dishes				
vacuum the carpet				
wipe the counter				
scrub the sink				
put away the toys				
Other: _____				

Challenge Write a *To Do* list of your housework for this week.

 See page 275 for listening practice.

1. **Look in your dictionary. What can you use to clean the following? There may be more correct answers than you can write here.**

Windows	Floor	Dishes
glass cleaner	_____	_____
_____	_____	_____
_____	_____	_____
_____	_____	_____
	_____	
	_____	

2. **Match each item with the correct coupon.**

TO BUY

_4_ a. feather duster
___ b. steel-wool soap pads
___ c. sponges
___ d. bucket
___ e. cleanser
___ f. garbage bags
___ g. dishwashing liquid
___ h. rubber gloves
___ i. vacuum cleaner bags
___ j. disinfectant wipes

1. 50-pack $2.99 Strongy 50 lg
2. 500 mL SPARKLE $1.89
3. 10 L $1.99
4. $1.99
5. 3/ $1.00 Cleanest
6. 99¢/pair
7. $3.29
8. pk of 12 $1.99
9. $1.59 SCRUB EZ
10. 2-pack $3.19

3. **What about you? Look at the cleaning supplies in Exercise 2. Which ones do you have? What do you use them for?**

Example: *feather duster—dust the desk*

Challenge Look in a store, online, or at newspaper ads. Write the prices of some cleaning supplies that you use.

1. Look in your dictionary. Who said the following things?

a. | I'm up on the roof. | _roofer_

b. | Goodbye, termites! | _____

c. | I'm turning on the power again. | _____

d. | I'll fix the toilet next. | _____

e. | I'm fixing the lock on the front door. | _____

f. | There's one more step to repair. | _____

g. | I'm putting in new windows. | _____

2. Look at John's bathroom. There are six problems. Find and circle five more.

3. Look at Exercise 2. *True* or *False*? Correct the underlined words in the false sentences.

        bathtub

a. The ~~sink~~ faucet is dripping. _____false_____

b. The <u>window</u> is broken. _____

c. There are <u>ants</u> near the sink. _____

d. The <u>light</u> isn't working. _____

e. The <u>sink</u> is overflowing. _____

f. The <u>wall</u> is cracked. _____

4. **Look at Exercise 2 and the ads below. Who should John call? Include the repair person, the problem(s), and the phone number on the list. (Hint: John will use some companies for more than one problem.)**

Challenge Look at the problems in Exercise 2. Who fixes them in your home? Make a list.
Example: *toilet stopped up—my son*

Go to page 244 for Another Look (Unit 3). | See page 276 for listening practice. 63

1. Look in your dictionary. *True* or *False*?

a. Sally and Tina are roommates.   _____true_____

b. They had a party in Apartment 3B.   _____

c. A DJ played music.   _____

d. Some people danced.   _____

e. Sally and Tina were irritated by the noise.   _____

f. The neighbours cleaned up the mess in the hallway.   _____

g. Sally and Tina gave an invitation to the woman in Apartment 2C. _____

2. Look at the pictures. Check (✓) the answers.

Friday Night   Saturday Night

	Friday Night	Saturday Night
a. The party was in the rec room.	✓	☐
b. There was a DJ at the party.	☐	☐
c. The music was loud.	☐	☐
d. There was a mess on the floor.	☐	☐
e. People danced.	☐	☐
f. There was a lot of noise.	☐	☐
g. The roommates were at the party.	☐	☐
h. A neighbour was irritated.	☐	☐

3. **Look at the top picture on page 65 in your dictionary. Circle the words to complete the sentences.**

   a. The man is Sally and Tina's (neighbour)/ roommate.

   b. He's <u>at the party</u> / in his bedroom.

   c. He's <u>happy / irritated</u>.

   d. It's <u>before / after</u> midnight.

   e. Sally and Tina didn't give him <u>an invitation / the rules</u> to the party.

   f. He can't sleep because of the <u>mess / noise</u>.

4. **Complete the sign. Use the words in the box.**

dance	DJs	mess	music	noise	parties	~~Rules~~

   # Building <u>Rules</u>
   a.

   - No loud _____ after 10:00 p.m.
     b.
   - Large _____ in rec room only.
     c.
   - Please be quiet in the hallways. No _____!
     d.
   - Please clean up your _____ in public areas.
     e.
   - You can _____ in your apartment, but you must have carpet.
     f.
   - No _____ at apartment parties.
     g.

   Thank you,
   The Manager

Challenge Look at the rules in Exercise 4 and the parties in Exercise 2.
Did the people follow the rules? Talk about it with a partner.

1. Look in your dictionary. Where are the following items? Check (✓) the answers.

a. fish	✓	☐	☐
b. rice	☐	☐	☐
c. butter	☐	☐	☐
d. meat	☐	☐	☐
e. bread	☐	☐	☐
f. pasta	☐	☐	☐
g. milk	☐	☐	☐

2. Complete Shao-fen's shopping list. Use your dictionary for help.

✓ **a.** e _g_ _g_ s
☐ **b.** ___ r ___ i t
☐ **c.** v ___ g e ___ a ___ l ___ s
☐ **d.** r ___ ___ e
☐ **e.** c ___ ___ e ___ e
☐ **f.** ___ r e ___ d
☐ **g.** ___ a ___ ___ a
☐ **h.** ___ h ___ c k ___ n

Shao-fen

3. Look at the food that Shao-fen bought at the market. Check (✓) the items she bought on the shopping list in Exercise 2.

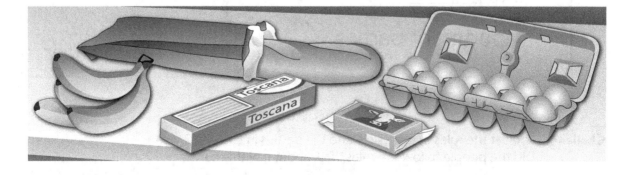

4. Look in your dictionary. *True* or *False*?

a. There are four grocery bags in the kitchen. ___false___

b. There's a shopping list on the table. _____

c. The word *butter* is on the shopping list. _____

d. There are coupons on the table. _____

e. There are eggs on the table. _____

f. There are vegetables in the refrigerator. _____

g. There's fruit in the refrigerator. _____

5. Complete the coupons. Write the names of the foods.

a.

SAVE 75¢
on one 2-litre bottle
or two 1-litre bottles
of Dairy Fresh
___milk___

☐ SELECT THIS COUPON

b.

SAVE 50¢
on Large or
Extra Large

_____

☐ SELECT THIS COUPON

c.

SAVE 75¢
on all Happy Cow

_____
250 g or larger

☐ SELECT THIS COUPON

d.

SAVE 55¢
on any box of
Caroline's white
or brown

_____

☐ SELECT THIS COUPON

e.

SAVE $1
on any (2) boxes
of DeRosa's

_____

☐ SELECT THIS COUPON

f.

SAVE 45¢
on all Arnie's

_____

☐ SELECT THIS COUPON

6. What about you? Do you use store coupons?

☐ Yes   ☐ No   If *yes*, for what items? _____

Challenge Look in your dictionary. Which foods do you like? Make a list. Compare lists with a classmate. Do you and your classmate like the same things?

1. Look in your dictionary. Write the name of the fruit.

a. They're to the right of the figs.   _____dates_____

b. They're to the left of the tangerines.   _____

c. They're below the peaches.   _____

d. They're above the mangoes.   _____

e. They're to the right of the raspberries.   _____

f. One is ripe, one is unripe, and one is rotten.   _____

2. Complete the online order form. Use the words in the box.

~~apples~~	grapefruit	grapes	kiwi	lemons
limes	oranges	pears	pineapples	strawberries

www.BobsGrocery.ca   Search

Specials

This Week's Specials   Checkout

OPEN

a.	b.	c.	d.	e.
Crisp Granny Smith _apples_	New Zealand	Bartlett	Juicy Florida	Pink
3 / $1	$1.09 / kg	3 kg bag $2.99	3 kg bag $2.99	2 / $1

f.	g.	h.	i.	j.
		Sweet ripe	Fresh Hawaiian	Large Bunch Seedless
Your choice _____ or _____				
4 / $1		$3.99 / box	$5 each	$2.29 / kg

3. What about you? Make a shopping list using the fruit in Exercise 2. How much or how many will you buy? How much will it cost?

Example: *6 apples—$2.00*

Challenge Make a list of fruit from your native country.

1. **Look in your dictionary. Which vegetables are the following colours? Put them in the correct columns.**

Yellow / Orange	Green		Red
sweet potatoes	_____	_____	_____
_____	_____	_____	_____
_____	_____	_____	_____
_____	_____	_____	_____
_____	_____	_____	
	_____	_____	
	_____	_____	
	_____	_____	

2. **Look at the chart. Which has more vitamin A? Circle the correct answer.**

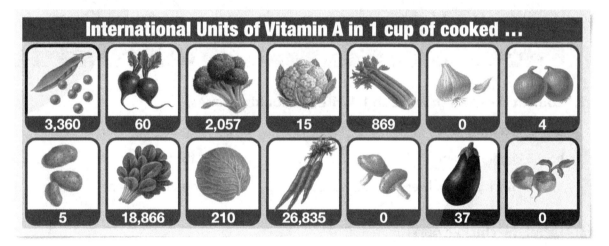

International Units of Vitamin A in 1 cup of cooked …

| 3,360 | 60 | 2,057 | 15 | 869 | 0 | 4 |
| 5 | 18,866 | 210 | 26,835 | 0 | 37 | 0 |

a. cabbage / ⟨spinach⟩   **d.** carrots / celery   **g.** broccoli / cauliflower

b. beets / turnips   **e.** garlic / potatoes   **h.** spinach / celery

c. mushrooms / onions   **f.** turnips / eggplant   **i.** beets / peas

3. **What about you? How often do you eat these vegetables in a week? Circle the numbers.**

carrots	0	1	2	3	4	more than 4 times a week
broccoli	0	1	2	3	4	more than 4 times a week
spinach	0	1	2	3	4	more than 4 times a week

Challenge Make a list of vegetables from your native country.

See page 277 for listening practice.

1. Look in your dictionary. Label the foods in the chart.

		Size	Cooking time	Method
	a. ___lamb___	2.2–3.6 kilograms	60 min./kg	oven
	b. _____	1/2" thick	3 min.*	broiler
	c. _____	1 1/2" thick	10 min.*	broiler
	d. _____	3.6–9 kilograms	40 min./kg	oven
	e. _____	3.6–5.4 kilograms	3–4 hours	oven
	f. _____	1–1.3 kilograms	1 1/4 hours	oven

*each side

2. Look at the chart in Exercise 1. Write the cooking times.

a. 4.5 kilogram turkey   ___3–4 hours___

b. 4.5 kilogram ham   _____

c. 1/2"-thick piece of liver   _____

d. 2.7 kilogram leg of lamb   _____

e. 1-1/2" thick steak   _____

f. 1.3 kilogram chicken   _____

3. Label the chicken parts.

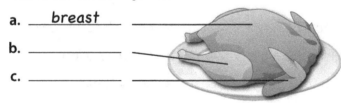

a. ___breast___   _____

b. _____

c. _____

4. What about you? Check (✓) the meat and poultry you eat.

☐ veal cutlets   ☐ bacon   ☐ duck   ☐ lamb chops

☐ tripe   ☐ beef ribs   ☐ pork chops   ☐ sausage

Challenge Take a survey. Ask five people which meats and poultry they eat.

1. Look in your dictionary. Write the names of the seafood.

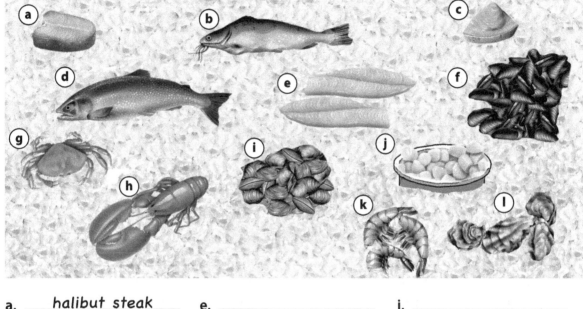

a. _____halibut steak_____   e. _____   i. _____

b. _____   f. _____   j. _____

c. _____   g. _____   k. _____

d. _____   h. _____   l. _____

2. Look at the sandwich. Complete the order form. Check (✓) the correct boxes.

Sandwich Order		
Meat	**Cheese**	**Bread**
✓ smoked turkey	☐ processed	☐ white
☐ roast beef	☐ mozzarella	☐ wheat
☐ corned beef	☐ Swiss	☐ rye
☐ salami	☐ cheddar	
☐ pastrami		

3. What about you? Complete your order with the food on the form in Exercise 2.

I'd like a _____ sandwich with _____ cheese on _____ bread.

Challenge Ask five classmates what they want from the deli. Write their orders.

1. **Look in your dictionary. *True* or *False*?**

   a. A customer is buying pet food.   _____true_____

   b. The manager is in aisle 3A.   _____

   c. The grocery clerk is in the produce section.   _____

   d. There's a scale in the dairy section.   _____

   e. There are five customers in line.   _____

   f. You can get frozen vegetables in aisle 2B.   _____

   g. The bagger is near the cashier.   _____

   h. The self-checkout doesn't have a cash register.   _____

2. **Complete the conversations. Use the words in the box.**

~~Bagger~~	bottle return	cart	checkouts
~~Customer~~	manager	scale	self-checkout

   __Customer__ : Excuse me. Where do I take these empty pop bottles?
        a.

   Grocery Clerk: To the _____. Near aisle 1.
                 b.

   Amy: I'll get a shopping basket.

   Jason: Get a _____. We have a lot on our list!
              c.

   Jason: We need two kilograms of potatoes. Is this enough?

   Amy: There's a _____ over there. We can weigh them.
                d.

   Jason: Look at the dates on these frozen dinners.

   Amy: They're all too old. Let's tell the _____.
                     e.

   Amy: Wow! Look at the lines at the _____.
                    f.

   Jason: I see. But I don't like to use the _____. I like to talk to a person.
                        g.

   Amy: Can we have four bags, please?

   _____: Sure. That will be 20 cents.
       h.

3. Look at the things Amy and Jason bought. Check (✓) the items on the shopping list.

Grocery List

- ☑ potatoes
- ☐ tuna
- ☐ aluminum foil
- ☐ bagels
- ☐ yogourt
- ☐ potato chips
- ☐ beans

- ☐ soup
- ☐ cookies
- ☐ nuts
- ☐ margarine
- ☐ sugar
- ☐ ice cream
- ☐ oil

- ☐ plastic wrap
- ☐ apple juice
- ☐ sour cream
- ☐ coffee
- ☐ cake
- ☐ chocolate bars

4. Put the items from the list in Exercise 3 in the correct category. Use your dictionary for help.

Canned Foods	Dairy	Snack Foods
_____	_____	_____
_____	_____	_____
_____	_____	_____

Baking Products	Beverages	Baked Goods
_____	_____	_____
_____	_____	_____
		_____

Grocery Products	Produce	Frozen Foods
_____	_____potatoes_____	_____
_____		

Challenge Make a shopping list for yourself. Write the section for each item.
  Example: *scallops—seafood section*

1. **Look at pages 72 and 73 in your dictionary. What is the container or packaging for the following items?**

   a. pinto beans _____can_____   c. sour cream _____

   b. plastic storage bags _____   d. potato chips _____

2. **Complete these coupons. Use the words in the box.**

bag	bottle	carton	loaf
six-pack	package	roll	~~tube~~

   a.

   2/$3 **Bright's toothpaste**

   100 mL
   ___tube___

   Limit 2

   b.
   BUY ONE GET ONE FREE.
   Smart's Potato Chips, low salt
   200 g _____
   Limit 1 free item

   c.
   Special!
   2 L orange juice
   $3.10 / _____

   d.

   $1.99 **Stop and Save rye bread**
   450 g _____
   Limit 1 per customer

   e.

   SAVE 50 cents
   Cola
   one _____
   Regular or diet

   f.
   SPECIAL! Chip's cookies (all varieties)
   350–450 g _____
   $2.99

   g.
   BUY ONE GET ONE FREE.
   Maine Spring Water
   500 mL _____

   h.

   100 sheets _____
   Strongy Paper Towels
   3/$2.99

3. **Write a shopping list. Use all the coupons in Exercise 2.**

   Example: *2 tubes of toothpaste*

   Challenge Which foods do you think are in your refrigerator? Make a list. Then check your answers at home. **Example:** *a bottle of pop*

1. Look in your dictionary. Write the words.

a. g _____gram_____

b. kg _____

c. mL _____

d. L _____

e. c. _____

f. tsp. _____

g. tbsp. _____

h. fl. oz _____

2. Write the weight or measurement.

a. _____680 grams of potatoes_____

b. _____

c. _____

d. _____

e. _____

f. _____

3. What about you? How much of the following do you eat or drink every week?

a. cheese _____

b. water _____

c. fish _____

d. sugar _____

Challenge Look at page 254 in this book. Follow the instructions.

1. **Look in your dictionary.** *True* or *False*? **Correct the <u>underlined</u> words in the false sentences.**

   counters
   a. Clean the kitchen ~~windows~~. *false*   d. Cook <u>meat</u> to 74°C. _____

   b. Separate carrots and <u>meat</u>. _____   e. Chill leftovers in the <u>refrigerator</u>. _____

   c. Cook <u>chicken</u> to 70°C. _____

2. **Look at the pictures. Which preparation has the most calories? Number them in order. (1 = the most calories)**

Calories in 85 gram Chicken Breast

150	161	222
172	168	175

   ____ a. boiled   ____ c. grilled   *1* e. fried

   ____ b. broiled   ____ d. roasted   ____ f. stir-fried

3. **What about you? Label the preparations and check (✓) the ways you like to eat eggs.**

   a.   ☐   b.   ☐

   c.   ☐   d.   ☐

   e.   ☐   f.    ☐

4. Look in your dictionary. Read the recipe. <u>Underline</u> all the food preparation words.

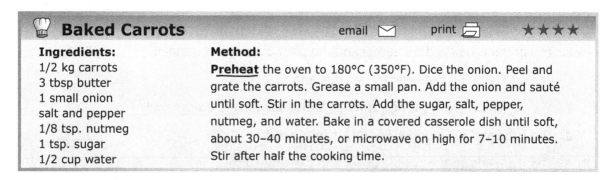

🍳 **Baked Carrots** email ✉ print 🖨 ★★★★

Ingredients:
1/2 kg carrots
3 tbsp butter
1 small onion
salt and pepper
1/8 tsp. nutmeg
1 tsp. sugar
1/2 cup water

Method:
<u>Preheat</u> the oven to 180°C (350°F). Dice the onion. Peel and grate the carrots. Grease a small pan. Add the onion and sauté until soft. Stir in the carrots. Add the sugar, salt, pepper, nutmeg, and water. Bake in a covered casserole dish until soft, about 30–40 minutes, or microwave on high for 7–10 minutes. Stir after half the cooking time.

5. Look at the recipe in Exercise 4. Number the pictures in order.

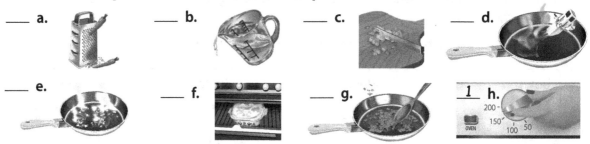

___ a. ___ b. ___ c. ___ d.

___ e. ___ f. ___ g. ___ h.

6. Look at the pictures. Circle the words to complete the recipe.

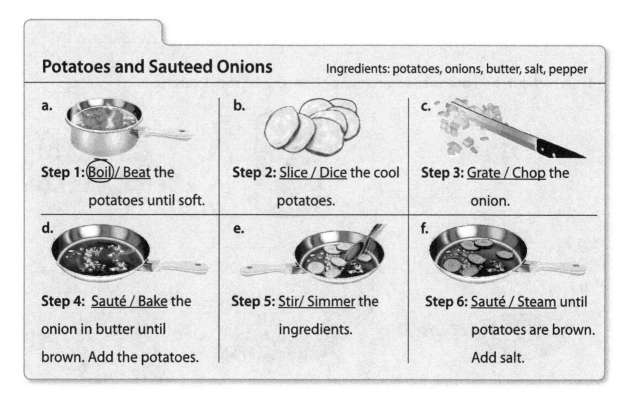

Potatoes and Sauteed Onions Ingredients: potatoes, onions, butter, salt, pepper

a.
Step 1: (Boil)/ Beat the potatoes until soft.

b.
Step 2: Slice / Dice the cool potatoes.

c.
Step 3: Grate / Chop the onion.

d.
Step 4: Sauté / Bake the onion in butter until brown. Add the potatoes.

e.
Step 5: Stir/ Simmer the ingredients.

f.
Step 6: Sauté / Steam until potatoes are brown. Add salt.

Challenge Write the recipe for one of your favourite foods. Share it with a classmate.

1. **Look in your dictionary.** *True* or *False*?

   a. The grater is below the steamer and the plastic storage container.   _____*false*_____

   b. The egg beater is between the spatula and the whisk.   _____

   c. The vegetable peeler, tongs, strainer, and saucepan are on the wall.   _____

   d. The ladle and the wooden spoon are in the pot.   _____

   e. There are lids on the double boiler and casserole dish.   _____

   f. The frying pan is next to the roasting pan.   _____

   g. The kitchen timer is near the colander and the paring knife.   _____

2. **Complete the two-part words. Use the words in the box.**

bowl	holders	knife	opener
~~pan~~	pin	press	sheet

   a. cake   _____*pan*_____   **e.** rolling   _____

   b. mixing   _____   **f.** cookie   _____

   c. garlic   _____   **g.** can   _____

   d. pot   _____   **h.** carving   _____

3. **Which kitchen utensils do you need? Use words from Exercise 2.**

   a. _____*garlic press*_____   **b.** _____   **c.** _____

   d. _____   **e.** _____   **f.** _____

Challenge List the three most important kitchen utensils. Why are they important?
         Example: *pot—to cook spaghetti, soup, and vegetables*

1. Look in your dictionary. *True* or *False*? Correct the underlined words in the false sentences.

                           doughnuts

a. There are muffins and ~~onion rings~~ on the counter.   ____*false*____

b. The restaurant has <u>pizza</u>.   _____

c. The <u>counter person</u> is talking to a woman.   _____

d. The <u>plastic utensils</u> are next to the salad bar.   _____

e. A woman is drinking <u>a milkshake</u> with a straw.   _____

f. A man is using <u>sugar substitute</u>.   _____

2. Look at the orders. Write the food.

a.	Quick & Tasty Receipt	
	Chicken sandwich	
	Thank You	

b.	Quick & Tasty Receipt	
	Thank You	

3. What about you? Look at the fast food in your dictionary. Tell a classmate your order.

Example: *I'd like a cheeseburger.*

—|**Challenge** Look at the fast food in your dictionary. Which foods are the most healthy? Make a list.

1. Look in your dictionary. Complete the chart. Do not include sandwiches or salads.

meat	vegetables	breads	hot beverages
bacon			

2. Look at the ingredients. Write the food.

a. _____club sandwich_____

b. _____

c. _____

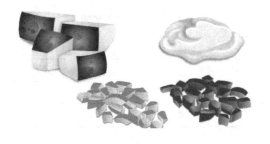

d. _____

e. _____

f. _____

3. Cross out the word that doesn't belong.

a. **Potatoes**   baked potato   hash browns   mashed potatoes   ~~rice~~

b. **Breads**   garlic bread   roll   pie   toast

c. **Beverages**   soup   coffee   low-fat milk   tea

d. **Breakfast food** biscuits   layer cake   pancakes   waffles

e. **Side salads**   chef's salad   coleslaw   pasta salad   potato salad

f. **Desserts**   cheesecake   layer cake   pie   hot cereal

4. Look at the food. Complete the orders.

a.   FOOD ORDER FORM

roast chicken

_____

_____

_____

_____

Thank You!

b.   FOOD ORDER FORM

_____

_____

_____

_____

_____

_____

Thank You!

5. What about you? What's your favourite . . .

soup? _____   dessert? _____   hot beverage? _____

Challenge Show five people the coffee shop menu in your dictionary. Write their orders.

See page 281 for listening practice.

1. Look in your dictionary. Who does the following?

   a. washes dishes   _dishwasher_

   b. leaves a tip   _____

   c. takes the orders   _____

   d. cooks food   _____

   e. seats the customers   _____

   f. orders from the menu   _____

2. Look in your dictionary. Circle the answers.

   a. The patrons are in the dish room / (dining room).

   b. The baby is in the booth / high chair.

   c. The chef is in the dish room / kitchen.

   d. The hostess is in the dining room / kitchen.

   e. The server pours the water in the dish room / dining room.

3. Look at the order and the place setting. Check (✓) the items the diner needs.

GUEST BILL

Date	Table	Guests	Server	
				410121

onion soup
house salad
steak
broccoli
mashed potatoes
garlic bread
half bottle of red wine
coffee

Total

Thank you! Please come again.

☐ dinner plate   ☐ wine glass   ☐ dinner fork

✓ salad plate   ☐ cup   ☐ steak knife

☐ soup bowl   ☐ saucer   ☐ knife

☐ bread-and-butter plate   ☐ napkin   ☐ teaspoon

☐ water glass   ☐ salad fork   ☐ soup spoon

4. Look at the menu. Complete the check.

The Bistro
✑ MENU ✑

Soup of the day	$4.50
House salad	$3.50
Fish of the day	$15.50
Chicken á l'orange	$12.50
Sirloin steak	$19.00
Vegetables	$2.50
Potatoes	$2.50
Cherry pie	$4.00
with ice cream	$5.00
Coconut cake	$4.50
Coffee or tea	$1.50

The Bistro
242 West Street 555-0700
GUEST BILL

				832000

black bean soup	$4.50
house salad	_____
grilled salmon	_____
peas	_____
french fries	_____
cherry pie w/vanilla ice cream	_____
coffee	_____
Subtotal	_____
Tax (5%)	_____
Total	_____

THANK YOU!

5. In Canada, most restaurant patrons leave a tip for the server when they pay the bill. The tip is often 15% of the subtotal. Look at the bill in Exercise 4. Circle the answers and complete the sentences.

a. The subtotal is __$35.00__ .   (⃝$35.00) $36.75 $40.25

b. A 15% tip is _____ . $1.75 $5.25 $4.72

c. Patrons leave the tip on the _____ .   menu   table   dinner plate

6. What about you? Do restaurant patrons leave tips for the server in your

native country? _____

If *yes*, how much? _____

Where do they leave it? _____

Challenge Look at the menu in Exercise 4. Order a meal. Figure out the subtotal, 5% tax, the total, and a 15% tip.

1. Look in your dictionary. *True* or *False*?

a. There's live music at the farmers' market. _____true_____

b. The avocados are with the fruit. _____

c. A vendor is counting watermelons. _____

d. You can find the herb *dill* at the farmers' market. _____

e. There are free samples of vegetables. _____

f. The avocados are organic. _____

g. The lemonade is sweet. _____

2. Look at the signs. Match.

1. Sweet!

2. TAKE ONE!

3.  Organic

4. FRESH!

5. Basil

_____ **a.** herb   _____ **c.** samples   _____ **e.** vegetables

_____ **b.** organic   _1_ **d.** strawberries

3. Complete the chart. Use the words in the box.

~~avocados~~   dill   Herbs   lemonade   Vegetables   Vendors   watermelon   zucchini

Fruit		Beverages		
avocados	peppers		Green Farms	parsley
strawberries		pop	Cara's Bakery	
	onions	milk	Hot Food	basil

84

4. Look in your dictionary. Circle the words to complete the flyer.

Welcome to
Greenview (Farmers) / Fish Market
a.

Right now we have fresh products such as the following:
- vegetables (tomatoes / turnips, lettuce, zucchini)
  b.
- fruits (avocados / apples, strawberries, apricots,
  c.
  peaches / pineapples)
  d.
- fish / herbs (basil, dill, parsley, chives)
  e.
- local cheese / ice cream (Swiss, cheddar, mozzarella)
  f.

We also have certified organic / sour produce.
g.

Free samples / vendors of many items! (Take one, you'll like it!)
h.

Some of our samples / vendors include the following:
i.
- Green Farms (fresh fruits / vegetables)
  j.
- The Lemonade / Live Music Stand (sweet / sour, but good!)
  k.   l.
- Cara's Bakery (freshly baked apple pies / pancakes, doughnuts,
  m.
  and cupcakes: sweet / sour and delicious!)
  n.
- Hot Food (sandwiches / tacos and much more!)
  o.
Listen to live music / vendors (featuring The Two-Step Band)!
p.

Time: Saturdays 8:00 a.m. – 2:00 p.m.
Place: Lakeside Park

5. What about you? Imagine you are at the farmers' market. Check (✓) the things you will do there. Then, compare answers with a classmate.

- [ ] listen to live music
- [ ] buy organic vegetables
- [ ] drink lemonade
- [ ] have lunch
- [ ] speak to the vendors
- [ ] eat samples
- [ ] buy sweets
- [ ] meet friends

Challenge Make a shopping list for the farmers' market in your dictionary.

Everyday Clothes

1. **Look in your dictionary. Which clothing items are the following colours?**

   a. green ____dress____ and _____

   b. dark blue _____, _____, and _____

   c. red _____

   d. yellow _____ and _____

   e. white _____, _____, _____, _____, and _____

   f. pink _____

   g. orange _____

   h. beige _____

2. **Look at the picture of Courtney and Nicholas. Read the school clothing rules. Complete the sentences.**

Courtney

Nicholas

CLOTHING RULES

Wear…	Don't wear…
shirts	T-shirts
blouses	jeans
pants	baseball caps
skirts	athletic shoes
dresses	
socks	

What's OK?

a. Courtney is wearing a ____blouse____.

b. Nicholas is wearing _____.

c. He's also wearing _____.

What's NOT OK?

d. Courtney is wearing _____ and _____.

e. Nicholas is wearing a _____ and a _____.

3. **What about you? What are you wearing today?**

_____

4. Look in your dictionary. *True* or *False*?

a. The man in the blue shirt is wearing jeans. _____true_____

b. The woman with white shoes is wearing socks. _____

c. The girl with the baseball cap is tying her shoes. _____

d. The woman in the skirt is putting on a sweater. _____

e. The woman with the sweater has a handbag. _____

f. The man in the green shirt and slacks has tickets. _____

5. Look in your dictionary. Circle the words to complete the conversation.

Sun: Clio? I'm in front of the theatre. Where are you? It's 7:45!

Clio: Sorry. I'm still getting dressed. What are you wearing?

Sun: A blue (blouse)/ T-shirt and a white baseball cap / skirt.
                      a.   **b.**

Clio: Is it cold out? Do I need a handbag / sweater?
                                        c.

Sun: Maybe. It *is* a little cool. What are you wearing?

Clio: Right now I'm wearing a dress / a suit, but maybe I'll put on pants / socks.
                                          d.   **e.**

Sun: OK. But hurry! The concert starts at 8:15!

6. Cross out the word that doesn't belong.

a. You wear it on top. ~~handbag~~   T-shirt   sweater

b. They're for your feet.   shoes   socks   skirt

c. It's only for women.   dress   blouse   suit

d. You wear it on bottom.   jeans   shirt   pants

7. What about you? Complete the checklist. Do you wear the following clothes?

	Yes	No	If *yes*, where?
jeans	☐	☐	_____
athletic shoes	☐	☐	_____
a T-shirt	☐	☐	_____
a suit	☐	☐	_____
a sweater	☐	☐	_____
a baseball cap	☐	☐	_____

Challenge Look in your dictionary. Imagine you have tickets for the concert. What are you going to wear? Tell a partner.

1. Look in your dictionary. Circle the words to complete the sentences.

a. The woman's (business suit) briefcase is purple.

b. The cardigan / pullover sweater is green.

c. The evening gown / uniform is turquoise.

d. The tank top / sweatshirt is gray.

e. The overalls / sweatpants are red.

f. The knit top / sports shirt is blue and white.

g. The cocktail / maternity dress is orange.

2. Which clothes do women or men usually wear? Which clothes can both wear? Put the words from the box in the correct spaces in the circles.

~~business suit~~	vest	shorts	cardigan sweater
uniform	tie	evening gown	sweatpants
pullover sweater	sandals	sports jacket	tuxedo
maternity dress	tank top	cocktail dress	capris

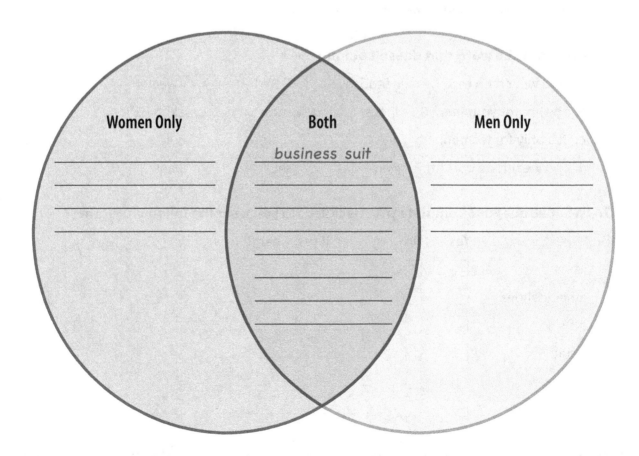

Women Only   Both   Men Only

business suit

3. **Look at the picture. Write the names of the clothing items on the list. Write the colour, too.**

Packing Log

to pack for Montreal Wedding

a _tank top_____

   and _____

b _____

   and _____

c _____

   and _____

d _____

   and _____

4. **Match the activity with the clothes from Exercise 3.**

HOTEL MONTREAL
ALEXANDRA PLACE
MONTREAL

SATURDAY

_c_ 1. Meet Ming in exercise room   7:30 a.m.

___ 2. Lunch near swimming pool   12:00 p.m.

___ 3. Formal dinner at the Grill   6:00 p.m.

___ 4. Wedding party at the   9:00 p.m.
      Grand Hotel Ballroom

5. **What about you? Where do you wear these clothes? Check (✓) the columns.**

	At School	At Work	At Home	At a Party	Never
pullover sweater					
vest					
sweatpants					
tuxedo or gown					
uniform					
cap					

Challenge What casual clothes do you have? Work clothes? Formal clothes? Exercise wear? Give two examples for each type of clothes.

See page 282 for listening practice. **89**

1. Look in your dictionary. *True* **or** *False***?**

    a. The man with the headwrap is wearing a jacket.   __true__

    b. The man with the down jacket is wearing earmuffs.   _____

    c. The woman in the poncho is wearing yellow rain boots.   _____

    d. The man with sunglasses is wearing a trench coat.   _____

2. Look at the ad. Circle the words to complete the sentences.

Dress for the Snow

Jessica is wearing a dark <u>down vest</u> / (<u>parka,</u>)
                a.

white <u>earmuffs</u> / <u>headband</u>, and a pair of
         b.

<u>gloves</u> / <u>mittens</u>. Justin is wearing a blue
        c.

<u>down jacket</u> / <u>coat</u>, a dark ski <u>hat</u> / <u>mask</u>, and
        d.   **e.**

a striped <u>winter scarf</u> / <u>hat</u>.
        f.

DRESS FOR THE SUN

Kimberly is wearing a <u>headwrap</u> / <u>straw hat</u>,
            g.

a dark <u>swimming trunks</u> / <u>swimsuit</u>, and a light
         h.

<u>cover-up</u> / <u>windbreaker</u>. Her <u>raincoat</u> / <u>umbrella</u>
    i.   **j.**

and <u>leggings</u> / <u>sunglasses</u> protect her from the sun.
      k.

3. What about you? Circle the words to complete the sentences.

    a. I <u>am</u> / <u>am not</u> wearing a jacket or coat today.

    b. I <u>wear</u> / <u>don't wear</u> sunglasses.

    c. I <u>sometimes</u> / <u>never</u> wear a hat.

Challenge Look at the clothes in your dictionary. List eight items you have. When do you wear
them? **Example:** *gloves—for cold weather*

1. **Look in your dictionary. Circle the words to complete the sentences.**

   a. The (pyjamas) / tights are pink.

   b. The slippers / crew socks are grey.

   c. The thermal undershirt / blanket sleeper is yellow.

   d. The robe / nightshirt is blue and white.

   e. The body shaper / nightgown is beige.

2. **Look at the ad. Complete the bill.**

Underneath It All
Semi-annual Sale
Hours: M – F 10:00 – 6:00 • Weekends 10:00 – 8:00

3 / $10.00	3 / $12.00	$6.50	4 / $18.00	$7.00
2 / $6.00	$3.50	3 / $13.50	$5.00	$25.00
$2.50	$9.00	$18.00	$15.00	

230 Green St. Tel.: 555-5431 Fax: 555-6548
www.unia.ca

```
        UNDERNEATH
          IT ALL
- - - - - - - - - - - - - - - - - - -
2  ____bras____      $50.00
1  _____      $ 9.00
2  _____      $36.00
3 PR._____    $12.00
2 PR._____    $ 6.00
8 PR._____    $36.00

           TOTAL $149.00
```

Challenge Choose clothes from the ad in Exercise 2. Write a bill. Figure out the total.

Workplace Clothing

1. **Look in your dictionary. Put the words in the correct column.**

For Your Head	For Your Face	For Your Hands
hard hat	_____	_____
_____	_____	_____
_____	_____	_____
_____	_____	**For Your Feet**
_____	_____	_____
_____		
_____		
_____		

2. **Look at the online catalogue. Write the names of the workplace clothing. Use the words on the left side of the catalogue page.**

3. **Look in your dictionary. *True* or *False*? Correct the underlined words in the false sentences.**

   a. The construction worker is wearing a ~~polo~~ *work* shirt.   ___*false*___

   b. The road worker is wearing <u>jeans</u>.   _____

   c. The farmhand is wearing <u>work gloves</u>.   _____

   d. The salesperson is wearing a <u>badge</u>.   _____

   e. The manager is wearing a <u>blazer</u>.   _____

   f. The counterperson is wearing a <u>chef's hat</u>.   _____

   g. The nurse is wearing <u>scrubs</u>.   _____

   h. The security guard has a <u>name tag</u>.   _____

   i. The medical technician is wearing a <u>lab coat</u>.   _____

   j. The surgeon is wearing a <u>surgical scrub cap</u>.   _____

4. **Look at the online catalogue in Exercise 2. What items will people buy? Complete the chart.**

Job	Quantity	Item	Item Price	Total
a. road worker	2 pairs	steel toe boots	$75	$150
	1 pair	_____	$80	_____
b. construction worker	1	_____	$32	_____
	2	safety vests	_____	_____
	1 box	_____	_____	_____

5. **What about you? Check (✓) the clothing you have. Do you wear the clothing for work?**

		For Work	Not for Work
☐	safety glasses	☐	☐
☐	waist apron	☐	☐
☐	blazer	☐	☐
☐	polo shirt	☐	☐
☐	work gloves	☐	☐
☐	helmet	☐	☐
☐	hairnet	☐	☐

Challenge Look at pages 166 and 167 in your dictionary. List three people's work clothing.
    Example: *the dental assistant—a face mask and disposable gloves*

1. **Look at the top picture in your dictionary. How many of the following can you see?**

   a. salesclerks   <u>3</u>   **d.** customers trying on shoes   ___

   b. customers waiting in line   ___   **e.** customers purchasing jewellery   ___

   c. hats   ___   **f.** display cases   ___

2. **Look at the pictures. Label the items. Use the words in the box.**

backpack	bracelet	pin	change purse	earrings	~~wallet~~
locket	cellphone holder	ring	shoulder bag	tote bag	watch

   a. ____wallet____   **b.** _____   **c.** _____   **d.** _____

   e. _____   **f.** _____   **g.** _____   **h.** _____

   i. _____   **j.** _____   **k.** _____   **l.** _____

3. **Look at the answers in Exercise 2. Put the words in the correct columns.**

Jewellery Department		Other Accessories	
_____	_____	___wallet___	_____
_____	_____	_____	_____
_____	_____	_____	_____

4. Cross out the word that doesn't belong.

a. Things you wear around your neck   necklace   ~~belt~~   scarf   locket

b. Types of necklaces   beads   buckles   chain   string of pearls

c. Things you keep a change purse in   backpack   handbag   wallet   tote bag

d. Types of shoes   oxfords   boots   pumps   shoelaces

e. Parts of a shoe   sole   suspenders   heel   toe

5. Complete the ad. Use the words in the box.

| ~~pumps~~   flats   boots   hiking boots   loafers   oxfords   tennis shoes   high heels |

SALE

The Good Sole

Save 20% on men's and women's shoes!

a. _____pumps_____

b. _____

c. _____

d. _____

e. _____

f. _____

g. _____

h. _____

Located at the Maple City Mall
East Elm St.

6. What about you? Check (✓) the items you have.

☐ chain   ☐ watch   ☐ pierced earrings

☐ clip-on earrings   ☐ belt buckle   ☐ cellphone holder

Challenge   List the kinds of shoes you have. When do you wear them?
          Example: *boots—I wear them in cold or wet weather.*

See page 283 for listening practice.

Describing Clothes

1. Look at the T-shirts in your dictionary. *True* or *False*?

    a. They come in six sizes.   ____*true*____   **d.** They are short-sleeved.   _____

    b. They have a V-neck.   _____   **e.** They are checked.   _____

    c. They are solid blue.   _____   **f.** They are stained.   _____

2. Look in your dictionary. Match the opposites.

    _5_ **a.** big   **1.** plain

    ___ **b.** fancy   **2.** wide

    ___ **c.** heavy   **3.** long

    ___ **d.** loose   **4.** tight

    ___ **e.** narrow   **5.** small

    ___ **f.** high   **6.** print

    ___ **g.** short   **7.** low

    ___ **h.** solid   **8.** light

3. Look at the picture. Describe the problems.

    a. His jeans are too ____*baggy*____ and too _____.

    b. His sweater is too _____ and the sleeves are _____.

    c. His jacket sleeve is _____ and a button _____.

4. Look at the order form. Circle the words to complete the statements.

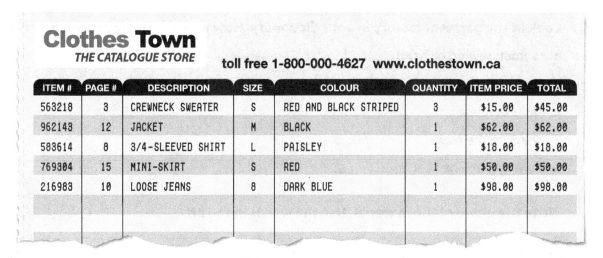

Clothes Town
THE CATALOGUE STORE   toll free 1-800-000-4627 www.clothestown.ca

ITEM #	PAGE #	DESCRIPTION	SIZE	COLOUR	QUANTITY	ITEM PRICE	TOTAL
563218	3	CREWNECK SWEATER	S	RED AND BLACK STRIPED	3	$15.00	$45.00
962143	12	JACKET	M	BLACK	1	$62.00	$62.00
583614	8	3/4-SLEEVED SHIRT	L	PAISLEY	1	$18.00	$18.00
769304	15	MINI-SKIRT	S	RED	1	$50.00	$50.00
216983	10	LOOSE JEANS	8	DARK BLUE	1	$98.00	$98.00

a. The customer wants extra-small / **small** crewneck sweaters.

b. She's ordering a long / large paisley shirt.

c. It's a 3/4-sleeved / sleeveless shirt.

d. She also wants a plaid / medium jacket.

e. The skirt is short / long.

f. The jeans are expensive / tight.

5. What about you? Look at the ad. Choose two items to order. Add them to the order form in Exercise 4.

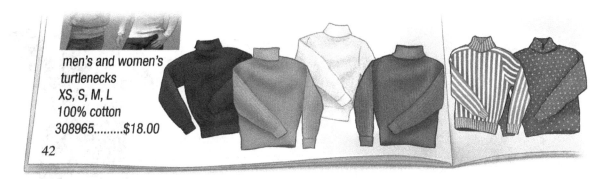

men's and women's
turtlenecks
XS, S, M, L
100% cotton
308965.........$18.00

42

6. What about you? Describe a problem you have or had with your clothes.

Example: *My jacket zipper is broken.*

_____

Challenge Describe the clothes you are wearing today. Include the colour, style, and pattern.
Example: *I'm wearing tight black jeans, a red and white striped shirt, and a light jacket.*

1. Look at the garment factory in your dictionary. How many of the following are there?

    a. women sewing by hand   _1_

    b. women sewing by machine   ____

    c. bolts of fabric   ____

    d. shirts on the rack   ____

    e. sewing machine needles   ____

2. Write the name of the material. Use the words in the box.

cotton	~~cashmere~~	leather	linen	silk	wool

a. ____cashmere____   **b.** _____   **c.** _____

d. _____   **e.** _____   **f.** _____

3. What about you? What materials are you wearing today? Write three sentences.

    Example: *I'm wearing a cotton sweater.*

    _____

    _____

    _____

4. Look in your dictionary. Cross out the word that doesn't belong.

a. Closures	zipper	snap	buckle	~~ribbon~~
b. Trim	thread	sequins	fringe	beads
c. Material	cashmere	pattern	leather	nylon
d. Sewing machine parts	bobbin	rack	needle	feed dog

5. Look at the picture. Circle the words to complete the sentences.

Vilma is wearing a (denim) / wool jacket with buttons / snaps. Her jacket has beautiful
               a.   **b.**

appliqués / sequins on it. Her husband, Enrique, is wearing a corduroy / suede jacket with
            c.   **d.**

fringe / ribbon. It's cold outside, but his jacket buckle / zipper is open. Their daughter,
   e.   **f.**

Rosa, is wearing a lace /velvet jacket with beads / thread. Her jacket is closed with
              g.   **h.**

hooks and eyes / buttons.
     i.

6. What about you? What type of closures do your clothes have?

Example: *My shirt has buttons. My jeans have a zipper.*

Challenge Look at pages 86 and 87 in your dictionary. Describe two people's clothing. Include the fabric, material, closures, and trim. **Example:** *One man is wearing blue denim jeans with a zipper and button, a light blue cotton shirt with buttons, and brown leather loafers.*

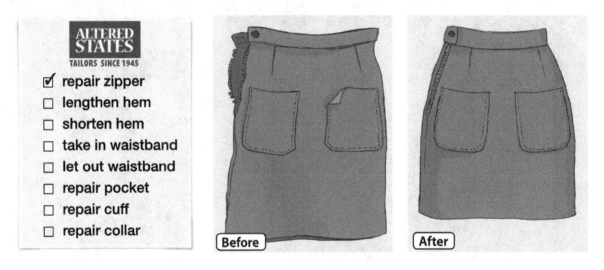

Making Alterations

1. Look in your dictionary. Who is doing the following things? Check (✓) the answers.

	Dressmaker	Tailor
a. working in the alterations shop	✓	✓
b. working on a dress	☐	☐
c. using a sewing machine	☐	☐
d. using a dummy	☐	☐
e. using a tape measure	☐	☐
f. using thread	☐	☐

2. Look at the pictures. Check (✓) the alterations the tailor made.

ALTERED STATES
TAILORS SINCE 1945

- ☑ repair zipper
- ☐ lengthen hem
- ☐ shorten hem
- ☐ take in waistband
- ☐ let out waistband
- ☐ repair pocket
- ☐ repair cuff
- ☐ repair collar

Before

After

3. List the items in the sewing basket.

tape measure _____ _____

_____ _____

_____ _____

_____ _____

_____

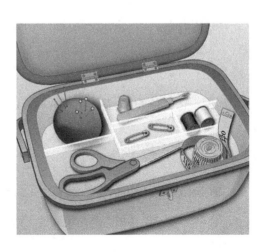

Challenge Look at the boy on page 96 of this workbook. What alterations do his clothes need? Discuss them with a classmate. **Example:** *He needs to shorten his pants.*

1. Look in your dictionary. Where are the following things? Use _in_ or _on_ in your answers.

    a. iron   _on the ironing board_

    b. fabric softener   _____

    c. spray starch   _____

    d. wet polo shirt   _____

    e. laundry   _____

    f. clothespins   _____

2. Look at the pictures. Write the instructions. Use the sentences in the box.

Clean the lint trap.	Fold the laundry.	Unload the washer.
~~Sort the laundry.~~	Load the washer.	Add the detergent.

a.   _Sort the laundry._   **b.** _____   **c.** _____

d. _____   **e.** _____   **f.** _____

3. What about you? Do you do the laundry in your family? Check (✓) the items you use.

☐ iron   ☐ hanger   ☐ clothespins

☐ ironing board   ☐ spray starch   ☐ dryer sheets

☐ clothesline   ☐ fabric softener   ☐ bleach

Challenge Which clothes do you iron? Which clothes do you hang up?

1. **Look in your dictionary. *True* or *False*?**

   a. You can buy new clothing at the garage sale.   _____*false*_____

   b. The flyer has information about the prices.   _____

   c. A woman is bargaining for an orange sweatshirt.   _____

   d. The sweatshirt has a blue sticker on it.   _____

   e. She buys the sweatshirt for 75 cents.   _____

   f. Some customers are browsing.   _____

   g. You can buy the folding card table and folding chair.   _____

   h. The VCR is new.   _____

   i. A customer buys the clock radio.   _____

2. **Look at the price list and the item stickers. Complete the sentences.**

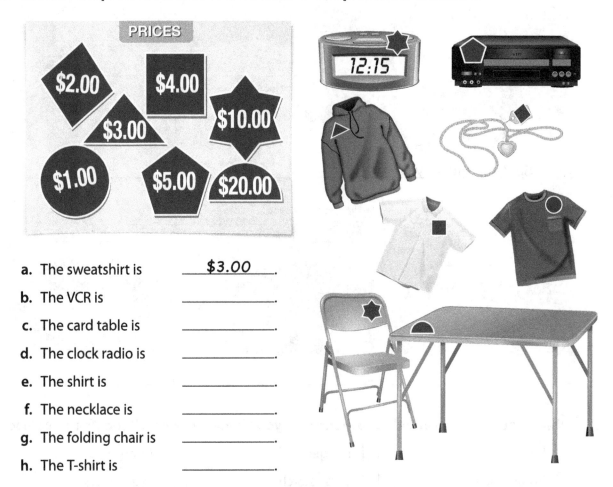

   a. The sweatshirt is   _____$3.00_____.

   b. The VCR is   _____.

   c. The card table is   _____.

   d. The clock radio is   _____.

   e. The shirt is   _____.

   f. The necklace is   _____.

   g. The folding chair is   _____.

   h. The T-shirt is   _____.

3. **What about you? Look in your dictionary. Imagine you are at the garage sale. What will you buy? What price do you want to pay for it? Tell a partner.**

4. Look in your dictionary. Check (✓) the items you can buy at the garage sale.

☐ belt	☐ socks	☐ necklace
✓ books	☐ sports jacket	☐ sewing machine
☐ bracelet	☐ straw hat	☐ shoes
☐ briefcase	☐ necklace	☐ sweatshirt
☐ clock radio	☐ hard hat	☐ T-shirt
☐ folding card table	☐ ironing board	☐ VCR
☐ purse	☐ jeans	☐ pin cushion

5. Complete the flyer. Use the words in the box.

bargain	browse	clock radios	folding card tables	folding chairs
~~Garage Sale~~	sweatshirts	sticker	Used Clothing	VCRs

We're having a ___Garage Sale___ !
a.

63 Elm Street
Saturday, September 22
Noon–5 p.m.

Come and _____ ! It's free to look!
b.

_____   Electronics   Furniture
c.

sweaters   _____   _____
                  d.   **f.**

jeans   _____   _____
                  e.   **g.**

_____
h.

See something you want? Each item has a coloured

_____ , but you can _____ !
     i.   **j.**

Challenge Work with a partner. Imagine you are going to have a garage sale. What items will you sell? Make a flyer. Use the flyer in Exercise 5 as an example.

1. Look in your dictionary. How many of the following do you see?

a. heads _11_

b. feet ___

c. hands ___

d. backs ___

e. eyes ___

f. ears ___

g. shoulders ___

2. Look at the pictures. Where on the body do you find them? Match.

1.

2.

3.

4.

5.

6.

7.

8.

___ a. hair

___ b. neck

___ c. feet

___ d. ears

___ e. eyes

___ f. nose

_1_ g. hands

___ h. finger

3. **How many of the following body parts do people usually have?**

a. People have _____ fingers.

b. People have _____ eyes.

c. People have _____ nose.

d. People have _____ arms.

e. People have _____ head.

f. People have _____ ears.

g. People have _____ toes.

h. People have _____ mouth.

4. **Look at the medical chart.** *True* or *False*?

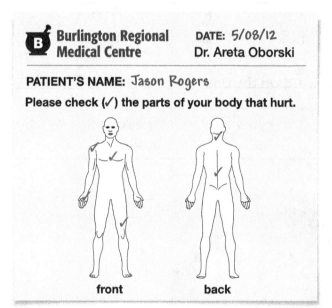

a. Jason's head hurts. _____ *false* _____

b. His right hand hurts. _____

c. His left shoulder hurts. _____

d. He has a pain in his neck. _____

e. His leg hurts. _____

f. He has a pain in his chest. _____

g. His back hurts. _____

Challenge Which parts of the body do these doctors help? Look online or ask a classmate.

podiatrist _____ ophthalmologist _____ chiropractor _____

105

1. Look in your dictionary. Cross out the word that doesn't belong.

a. **The face**	forehead	jaw	chin	~~toe~~
b. **Inside the body**	liver	intestines	abdomen	stomach
c. **The leg and foot**	knee	heel	ankle	tongue
d. **The skeleton**	pelvis	brain	skull	rib cage
e. **The hand**	thumb	shin	palm	wrist
f. **The senses**	taste	hear	lip	smell

2. Label the parts of the face. Use the words in the box.

eyebrow	eyelashes	eyelid	cheek	chin
~~forehead~~	jaw	lip	teeth	

a. ___forehead___

b. _____

c. _____

d. _____

e. _____

f. _____

g. _____

h. _____

i. _____

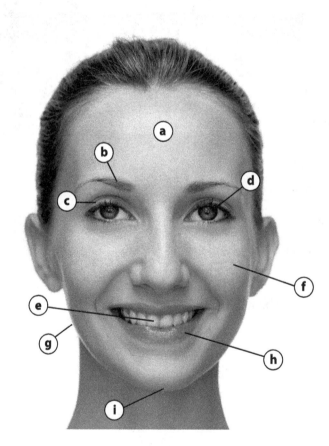

3. **Look at the picture. Check (✓) the parts of the body that are NOT covered by clothes.**

✓	arms	☐	buttocks
☐	calves	☐	chest
☐	elbows	☐	fingers
☐	feet	☐	forearms
☐	hands	☐	head
☐	knees	☐	legs
☐	lower back	☐	shins
☐	shoulder blades	☐	jaw

4. **Match.**

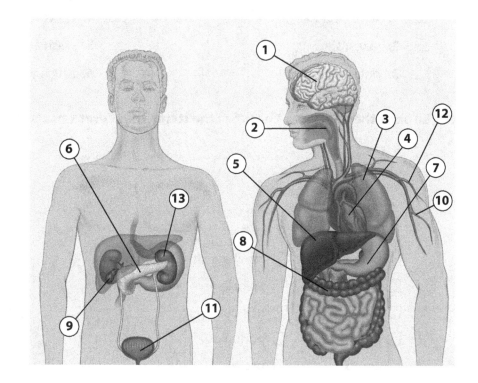

_4_ **a.** heart

___ **b.** kidney

___ **c.** lung

___ **d.** liver

___ **e.** gallbladder

___ **f.** bladder

___ **g.** throat

___ **h.** stomach

___ **i.** pancreas

___ **j.** brain

___ **k.** intestines

___ **l.** artery

___ **m.** vein

5. **What about you? <u>Underline</u> the words for parts of the body that are NOT OK for men to show on the street in your native country. Circle the words for parts of the body that are NOT OK for women to show.**

arms	abdomen	elbows	face	mouth
ankles	chest	knees	calves	feet

Challenge Choose five parts of the body. What are their functions?
Example: *brain—We use it to think.*

1. Look in your dictionary. Cross out the word that doesn't belong.

a. shower cap	soap	~~hairspray~~	bath powder
b. electric shaver	razorblades	aftershave	sunscreen
c. hair clip	emery board	nail polish	nail clipper
d. barrettes	eyebrow pencil	bobby pins	hair gel
e. blush	foundation	eyeliner	deodorant
f. body lotion	shampoo	blow dryer	conditioner
g. toothbrush	comb	dental floss	toothpaste

2. Look at Exercise 1. Write the letter of the items that you need for these activities.

_d_ **1.** style your hair   ___ **4.** shave

___ **2.** take a shower   ___ **5.** wash and dry your hair

___ **3.** put on makeup   ___ **6.** brush your teeth

3. Look at the checklist. Check (✓) the items that Teresa packed.

Travel Packing List

to pack for _Vancouver_

☑ bath powder	☐ mouthwash
☐ blow dryer	☐ nail clipper
☐ bobby pins	☐ nail polish
☐ brush	☐ perfume
☐ comb	☐ razor
☐ conditioner	☐ shampoo
☐ curling iron	☐ shaving cream
☐ dental floss	☐ shower cap
☐ deodorant	☐ soap
☐ emery board	☐ sunscreen
☐ lipstick	☐ toothbrush
☐ mascara	☐ toothpaste

4. Teresa is at the hotel. Go back to the checklist in Exercise 3. Check (✓) the additional items that Teresa has now.

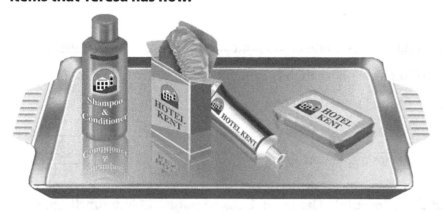

5. What does Teresa still need? Complete her shopping list.

HOTEL KENT

TO BUY

bobby pins

_____

_____

_____

_____

_____

6. What about you? How often do you use the following products? Check (✓) the columns.

	Every Day	Sometimes	Never
sunblock			
shower gel			
perfume or cologne			
hairspray			
dental floss			
body lotion or moisturizer			
mouthwash			
Other: _____			

Challenge List the personal hygiene items you take with you when you travel.

See page 285 for listening practice.

1. Look in your dictionary. *True* or *False*?

a. The man in picture 11 has an insect bite on his right arm.   <u>   true   </u>

b. The man in picture 13 has a cut on his thumb.   <u>   </u>

c. The man in picture 15 has a blister on his hand.   <u>   </u>

d. The woman in picture 16 has a swollen toe.   <u>   </u>

e. The woman in picture 18 has a sprained ankle.   <u>   </u>

2. Look at Tania's medicine. Complete the form. Look at page 113 in your dictionary for help.

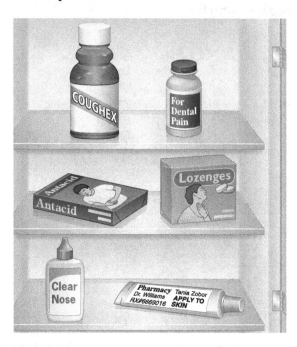

DATE: 3/5/12

PATIENT'S NAME: Tania Zobor

Please check (✓) all your symptoms.

I OFTEN GET. . . .

☐ headaches	☐ sore throats
☐ earaches	☐ nasal congestion
☑ toothaches	☐ fevers
☐ stomach aches	☐ bruises
☐ backaches	☐ rashes
☐ bloody noses	☐ chills

I OFTEN. . . .

☐ cough   ☐ feel nauseous   ☐ vomit

☐ sneeze   ☐ feel dizzy

3. What about you? Complete the form. Use your own information or information about someone you know.

PATIENT'S NAME: _____   Please check (✓) all your symptoms.

I OFTEN GET. . . .			I OFTEN. . . .	
☐ headaches	☐ backaches	☐ fevers	☐ cough	☐ feel dizzy
☐ earaches	☐ bloody noses	☐ bruises	☐ sneeze	☐ vomit
☐ toothaches	☐ sore throats	☐ rashes	☐ feel nauseous	
☐ stomach aches	☐ nasal congestion	☐ chills		

Challenge Choose four health problems in Exercise 3. What can you do for them? Look at page 113 in your dictionary for help. **Example:** *headaches—Take pain reliever.*

1. **Look at the bottom picture in your dictionary. Write the illness or medical condition.**

    a. lungs   _____TB_____ and _____

    b. heart and arteries   _____ and _____

    c. pancreas   _____

    d. brain   _____

    e. blood   _____

2. **Look at the photos of Mehmet when he was a child. Complete the form.**

Nov. 1961   Jan. 1963   Dec. 1969   May 1974

EDG EARLY DIAGNOSIS CENTRE   NAME: _Mehmet Caner_   DATE OF BIRTH: _April 18, 1959_

CHECK (✓) THE ILLNESSES OR CONDITIONS YOU HAD AS A CHILD.

☐ DIABETES	☐ CHICKEN POX	☐ MUMPS
☐ INTESTINAL PARASITES	☐ ASTHMA	☐ ALLERGIES
☑ EAR INFECTIONS	☐ STREP THROAT	

3. **What about you? Complete the form. Use your own information or information about someone you know.**

EDG EARLY DIAGNOSIS CENTRE   NAME: DATE OF BIRTH:

CHECK (✓) THE ILLNESSES OR CONDITIONS YOU HAD AS A CHILD.

☐ DIABETES	☐ CHICKEN POX	☐ MUMPS
☐ INTESTINAL PARASITES	☐ ASTHMA	☐ ALLERGIES
☐ EAR INFECTIONS	☐ STREP THROAT	

Challenge List the things you do when you have a cold or flu. **Example:** _drink hot water with lemon_

1. Look in your dictionary. *True* or *False?* **Correct the** <u>underlined</u> **words in the false sentences.**

prescription medication

a. The pharmacist is giving a customer <u>a ~~prescription~~</u>.   *false*

b. The humidifier is above the <u>heating pad</u>.   _____

c. The <u>hot water bottle</u> is next to the air purifier.   _____

d. There is a pair of crutches and three <u>wheelchairs</u>.   _____

e. A customer is wearing a sling and <u>a cast</u>.   _____

2. Complete the medical warning labels. Use the sentences in the box.

> Take with dairy products.   Do not take with dairy products.   Finish all medication.
> ~~Do not drive or operate heavy machinery.~~   Take with food or milk.   Do not drink alcohol.

a.

Do not drive or operate
heavy machinery.
when taking this medicine

b.

_____
_____

c.

_____
_____

d.

IMPORTANT

_____
_____

e.

_____

f.

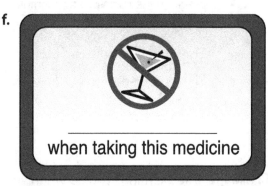

_____
when taking this medicine

3. **Look at the picture. Circle the words to complete the sentences.**

a. Brian got over-the-counter /(prescription)
   medication.

b. The name of the pharmacist / pharmacy
   is Duggen Drugs.

c. The bottle contains capsules / tablets.

d. The prescription number is 20 / 639180.

e. The prescription / warning label says,
   "Do not take with dairy products."

f. Brian can't drink water / eat cheese
   with this medicine.

g. The medicine isn't good after
   September 2010 / March 2011.

h. The dosage is two / four capsules every day.

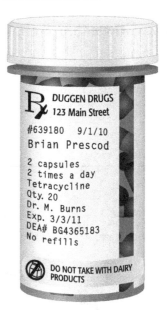

4. **What about you? Check (✓) the items you think are in your medicine cabinet.**
   Then, check your answers at home.

- [ ] pain reliever
- [ ] cold tablets
- [ ] antacid
- [ ] cream
- [ ] cough syrup
- [ ] throat lozenges
- [ ] nasal spray
- [ ] ointment
- [ ] eye drops
- [ ] vitamins

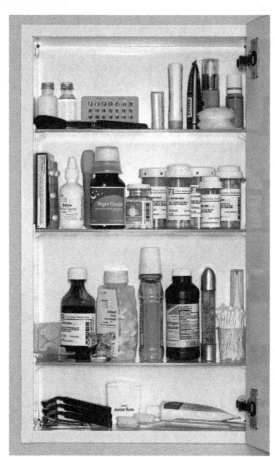

Challenge Look at some prescription or over-the-counter medications in your medicine cabinet.
What's the dosage? The expiration date? Is there a warning label? Make a list.

See page 287 for listening practice.

1. Look in your dictionary. Complete the poster.

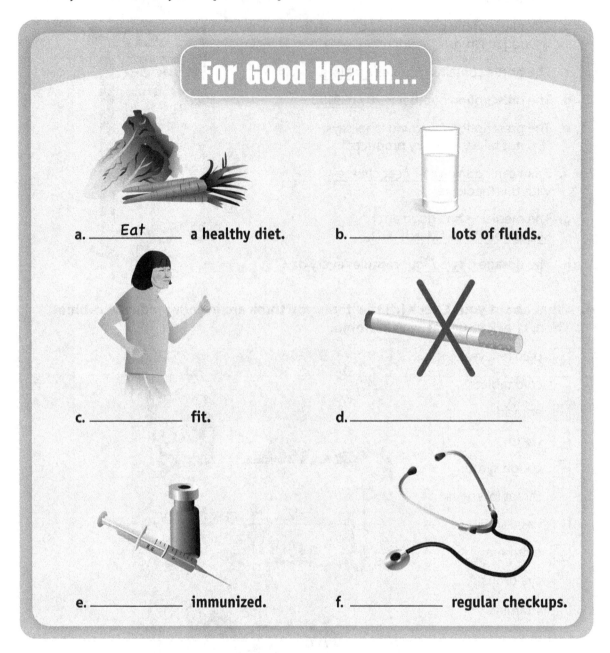

For Good Health...

a. ___Eat___ a healthy diet.

b. _____ lots of fluids.

c. _____ fit.

d. _____

e. _____ immunized.

f. _____ regular checkups.

2. Look at the doctor's notes. *True* or *False*?

a. The patient sought* medical attention. ___true___

b. The patient should get bed rest. _____

c. She doesn't need to take medicine. _____

d. She must stop smoking. _____

e. She should drink more fluids. _____

*sought = past tense of *seek*

From the desk of Dr. Mary Burns

Stay in bed.

Fill prescription for antibiotics.

Drink a lot of water or juice.

NO more smoking!!

Call for Appointment in __2 weeks__.

3. Look in your dictionary. Complete the chart.

Problem	Doctor	Help
a. vision problems		glasses or contact lenses
b.		hearing aid
c. stress or		talk therapy or
d. knee pain		

4. Match.

_7_ **a.** I see my doctor every January.

____ **b.** I'd like some more vegetables, please.

____ **c.** I exercise every day.

____ **d.** No cigarettes for me, thanks.

____ **e.** I always get a flu vaccination.

____ **f.** I'll have another glass of water, please.

____ **g.** I need to see the doctor today.

____ **h.** It's time for my pills.

1. Eat a healthy diet.

2. Seek medical attention.

3. Get immunized.

4. Don't smoke.

5. Take medicine

6. Drink fluids.

7. Have regular checkups.

8. Stay fit.

5. What about you? Check (✓) the things you do. Explain.

Example: *stay fit—I exercise four times a week.*

☐ stay fit _____

☐ eat a healthy diet _____

☐ get immunized _____

☐ drink fluids _____

☐ have regular checkups _____

☐ follow medical advice _____

☐ Other: _____

Challenge List three other kinds of doctors. What problems do they treat?
Example: *orthopedist—for problems with bones*

See page 288 for listening practice.

1. Look in your dictionary. *True* or *False*?

a. A paramedic is helping an unconscious woman.   _____true_____

b. The woman in the red sweater is in shock.   _____

c. The man near the bookcase is hurt.   _____

d. The boy in the dark blue shirt is having an allergic reaction.   _____

e. The child in the swimming pool is getting frostbite.   _____

f. The woman at the table is choking.   _____

g. The boy in the doctor's office broke a leg.   _____

h. The man holding his chest is having a heart attack.   _____

2. Look at the chart. How did the people injure themselves? Circle the words.

Number of Injuries in Canada in a Year		
Product	**Estimated Injuries**	**People probably . . . .**
a. Stairs	207, 404	had an allergic reaction / fell
b. Bikes	53,510	overdosed / fell
c. Bathtubs / Showers	30,488	broke bones / got frostbite
d. TVs	5,347	were in shock / got an electric shock
e. Razors	3,661	bled / couldn't breathe
f. Stoves / Ovens	4,335	burned themselves / choked
g. Irons	1,281	drowned / burned themselves

3. What about you? Check (✓) the emergencies that have happened to you. When or where did they happen?

Emergency   When or Where

☐ I had an allergic reaction to _____.   _____

☐ I fell.   _____

☐ I broke my _____.   _____

☐ Other: _____.   _____

Challenge Write a paragraph about an emergency from Exercise 3. What treatment did you (or someone you know) get? Look at page 117 in your dictionary for help.

1. **Look in your dictionary. Write the first aid item for these conditions.**

   a. rash on hand   <u>antihistamine cream</u>

   b. broken finger   _____

   c. swollen foot   _____ or _____

   d. infected cut   _____ or _____

2. **Look at Chen's first aid kit. Check (✓) the items he has.**

   ⊕ FAMILY FIRST AID AND EMERGENCY PREPAREDNESS

☑ adhesive bandages	☐ first aid manual
☐ antihistamine cream	☐ antibacterial ointment
☐ elastic bandage	☐ hydrogen peroxide
☐ splint	☐ ice pack
☐ sterile pad	☐ sterile tape
☐ gauze	☐ tweezers

3. **What about you? Check (✓) the first aid items you have at home. Then, check (✓) the things you can do.**

At home I have	
☐ adhesive bandages	☐ first aid manual
☐ antihistamine cream	☐ antibacterial ointment
☐ elastic bandages	☐ hydrogen peroxide
☐ splints	☐ ice packs
☐ sterile pads	☐ sterile tape
☐ gauze	☐ tweezers

I can do . . . .
☐ CPR
☐ rescue breathing
☐ the Heimlich manoeuvre

Challenge Look at the items in Exercise 3. What can you use them for?
         Example: _adhesive bandages—cuts_

1. Look in your dictionary. Who is doing the following things? Check (✓) the columns.

	Patient	Receptionist	Doctor	Nurse
a. going to an appointment	✓			
b. checking blood pressure				
c. holding a thermometer				
d. examining the throat				
e. holding a health card				
f. sitting on the examination table				
g. holding a health history form				
h. using a stethoscope				

2. Look at the doctor's notes. Which medical instrument did the doctor use? Match.

	Dr. D. Ngoc Huynh

MEDICAL CENTER

DATE: 3/5/12

PATIENT'S NAME: Carla Vega

1. checked BP—120/80
2. took temp.— 37°C
3. listened to lungs—clear
4. gave flu immunization

___4___ **a.** syringe

_____ **b.** thermometer

_____ **c.** blood pressure gauge

_____ **d.** stethoscope

3. What about you? Think of the last time you saw the doctor. How long were you . . .

in the waiting room? _____

in the examining room? _____

on the examination table? _____

Did the doctor or nurse do the following? Check (✓) the answers.

☐ check your blood pressure ☐ draw blood

☐ examine your eyes ☐ take your temperature

Challenge Find out about health insurance in other countries. Which countries have national health insurance? Who can get it?

1. Circle the words to complete the sentences.

a. (A dental assistant)/ An orthodontist helps the dentist.

b. A dental hygienist uses <u>dental instruments / fillings</u> to clean teeth.

c. <u>An orthodontist / A dentist</u> gives people braces.

d. <u>A crown / Plaque</u> causes gum disease.

e. The dentist takes X-rays to help find <u>cavities / dentures</u>.

f. The dentist uses a syringe to <u>drill a tooth / numb the mouth</u>.

g. The dentist numbs your mouth before <u>taking X-rays / pulling a tooth</u>.

2. Label the pictures. Use the words in the box.

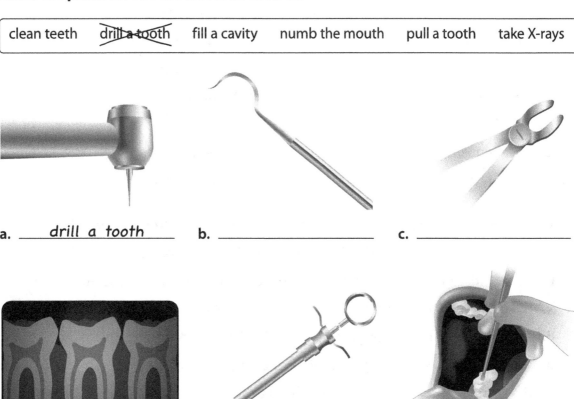

| clean teeth | ~~drill a tooth~~ | fill a cavity | numb the mouth | pull a tooth | take X-rays |

a. ____drill a tooth____   b. _____   c. _____

d. _____   e. _____   f. _____

Challenge How can you try to prevent gum disease? Write three sentences.
Example: *Go to the dentist two times a year.*

119

1. Look in your dictionary. Match.

_5_ **a.** general health problems

___ **b.** heart

___ **c.** cancer

___ **d.** depression

___ **e.** eyes

___ **f.** children

___ **g.** pregnant women

___ **h.** X-rays

1. radiologist

2. oncologist

3. ophthalmologist

4. psychiatrist

5. internist

6. pediatrician

7. cardiologist

8. obstetrician

2. Circle the words to complete the sentences. Use your dictionary for help.

a. The internist / (surgical nurse) helps the surgeon during an operation.

b. The anesthesiologist / radiologist makes the patient "sleep" on the operating table.

c. The paramedic / pediatrician takes the patient out of the ambulance.

d. The oncologist / phlebotomist takes the patient's blood for blood tests.

e. The admissions clerk / volunteer works in the hospital for no pay.

f. The nursing assistant / dietician plans the patient's food.

g. The administrator / orderly takes the patient from place to place.

h. The registered nurse / surgical nurse checks the patient's IV.

i. The registered practical nurse / phlebotomist takes the patient's blood pressure.

3. Write the full forms. Use your dictionary for help.

a. IV _____intravenous drip_____ **b.** RPN _____

c. RN _____

4. **Look at the hospital room in your dictionary. *True* or *False*?**

   a. The patient is on a stretcher.   _____false_____

   b. There's a bedpan near the bed.   _____

   c. The volunteer is carrying medication.   _____

   d. The nurse is wearing a hospital gown.   _____

   e. There's medication on the over-bed table.   _____

   f. The vital signs monitor is near the hospital bed.   _____

   g. The patient is using the call button now.   _____

5. **Look at the picture and the supply list. Match.**

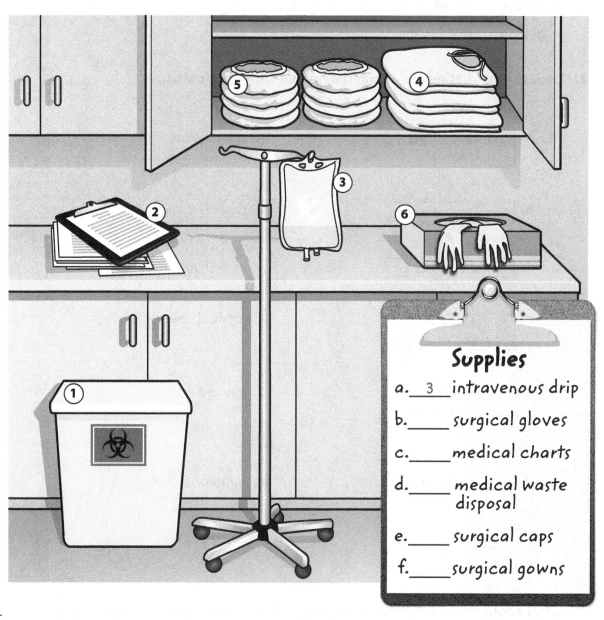

Supplies

a. __3__ intravenous drip

b. _____ surgical gloves

c. _____ medical charts

d. _____ medical waste disposal

e. _____ surgical caps

f. _____ surgical gowns

Challenge Find out the names of an internist, an ophthalmologist, and a pediatrician in your community. Make a list.

1. **Look in your dictionary. How many people are doing the following things? Write the number.**

   a. doing aerobic exercise   _4_

   b. doing yoga now   ___

   c. getting acupuncture   ___

   d. waiting to get a free eye exam   ___

   e. listening to the nutrition lecture   ___

   f. taking people's blood pressure   ___

   g. watching the Healthy Cooking demonstration   ___

   h. getting a medical exam   ___

2. **Look in your dictionary. Match the people with the booths.**

   Booth

   _4_ a. Do I have high blood pressure?   1. acupuncture

   ___ b. I need more vitamin D.   2. Healthy Cooking

   ___ c. How is my vision?   3. Good Foods Market

   ___ d. I need to eat sugar-free food.   4. medical screenings

   ___ e. I don't really understand nutrition labels.   5. free eye exam

   ___ f. I get a lot of headaches.   6. nutrition lecture

   ___ g. I need to relax.   7. Hatha yoga

3. **What about you? Look in your dictionary. Imagine you are at the health fair. Where will you go? Why? Tell a partner.**

4. Look in your dictionary. *True* or *False*? Correct the underlined words in the false sentences.

                clinic

a. The health fair is at a ~~hospital~~.   _____*false*_____

b. A nurse is checking a woman's <u>temperature</u>.   _____

c. People pay $5.00 for <u>a medical screening</u>.   _____

d. Four people are doing <u>yoga</u>.   _____

e. They sell <u>sugar-free</u> food at Healthy Cooking.   _____

f. The woman in line at the eye exam booth uses a <u>walker</u>.   _____

g. The acupuncture doctor is going to put a needle in the man's <u>hand</u>.   _____

5. Complete the flyer. Use the words in the box.

Acupuncture	aerobic exercise	demonstration	Health Clinic	Free
~~Health Fair~~	lecture	medical	nurse	
nutrition label	pulse	Sugar-free	yoga	

Fadool _Health Fair_
                         a.

_____ SCREENINGS
     b.

(A _____ will check your BLOOD PRESSURE and your _____.)
       c.   **d.**

_____ EYE EXAMS ($0 !!!) and there are _____ treatments.
     e.   **f.**

Free _____ : "What does that _____ really mean?"
        g.   **h.**

_____ cooking _____ at Healthy Cooking (Free samples!)
    i.   **j.**

Do _____ to DANCE MUSIC. Then STRETCH AND RELAX
      k.

with hatha _____.
         l.

When: Saturday, July 10, 9:00 – 4:00   **Where: Fadool** _____
                                                                        m.

Challenge Look at three nutrition labels. How much sugar does the food have? How much salt?
          Example: *La Rosa spaghetti sauce has 6 grams of sugar and 310 milligrams of salt in a half-cup serving.*

1. Look at page 124 in your dictionary. *True* or *False*?

a. The parking garage is next to the office building. _____ true _____

b. The bank is on the corner of Main and Grand. _____

c. The driver licensing office is on 5th Street. _____

d. There's a bus station across from the hotel. _____

e. There's a clock on the city hall building. _____

2. Match.

_3_ a.
| I'm taking the 5:10 to Edmonton. |

1. hotel

___ b.
| We need to get a marriage licence. |

2. office building

___ c.
| We'd like a room for two nights. |

3. bus station

___ d.
| I work on the fifth floor. |

4. parking garage

___ e.
| I need to deposit this check. |

5. driver licensing office

___ f.
| My car is on the second level. |

6. bank

___ g.
| I want to get a driver's licence. |

7. city hall

3. What about you? Write the street locations for these places in your community.

bus station _____ Elm and West 10th Street _____

bank _____

office building _____

city hall _____

4. Look in your dictionary. Complete the sentences.

a. The _____ *hospital* _____ is on 6th Street.

b. The _____ is next to the fire station.

c. There's a Chinese _____ on Main Street.

d. The _____ is on the corner of Main and Grand Avenue.

e. The _____ is to the right of the restaurant.

f. There's a _____ across from the hospital.

5. Look at the pictures. Where should the people go? Use the words in the box.

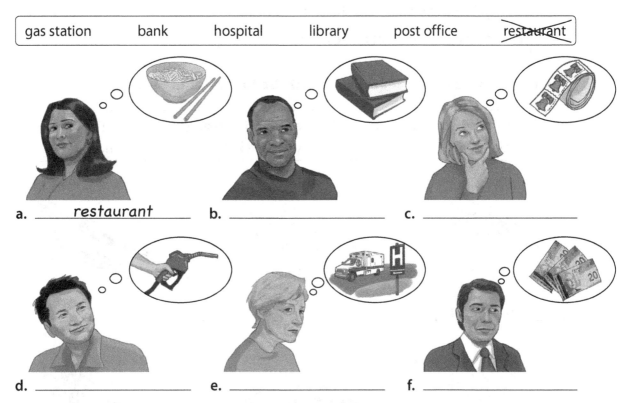

| gas station | bank | hospital | library | post office | ~~restaurant~~ |

a. _____ *restaurant* _____   b. _____   c. _____

d. _____   e. _____   f. _____

6. What about you? How often do you go to the following places? Check (✓) the columns.

	Often	Sometimes	Never
gas station			
library			
post office			
hospital			
courthouse			

Challenge Look in your dictionary. Choose four places. Why do you go there? Write sentences.
Example: *I go to the post office to buy stamps.*

1. **Look in your dictionary. Circle the words to complete the sentences.**

   a. There's a (furniture store) / coffee shop on Second and Oak.

   b. There's a <u>school / factory</u> on Third near Elm.

   c. The <u>mosque / synagogue</u> is on Second and Oak.

   d. There's a <u>car dealership / construction site</u> on Oak and First.

   e. The garbage truck is in front of the <u>home improvement store / office supply store</u>.

   f. The shopping mall is next to the <u>movie theatre / theatre</u>.

   g. There's a <u>bakery / cemetery</u> near the church.

   h. There are two people in front of the <u>bakery / gym</u>.

2. **Where do you go for the following items? Use the words in the box.**

home improvement store	car dealership	~~coffee shop~~	furniture store gym
office supply store	movie theatre	bakery	shopping mall

a. ___coffee shop___   b. _____   c. _____

d. _____   e. _____   f. _____

g. _____   h. _____   i. _____

3. Look at the map. Complete the notes.

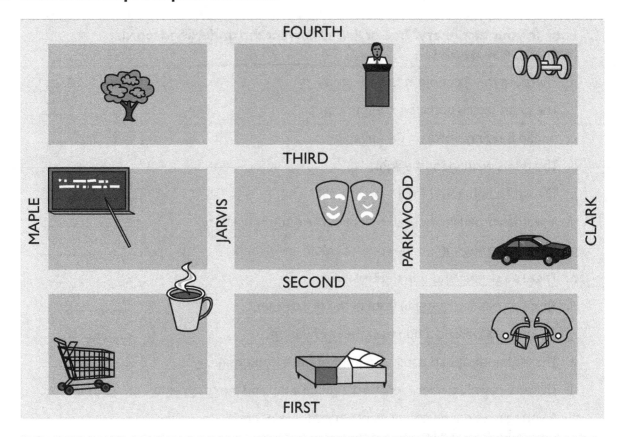

LOCATIONS

a. gym _____Fourth and Clark_____

b. theatre _____

c. stadium _____

d. convention centre _____

e. community college _____

f. car dealership _____

g. supermarket _____

h. coffee shop _____

i. motel _____

4. What about you? Does your community have the following places? Check (✓) the boxes.

☐ a stadium

☐ a movie theatre

☐ a convention centre

☐ skyscrapers

☐ factories

☐ a motel

☐ a community college

☐ a cemetery

Challenge Draw a street map of an area you know. Use some of the places in Exercises 2, 3, and 4.

See page 291 for listening practice.

An Intersection

1. **Look in your dictionary. *True* or *False*? Correct the underlined words in the false sentences.**

   a. There are ~~three~~ *two* people at the bus stop.   <u> *false* </u>

   b. The pharmacy is open <u>twenty-four</u> hours.   _____

   c. A man is riding a bike on <u>Green Street</u>.   _____

   d. The <u>bus</u> is waiting for the light.   _____

   e. The traffic light is <u>red</u> for the orange car.   _____

   f. A woman is parking her car in front of the <u>doughnut shop</u>.   _____

   g. There's a <u>street sign</u> on the corner of Main and Green.   _____

   h. There's a <u>street vendor</u> in the crosswalk.   _____

   i. There's a parking <u>meter</u> in front of the dry cleaners.   _____

   j. A woman is walking a dog near the <u>fire hydrant</u>.   _____

   k. There's handicapped parking in front of the <u>laundromat</u>.   _____

   l. There's a pay phone between the doughnut shop and the <u>copy centre</u>. _____

   m. A young man on the corner wants to cross Main Street. He's <u>waiting for the light</u>.   _____

2. **Match.**

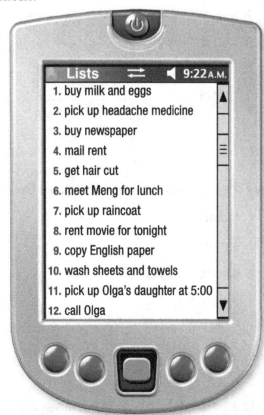

     ___ **a.** video store

     ___ **b.** pay phone

     ___ **c.** dry cleaners

     ___ **d.** copy centre

     ___ **e.** pharmacy

     ___ **f.** childcare centre

     ___ **g.** laundromat

     _1_ **h.** convenience store

     ___ **i.** barbershop

     ___ **j.** fast-food restaurant

     ___ **k.** newsstand

     ___ **l.** mailbox

Lists ⇄ 🔊 9:22 A.M.
1. buy milk and eggs
2. pick up headache medicine
3. buy newspaper
4. mail rent
5. get hair cut
6. meet Meng for lunch
7. pick up raincoat
8. rent movie for tonight
9. copy English paper
10. wash sheets and towels
11. pick up Olga's daughter at 5:00
12. call Olga

3. Cross out the word that doesn't belong.

a. **People** — pedestrian — street vendor — ~~corner~~

b. **Stores** — doughnut shop — mailbox — pharmacy

c. **Services for clothes** — street sign — laundromat — dry cleaners

d. **Transportation** — drive-through window — bus — bike

e. **Parts of the street** — curb — sidewalk — cart

f. **Things you put coins in** — pay phone — parking meter — fire hydrant

g. **Things that move** — bus — cart — crosswalk

4. Write the location of these signs.

a. _laundromat_

b. _____

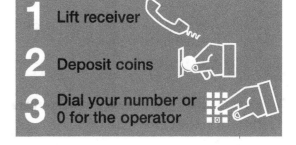

c. _____

d. _____

e. _____

f. _____

Challenge Look in your dictionary. Write the locations of five stores. **Example:** *The doughnut shop is on the corner of Main and Green.*

See page 292 for listening practice.

A Mall

1. Look in your dictionary. Complete the mall directory. Use the words in the box.

florist	jewellery store	nail salon	food court
travel agency	maternity store	hair salon	candy store
~~cellphone kiosk~~	ice cream shop	optician	~~pet store~~
toy store	electronics store	music store	shoe store

MALL DIRECTORY

	Floor
Department Store	1, 2
Entertainment / Music	
Food	

*Services are stores that do jobs for people or help people.

Services*	Floor
cellphone kiosk	1
Shoes / Accessories	
Specialty Stores	
pet store	1

2. Look at the mall directory in Exercise 1. Where can you buy these items (other than a department store)?

a. _____optician_____

b. _____

c. _____

d. _____

e. _____

f. _____

g. _____

h. _____

i. _____

3. **Look at this mall directory and map. Circle the words to complete the conversations.**

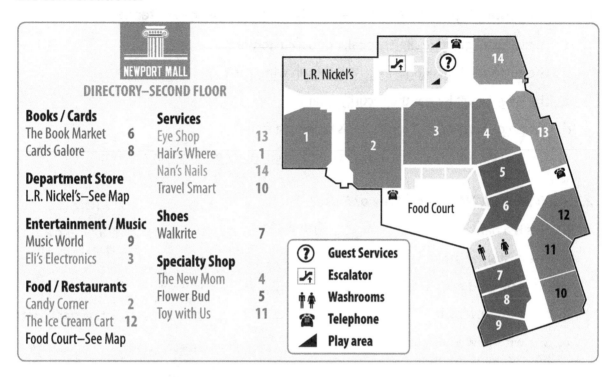

Customer 1: Excuse me. Where's the card store?

Guest Services: It's next to the <u>nail salon /</u> (shoe store.)
a.

Customer 2: Can you tell me where the hair salon is?

Guest Services: Sure. It's across from <u>the department store / guest services</u>.
b.

Customer 3: I'm looking for the <u>elevator / escalator</u>.
c.
Guest Services: It's next to Nickel's.

Customer 4: Hi. Where's the travel agency, please?

Guest Services: It's right over there. Next to the <u>toy / music</u> store.
d.

Customer 5: Excuse me. I'm looking for the candy store.

Guest Services: It's between the <u>music / electronics</u> store and the
e.
<u>hair salon / maternity store</u>.
f.

Customer 6: Excuse me. Is there an optician in this mall?

Guest Services: Yes. There's one across from the <u>florist / bookstore</u>.
g.

Challenge Look at the map in Exercise 3. Write the locations of Flower Bud, The Ice Cream Cart, and Guest Services.

1. Look in your dictionary. Circle the words to complete the sentences.

    a. The security guard / (teller) is speaking to a customer.

    b. The customer is making a deposit / withdrawing cash.

    c. The ATM / vault is near the security guard.

    d. The account manager / customer is holding a form.

    e. The two customers on the left are cashing a cheque / opening an account.

2. Look at the ATM receipt. *True* or *False*?

    a. This is a bank statement.   *false*

    b. The customer banked online.   _____

    c. Her ATM card ends in 6434.   _____

    d. She withdrew cash.   _____

    e. She withdrew $100 from her chequing account.   _____

    f. Her savings account number is 056588734.   _____

    g. Her balance is $623.40.   _____

```
--------------------------------------
           FIRST BANK
        54 CHURCH STREET
          BLENHEIM.ON
--------------------------------------

DATE: 05/06/09        TIME: 11:51
ATM: 045-3
CARD NUMBER:      ***********6434

TRANSACTION:          WITHDRAWAL
SERIAL NUM.:                 345
AMOUNT:                     $100
FROM SAVINGS:          056588734
BALANCE:                  $6,234
```

3. How do you use an ATM? Number these steps in order. (1 = the first thing you do)

    ____ **a.** enter your PIN

    ____ **b.** withdraw cash

    ____ **c.** remove your card

    _1_ **d.** insert your ATM card

4. What about you? Check (✓) the things you did last month.

    ☐ bank online   ☐ withdraw cash

    ☐ cash a cheque   ☐ make a deposit

    ☐ use an ATM   ☐ open an account

    ☐ use a passbook   ☐ read a bank statement

Challenge Which documents and valuables do people keep in a safety deposit box? Make a list.

1. **Look in your dictionary. Where can you find the following ?**

   a. titles and locations of library books   *online catalogue*

   b. magazines and newspapers   _____

   c. maps   _____

   d. DVDs, video cassettes, and audio books   _____

   e. the library clerk   _____

2. **Circle the words to complete the sentences.**

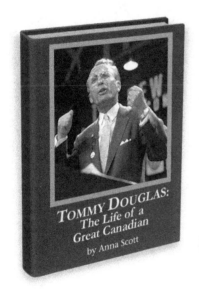

   a. The (author) / reference librarian is Anna Scott.

   b. The headline / title of the book is *Tommy Douglas: The Life of a Great Canadian*.

   c. This book is a biography / novel.

   d. You need a library card to check out / return the book.

   e. You return the book on May 16. The book is / is not late.

   f. The book is ten days late. The late fine is $.10 / $1.00.

3. **What about you? Check (✓) the items you would like to borrow from a library.**

   ☐ novels   ☐ video cassettes

   ☐ DVDs   ☐ picture books

   ☐ audio books   ☐ Other: _____

Challenge Find out about your school library or a public library in your community. For how long can you borrow the items in Exercise 3? Ask at the library or check online.

See page 294 for listening practice.   133

1. Look in your dictionary. Match.

_6_ **a.** registered mail

____ **b.** air mail

____ **c.** Xpresspost™

____ **d.** surface mail

____ **e.** Xpresspost bubble envelope™

____ **f.** Priority Courier™

1. for delivery tomorrow

2. for packages

3. for CDs

4. for two- to three-day delivery

5. for mail to other countries

6. for very important mail

2. Circle the words to complete the sentences.

a. This is a greeting card / <u>letter.</u>

b. The <u>envelope</u> / letter is white.

c. The mailing / <u>return</u> address is 46 Main Street, Chatham, ON N7H 1R2.

d. The postal form / <u>postmark</u> is December 15.

e. Alicia sent this Priority Courier™ / <u>registered mail</u>.

3. What about you? Address this envelope to your teacher. Use your school's address. Don't forget your return address.

4. Look in your dictionary. *True* **or** *False***?**

a. A postal clerk is using a scale. _____true_____

b. Letter carriers deliver packages and letters. _____

c. You can mail a letter in a PO box. _____

d. A Canadian mailbox is yellow. _____

e. Sonya wrote her return address on the envelope. _____

f. Cindy received a postcard from Sonya. _____

5. Put the sentences in order. Use your dictionary for help. (1 = the first thing you do)

____ a. Write a note in the card.

____ b. Put on a stamp.

____ c. Go to the stamp machine.

____ d. Find the mailbox.

_1_ e. Buy a greeting card.

____ f. Buy a book of stamps.

____ g. Mail the card.

____ h. Go to the post office.

____ i. Address the envelope.

6. What about you? Check (✓) the things you did last month.

☐ go to the post office   ☐ buy stamps

☐ receive a card   ☐ speak to a postal clerk

☐ address an envelope   ☐ read a letter from a friend

☐ mail a postcard   ☐ write back to a friend

☐ speak to the letter carrier   ☐ receive a package

☐ complete a postal form

Challenge Find out how much it costs to send a Priority Courier™ letter.

1. Look at page 136 in your dictionary. How many of the following things do you see?

a. people in the testing area   <u>3</u>

b. licensing clerks   _____

c. driving handbooks   _____

d. open windows   _____

e. closed windows   _____

f. people taking a vision exam   _____

2. Circle the words to complete the sentences.

a. This is a <u>driver's licence</u> / licence plate.

b. The driver's licence number is <u>020589 / 832643436</u>.

c. There's a <u>signature / photo</u> of Luisa Rodriguez.

d. The expiration date is <u>12-27-07 / 02-05-17</u>.

e. This is a <u>driver's licence / licence plate</u>.

f. It has two <u>driver's licence numbers / registration tags</u>.

g. The <u>expiration date / licence number</u> is August 2010.

3. What about you? Check (✓) the things you have.

☐ driver's licence

☐ licence plate

☐ registration stickers

☐ proof of insurance

4. **Look at page 137 in your dictionary. *True* or *False*?**

   a. Miguel wants to get a driver's licence.   _____true_____

   b. He needs a beginner's permit to take a driver education and training course.   _____

   c. He takes two tests.   _____

   d. He takes three courses.   _____

   e. He shows two forms of identification.   _____

   f. He pays the application fee with cash.   _____

   g. He passes the written test.   _____

   h. He studies the driving handbook.   _____

   i. He passes the driving test.   _____

5. **Which happens first? Fill in the first event.**

   1. ⬤ Study the driving handbook.
      Ⓑ Take a written test.

   2. Ⓐ Get your licence.
      Ⓑ Get a beginner's permit.

   3. Ⓐ Take a driver education and training course.
      Ⓑ Pass a vision exam.

   4. Ⓐ Take a driving test.
      Ⓑ Take a written test.

   5. Ⓐ Get your licence.
      Ⓑ Show your identification.

   6. Ⓐ Pay the application fee.
      Ⓑ Pass a driving test.

Challenge Answer these questions about your community.

   a. Where is the driver licensing office?   _____

   b. How much is the application fee?   _____

See page 295 for listening practice.

Government and Military Service

1. Fill in the blanks.

~~Governor General~~	prime minister	judges	Parliament of Canada	air force
House of Commons	senators	navy	chief justice	army

1. The __Governor General__ represents the sovereign in Canada.

2. The Supreme Court of Canada is composed of eight _____ and one _____.

3. People who want to be military pilots often join the _____.

4. The _____ is the leader of Canada.

5. The members of parliament meet in the _____.

6. The Senate is a political body that is made up of 105 people called _____.

7. The _____ fights military battles in the water.

8. Many people feel they serve their country by becoming soldiers in the _____.

9. Members of the House of Commons and the Senate make up the _____.

2. Cross out the word that doesn't belong.

1. **Federal Government**   senate   judges   chief justice   minister

2. **Military**   army   navy   cabinet   air force

3. **People**   sovereign   Governor General   prime minister   cabinet

4. **Government Bodies**   Parliament of Canada   minister   House of Commons   Senate

5. **Government Branches**   cabinet   Senate   Supreme Court of Canada   navy

3. Look in your dictionary. *True* or *False*? Correct the <u>underlined</u> words in the false sentences.

a. Dan Chen wants a job in ~~provincial~~ *city* government.   *false*

b. He wants to be a <u>premier</u>.   _____

c. Chen <u>runs for office</u>.   _____

d. Chen debates <u>his opponent</u>.   _____

e. Chen is happy with the <u>election results</u>.   _____

f. Chen <u>gets elected</u>.   _____

g. He now works in the <u>provincial capital</u>.   _____

h. Chen is <u>an elected official</u>.   _____

4. Circle the correct word to complete the sentence.

a. The highest member of city council is called the <u>lieutenant governor / mayor</u>.

b. The first step in becoming an elected official is to <u>run for office / get elected</u>.

c. The <u>premier / opponent</u> is the highest official of a province or territory.

d. Two candidates who are running for office often <u>debate / serve</u> in public about important issues.

e. To find the winner of the election, you check the <u>election results / political campaign</u>.

5. What about you? Answer the quiz questions.

Quiz: Canadian Government **Name:** _____

1. Who is the prime minister of Canada?

   _____

2. Who is the Governor General?

   _____

3. What is your provincial capital?

   _____

4. Who is the premier of your province?

   _____

5. How many members of legislative assembly does your province have?

   _____

6. Who is the mayor of your city?

Challenge For how long can the following people serve? Use an encyclopedia or the Internet to find the answers.

Prime Minister of Canada   _____

Chief Justice of the Supreme Court of Canada   _____

premier of your province   _____

1. Look in your dictionary. Check (✓) the civic responsibilities.

- ✓ help other
- ☐ obey Canadian laws
- ☐ vote in elections
- ☐ freedom of thought, belief, opinion and expression
- ☐ care for and protect our heritage and environment
- ☐ peaceful assembly

2. Label the pictures. Use the words in the box.

> freedom of association   freedom of thought, belief, opinion, and expression
> freedom of conscience and religion   ~~peaceful assembly~~

a. _peaceful assembly_

b. _____

c. _____

d. _____

3. Look at the forms. Then answer the questions below.

Name: Hassan Al Bahraini	Date of Birth: 8/13/97
Address: 25 Brock St.	Lived there 8 years
Windsor, ON N8O 1V8	Gender: M ☑ F ☐

Name: Yoko Tanaka	Date of Birth: 2/9/71
Address: 209 Gorham St.	Lived there 2 years
Toronto, ON M4B 1B4	Gender: M ☐ F ☑

Name: Ana Suarez	Date of Birth: 5/6/82
Address: 38 Opechee Dr.	Lived there 10 years
Ottawa, ON K1A 9V8	Gender: M ☐ F ☑

Name: Chen Lu	Date of Birth: 11/11/92
Address: 47 Bleecker St.	Lived there 1 year
Vancouver, BC V0T 1K2	Gender: M ☑ F ☐

a. Who lived in Canada for five or more years? __Hassan__ and __Ana__

b. Who is 18 years or older? _____, _____, and _____

c. Who can take a Canadian citizenship test? _____

Challenge List the ways people can stay informed about current events. **Example:** *read the paper*

1. **Look in your dictionary. Circle the words to complete the sentences.**

   a. The guard / ~~(police officer)~~ arrested the suspect.

   b. The suspect / witness wears handcuffs.

   c. The defence lawyer / Crown counsel is a man.

   d. The court reporter / judge says, "Guilty."

   e. There are ten / twelve people on the jury.

   f. The judge is in the courtroom / prison.

   g. The convict / bailiff is in prison.

2. **Complete the sentences with the words in the box. Then, number the events in order. (1 = the first event)**

court	defendant	~~jail~~	lawyer	released	suspect	trial	verdict

   ____ **a.** The defendant goes to ___*jail*___.

   ____ **b.** The defendant stands _____.

   ____ **c.** The judge sentences the _____.

   ____ **d.** The defendant appears in _____.

   ____ **e.** The convict is _____.

   ____ **f.** The judge reads the _____.

   _1_ **g.** The police officer arrests a _____.

   ____ **h.** The suspect hires a _____.

   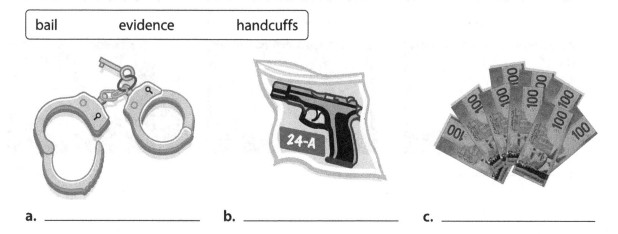

   SUPREME COURT OF CANADA

3. **Label the pictures. Use the words in the box.**

bail	evidence	handcuffs

   a. _____   **b.** _____   **c.** _____

Challenge Look in your dictionary. Tell the story. Begin: *The police officer arrested the suspect....*

1. Look in your dictionary. Read the TV movie descriptions. Circle the crime words.

8:00 P.M.	**TELEVISION GUIDE** ◀▶ ▼▲
2	**UNDER THE INFLUENCE** ('05) (Drunk driving) destroys two families.
4	**THE BREAK-IN** ('02) A burglary changes life in a small, quiet town.
5	**CRIMES AGAINST PROPERTY** ('09) Teenage boys commit vandalism.
7	**THE VICTIM** ('00) A man fights back after a mugging.
9	**THE FIVE-FINGER DISCOUNT** ('07) A young woman can't stop shoplifting.
11	**IT'S MY LIFE!** ('09) Identity theft causes big problems.
13	**KEEP THE CHANGE** ('05) An assault changes a man's life.
28	**EAST SIDE SAGA** ('09) A story of gang violence.
41	**WITH HIS GUN** ('99) A doctor tries to hide her husband's murder.

2. Match the TV movies with the descriptions in Exercise 1. Write the channel numbers.

a. _____28_____ b. _____ c. _____

d. _____ e. _____ f. _____

g. _____ h. _____ i. _____

Challenge Look at the movies in Exercise 1. Which do you want to see? Which don't you want to see? Why?

1. Look in your dictionary. Put the public safety tips in the correct columns.

At Home

Lock your doors.

_____

_____

_____

_____

On the Street

_____

_____

_____

_____

At the Airport

_____

At the Bank

_____

2. Give these people advice. Use the information from Exercise 1.

a. *Be aware of your surroundings.*

b. _____
_____

c. _____
_____

d. _____
_____

e. _____
_____

f. _____
_____

Challenge Make a list of things you do to be safe in public.

1. Look in your dictionary. Circle the emergency or disaster.

a. It covered almost half the house!   avalanche /(mudslide)

b. It's going to hit the farm!   tornado / volcanic eruption

c. We need rain.   drought / famine

d. Don't move. We're coming to get you!   flood / forest fire

e. The light was red! You didn't stop.   airplane crash / car accident

f. There's almost a foot of snow!   blizzard / explosion

2. Match.

1.

2.

3.

4.

5.

6.

7.

8.

____ **a.** car accident   ____ **c.** avalanche   _1_ **e.** airplane crash   ____ **g.** earthquake

____ **b.** fire   ____ **d.** flood   ____ **f.** hurricane   ____ **h.** tornado

3. Match.

a. _____3_____

b. _____

c. _____

d. _____

e. _____

f. _____

1. **EXTRA**
EXPLOSION ROCKS CITY CENTRE

2. **Strongville Chronicle**
FLOOD LEAVES THOUSANDS HOMELESS

3. **SUNDAY EDITION**
TIDAL WAVE HITS JAPAN

4. **Victoria Global**
Lost Child Home Safe

5. **Town Spirit**
Firefighters Fight Forest Fires

6. **EARTH MAGAZINE**
VOLCANIC ERUPTION AT MT. ST. HELENS

4. What about you? Check (✓) the natural disasters your province has experienced. Complete the chart.

Disaster	Which city?	When?
earthquake		
blizzard		
hurricane		
tornado		
flood		
Other: _____		

Challenge Find information about a natural disaster. Look online or in an almanac, encyclopedia, or newspaper. What kind of disaster was it? Where and when was it?

1. Look in your dictionary. Match.

Emergency Plan

___3___ **a.** Meet at Oak and Elm.

_____ **b.** Call Aunt Maria.

_____ **c.** Leave through the roof window.

_____ **d.** Turn off utilities in basement.

_____ **e.** Take Highway 401.

1. gas shut-off valve

2. escape route

3. meeting place

4. evacuation route

5. out-of-town contact

2. Carlos is starting a disaster kit. Check (✓) the items he has.

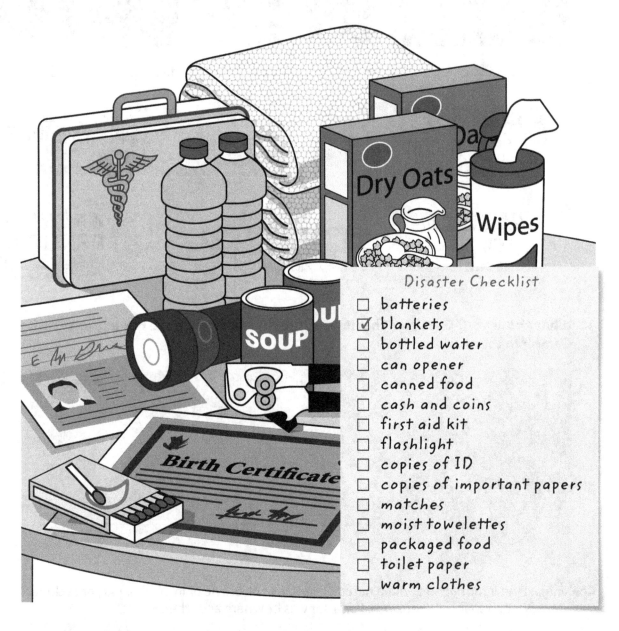

Disaster Checklist

- ☐ batteries
- ☑ blankets
- ☐ bottled water
- ☐ can opener
- ☐ canned food
- ☐ cash and coins
- ☐ first aid kit
- ☐ flashlight
- ☐ copies of ID
- ☐ copies of important papers
- ☐ matches
- ☐ moist towelettes
- ☐ packaged food
- ☐ toilet paper
- ☐ warm clothes

3. Look in your dictionary. Circle the answers.

a. | Stay under the table. | Seek shelter. / (Take cover.)

b. | Aunt Maria? It's me—Rosa! | Call out-of-town contacts. / Help people with disabilities.

c. | The radio says we need to go to a shelter. | Clean up debris. / Follow directions.

d. | How does it look outside? Did it start raining yet? | Evacuate the area. / Watch the weather.

e. | There are a lot of cars on the road. | Evacuate the area. / Stay away from windows.

f. | Don't worry. We're almost at the shelter. | Help people with disabilities. / Remain calm.

g. | The radio says there's a hurricane watch. | Pay attention to warnings. / Seek shelter.

4. What about you? Are you ready? Check (✓) the things you have for an emergency.

☐ can opener   ☐ first aid kit   ☐ flashlight

☐ copies of important papers   ☐ batteries   ☐ Other: _____

Challenge Make a list of other items for a disaster kit. **Example:** *medicine*

Go To Page 248 For Another Look (Unit 7). | See Page 299 for listening practice.

1. **Look in your dictionary. *True* or *False*?**

   a. Marta's street has problems. _____true_____

   b. There's graffiti on the stores. _____

   c. There's litter in front of the pharmacy. _____

   d. The hardware store is between the doughnut shop and the florist. _____

   e. The man in the hardware store is upset. _____

2. **Look at the pictures. Check (✓) the changes. Then, write sentences about each item on the list.**

OAK STREET ASSOCIATION

✓ repair street sign	☐ clean up graffiti
☐ repair curb	☐ repair streetlight
☐ repair sidewalk	☐ repair windows
☐ clean up litter	☐ paint stores

   a. *They repaired the street sign.* e. _____

   b. *They didn't* _____ f. _____

   c. _____ g. _____

   d. _____ h. _____

3. Look in your dictionary. Who does the following things? Check (✓) the columns.

	Marta Lopez	City Council	Volunteers	Citizens of City Centre	Hardware Store Manager
a. is upset	✓				✓
b. gives a speech					
c. signs the petition					
d. applauds Marta					
e. votes *yes*					
f. cleans up the street					
g. donates doughnuts					
h. donates paint					
i. changes Main Street					

4. Complete the letter to the City Centre City Council. Use the words in the box.

street	change	~~hardware store~~	graffiti	litter	volunteers

5/6/12

Dear Councillor:

I live in City Centre, and I am the owner of Hammers & More __hardware store__.
                                                       a.

I am very upset about the problems on my _____. There is _____
                                       b.   **c.**

on the buildings and _____ in the street. The streetlight in front of my store
                     d.

is broken, too. We have many _____ ready to help clean up the street, but
                             e.

we need your help. Please repair the streetlights. Together we can _____
                                                      f.

Main Street.

Sincerely yours,

Tom Lee

Tom Lee

5. What about you? Imagine you live in City Centre. How can you volunteer to help Main Street?

Challenge Imagine you own the pharmacy on Main Street. Write a letter to the City Centre City Council about the problems on your street.

1. Look in your dictionary. How many of the following do you see?

a. cars   _2_

b. bicycles   ___

c. trucks   ___

d. airplanes   ___

e. helicopters   ___

f. motorcycles   ___

g. people at the bus stop   ___

h. passengers leaving the subway station   ___

2. Look at the graph. Complete the sentences.

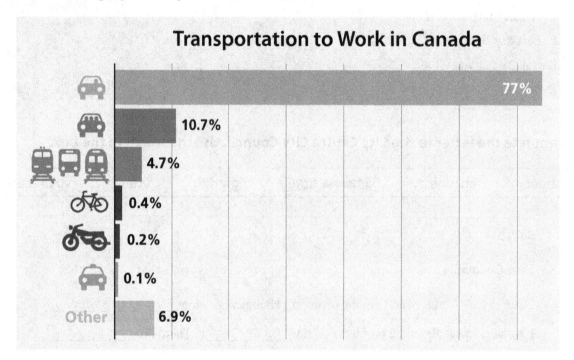

Transportation to Work in Canada

- 77%
- 10.7%
- 4.7%
- 0.4%
- 0.2%
- 0.1%
- Other 6.9%

a. Almost 80% of Canadians get to work alone in a _____ _car_ _____.

b. Almost 11% go to work in a _____ with other people.

c. Only 0.1% take a _____.

d. Only 0.2% ride a _____ to work.

e. Only 0.4% ride a _____ to work.

f. Almost 5% take a _____, _____, or _____ to work.

3. What about you? How do you get to the following places?

a. school   _____

b. work   _____

c. the supermarket   _____

d. Other: _____   _____

4. Look in your dictionary. _True_ or _False_?

a. A passenger is getting into a taxi. _____true_____

b. There is a bus at the bus stop. _____

c. Two people are entering the subway station. _____

d. There's a train near the airport. _____

e. There's a helicopter over the bus. _____

f. There are bicycles on the street. _____

g. The motorcycle is with the bicycles. _____

h. The bus stop is in front of Mario's Italian Deli. _____

5. Look at the pictures. Match.

1.
Hummingbird Air GATE B27
FLIGHT **128**
Date 6-28-08 SEAT 10C
Origin   Toronto
Destination   NYC
Boarding Pass

Hummingbird Air
Boarding Pass
Date 6-28-08
FLIGHT 128
SEAT 10C
Origin: Toronto
Destination: NYC

2.
Ride the Rocket.
THE BETTER WAY **A** ADULT
METROPASS

3.
CANADA
10

4.
DRIVER'S LICENCE
DL: 9999999
Class: 5****
SUNG, SAM, CHO
Issued: June 5, 2009
Expiry: June 5, 2014
65
1234-5678-90

5.
Riders
1
NOVAK/ANNA
EDMONTON, AB   VANCOUVER, BC
Carrier Train Date
2V   276   17 OCT 10
VANCOUVER, BC   EDMONTON, AB
Carrier Train Date
2V   276   22 OCT 10
$18   M XXXX939979   COACH CL

____ **a.** car   _1_ **b.** plane   ____ **c.** taxi   ____ **d.** train   ____ **e.** subway

6. What about you? How often do you take or ride the following? Check (✓) the columns.

	Often	Sometimes	Never
car			
taxi			
motorcycle			
truck			
train			
plane			
subway			
bus			
bicycle			
Other: _____			

Challenge Take a survey. How do your classmates come to school? **Example:** _Five students take the bus, two students . . . ._

Public Transportation

1. Look in your dictionary. Circle the words to complete the sentences.

a. There are three turnstiles /(riders) on the bus.

b. The girl on the bus has the fare / transfer in her hand.

c. The man is putting money / tokens into the vending machine.

d. The woman at the subway turnstile / in the subway car is paying the fare.

e. The ticket to Montreal is for a one-way trip / round trip.

f. The woman on the platform / track in the train station has a ticket.

g. The airport shuttle / town car is bright blue.

h. The taxi licence has a photo of the taxi driver / meter.

2. Cross out the word that doesn't belong.

a. Types of transportation	bus	shuttle	subway	~~track~~
b. People	rider	driver	transfer	conductor
c. Forms of payment	fare	track	token	fare card
d. Places to wait for transportation	subway car	platform	bus stop	taxi stand
e. Things with words	schedule	turnstile	transfer	fare card
f. Things with numbers	taxi licence	ticket	meter	rider

3. Look at the ticket. *True* or *False*?

a. This is a train ticket. ____true____

b. It shows the fare. _____

c. It's for a one-way trip. _____

d. It shows the track number. _____

YORK RAIL

CLASS	TICKET TYPE	ADULT	CHILD
COACH	ROUND TRIP	ONE	NONE
START DATE	NAME OF PASSENGER		PRICE
02 NOV 10	FOX/STEVE MR.		$16.88
FROM	VALID UNTIL		BAGGAGE
19TH AVE	10 NOV10		
TO	DATE OF PURCHASE		
SHEPPARD/YOUNG	10 AUG10		

ROUND TRIP/SPECIAL FARE
PASSENGER RECEIPT 13303 1226058975

4. What about you? Check (✓) the items you have or use.

☐ bus transfer   ☐ train ticket   ☐ taxi licence

☐ token   ☐ train schedule   ☐ Other: _____

☐ fare card   ☐ bus schedule

Challenge What public transportation can you take to the nearest airport? How much does it cost?

1. **Look in your dictionary. *True* or *False*?**

   a. A man is going under the bridge. ____false____

   b. There are two people walking down the steps. _____

   c. A woman is getting into a taxi. _____

   d. A man is getting out of a taxi. _____

   e. A red car is getting on the highway. _____

   f. A yellow car is getting off the highway. _____

   g. A taxi is driving through the tunnel. _____

2. **Look at the map. Circle the words to complete the directions.**

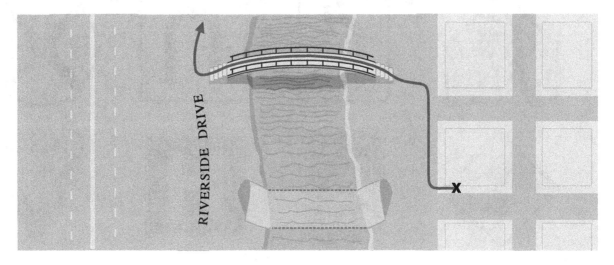

   Man: Excuse me. How do I get to Riverside Drive?

   Woman: Riverside Drive? Go around the (corner) / tunnel. Then go <u>down</u> / up the steps and
   a.   b.
   <u>over</u> / under the <u>bridge</u> / highway. Go down / <u>up</u> the steps and you'll be right on
   c.   d.   e.
   Riverside Drive.

   Man: Oh, so I have to go <u>across</u> / around the bridge?
   f.

   Woman: That's right.

3. **Read the conversation in Exercise 2 again. Circle the answer.**

   The man is <u>driving</u> / on a bus / walking.

   Challenge Write directions from your home to school.

1. Look at the intersection on pages 128 and 129 in your dictionary. *True* or *False*?

a. There's a stop sign at the intersection.   *false*

b. There's a no parking sign near the fire hydrant.   _____

c. There's a pedestrian crossing sign at Main and Green Streets.   _____

d. The bus is on a one-way street.   _____

e. There's handicapped parking in front of Al's Mini Mart.   _____

f. There are no speed limit signs.   _____

2. Look at the traffic signs. Match.

1.    2.    3.    4.

5.    6.    7.    8.

9.    10.    11.    12.

___ **a.** yield   ___ **g.** railroad crossing

___ **b.** road work   ___ **h.** no left turn

___ **c.** U-turn OK   _1_ **i.** school crossing

___ **d.** hospital   ___ **j.** right turn only

___ **e.** do not enter   ___ **k.** merge

___ **f.** pedestrian crossing   ___ **l.** handicapped parking

Challenge Draw three more traffic signs. Work with a partner. What do they mean?

154

1. **Look at pages 128 and 129 in your dictionary. Circle the words to complete the sentences.**

   a. The bicycle is going east / (west) on Green Street.

   b. It just went past Mel's / Print Quick.

   c. The orange car is going north / south.

   d. To get to the bus stop, the bus must turn right / left at the intersection.

   e. Dan's Drugstore is on the northwest / northeast corner.

2. **Look at the map. Use your pen or pencil to follow the directions to a shoe store. Put an X on the shoe store.**

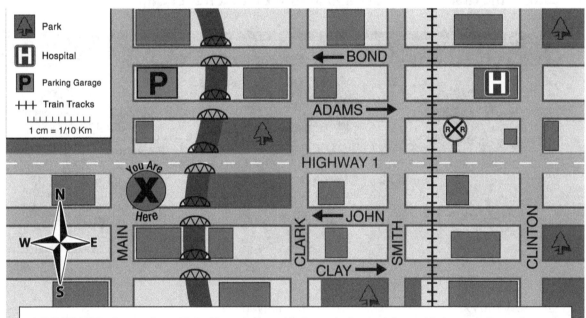

   DIRECTIONS: Go north on Main. Turn right on Highway 1. Go straight on Highway 1. Cross the tracks and continue to Clinton. Turn left. The store is on the left side of Clinton, but you can't make a U-turn there. So, continue north on Clinton. Go past the hospital. Turn left on Bond, left on Smith, and left again on Adams. Then turn right on Clinton. The shoe store is in the middle of the block, on the west side.

3. **Look at the map in Exercise 2. *True* or *False*?**

   a. This is an Internet map.   *false*

   b. The map has a key.   _____

   c. There is a symbol for schools.   _____

   d. One centimetre equals 1/10 of a kilometre.   _____

Challenge Give directions to a place near your school. Draw a map.

1. Look in your dictionary. Circle the words to complete the sentences.

a. The 2-door / <u>4-door</u> car is blue.

b. The <u>tanker / cargo van</u> is light brown.

c. The <u>dump truck / tow truck</u> is white.

d. The <u>moving van / tractor trailer</u> has a red cab.

e. The <u>camper / school bus</u> is yellow.

f. The <u>limo / cargo van</u> is white.

g. The <u>hybrid / RV</u> uses gas and electricity.

2. Look at the chart. Match the car models with the kinds of car.

A Car for Every Lifestyle ...

CLX Z4   Sol Aventura   Marvette

Venus XL   Charge Impact   Eton Grand Tour

<u> 5 </u> a. Venus XL   **1.** minivan

____ b. Marvette   **2.** SUV

____ c. Charge Impact   **3.** pickup truck

____ d. Eton Grand Tour   **4.** sports car

____ e. Sol Aventura   **5.** sedan

____ f. CLX Z4   **6.** convertible

3. What about you? Think about the last ten years. Check (✓) the vehicles you used.

☐ cargo van   ☐ tow truck   ☐ moving van

☐ dump truck   ☐ school bus   ☐ tractor trailer

Challenge Look at Exercise 2. Which car do you like? Why?
         Example: *I like the minivan because I have a big family.*

1. Look in your dictionary. *True* or *False*?

a. Juan is looking at car ads on the Internet and in the newspaper.   _____true_____

b. He buys the car. Then he takes the car to a mechanic.   _____

c. He asks the mechanic, "How many kilometres does it have?"   _____

d. He negotiates a price with the seller.   _____

e. He registers the car. Then he gets the title.   _____

f. He gets the title in the registration office.   _____

2. Match.

_4_ a.

1. Fill the tires with air.

___ b.

2. Go for an emissions test.

___ c.

3. Check the oil.

___ d.

4. Fill the tank with gas.

___ e.

5. Replace the windshield wipers.

3. What about you? Check (✓) the things you do.

☐ Look at car ads.   ☐ Put in coolant.

☐ Take the car to a mechanic.   ☐ Go for an emissions test.

☐ Fill the tank with gas.   ☐ Fill the tires with air.

Challenge What are other ways to buy a used car? **Example:** *from a friend*

1. **Look in your dictionary. What does the person need to use or check?**

   Page 158

   a. Turn left! _____turn signal_____

   b. It's raining. _____

   c. The battery is dead. _____

   d. It's getting dark outside. _____

   Page 159

   e. It's hot in here. _____

   f. Do we need gas? _____

   g. That car doesn't see us! _____

   h. You're going too slow. _____

   i. Stop at the next traffic light. _____

   j. It's cold in here. _____

   k. Let's listen to some music, OK? _____

   l. I forgot to charge my cellphone. _____

   m. What's the weather report for tomorrow? _____

   n. How fast are you going? _____

2. **Look at the diagrams of the rental car. An X shows a problem. Look at the list and check (✓) all the car parts that have problems.**

3. Put the words in the correct column. Use your dictionary for help.

~~accelerator~~   brake pedal   clutch   gearshift   horn
ignition   seat belt   steering wheel   stick shift

Things you use with your hands

_____

_____

_____

_____

_____

_____

Things you use with your feet

_____*accelerator*_____

_____

_____

4. Cross out the word that doesn't belong.

   a. For problems   lug wrench   jack   spare tire   ~~gas tank~~

   b. For safety   air bag   hazard lights front seat   seat belt

   c. To measure things oil gauge   speedometer   engine   temperature gauge

   d. To see other cars rear-view mirror windshield   muffler   side-view mirror

5. Circle the words to complete the sentences.

   a. You can keep maps in the (glove compartment)/ power outlet.

   b. The key is in the ignition / muffler.

   c. You should always wear a clutch / seat belt in the car.

   d. It's important to have a spare tire / steering wheel in the trunk.

   e. The radiator is inside the trunk / under the hood.

   f. Small children should sit in the front seat / back seat.

6. What about you? Check (✓) the items you would like in a car.

   ☐ CD player   ☐ stick shift

   ☐ air conditioner   ☐ automatic transmission

   ☐ child safety seat   ☐ Other: _____

Challenge Explain your choices in Exercise 6. **Example:** *I would like an air conditioner because it's more comfortable.*

1. Look in your dictionary. Who does the following?

   a. works at the check-in kiosk   _____ticket agent_____

   b. goes though security   _____

   c. examines your luggage in the screening area   _____

   d. helps passengers carry their baggage   _____

   e. is in the cockpit   _____

   f. helps passengers on the airplane   _____

   g. looks at your declaration form   _____

2. Circle the words to complete the conversations. Then, write where the people are. Use the words in the box.

~~airplane~~   airplane   baggage carousel   boarding area   cockpit   customs

Passenger 1: Where's your carry-on bag?

Passenger 2: Up there, in the overhead compartment / on the tray table.   _____airplane_____
                         a.

Passenger 3: Is our flight still on time?

Passenger 4: Let's check the arrival and departure monitors / turbulence.   _____
                                    b.

Customs Officer: Do you have anything to declare?

Passenger 1: Yes. Here's my declaration form / e-ticket.   _____
                         c.

Flight Attendant: You have a boarding pass / life vest under
                                    d.
                      your seat in case of emergency. Please look for the

                      nearest emergency exit / reclined seat now.   _____
                                    e.

Passenger 3: I don't see my e-ticket / luggage.
                         f.
Passenger 4: Don't worry. More bags are still coming out.   _____

Pilot: I hope you enjoyed your flight. We will land / take off in about ten minutes,
                                                        g.
          and we will be at the check-in kiosk / gate in about twenty minutes.   _____
                               h.

3. Look at page 160 in your dictionary. Match.

_3_ **a.** I just have this one bag.

____ **b.** Is this 14F?

____ **c.** Can I walk through now?

____ **d.** Now I just press PRINT.

____ **e.** OK. I'm pressing OFF. It won't ring now.

____ **f.** Here's my driver's licence.

____ **g.** Here it is! The large red one.

____ **h.** I think I ate too much! It's a little too tight.

____ **i.** Oh, good. It fits in the overhead compartment.

1. Stow your carry-on bag.

2. Claim your baggage.

3. Check your bags.

4. Find your seat.

5. Check in electronically.

6. Go through security.

7. Show your ID.

8. Turn off your cellphone.

9. Fasten your seatbelt.

4. Look at the picture. Check (✓) the things the passenger did.

✓ got her boarding pass	☐ found her seat	☐ landed
☐ stowed her carry-on bag	☐ read the emergency card	☐ took off
☐ fastened her seat belt	☐ boarded the plane	☐ checked in

Challenge List the things you can do to make a plane trip more comfortable.
Example: _wear comfortable clothing_

Go to page 249 for Another Look (Unit 8). | **See page 302 for listening practice.**

1. Look in your dictionary. _True_ or _False_?

a. They pack their bags in New York.   _____false_____

b. They ask a gas station attendant for directions.   _____

c. They see beautiful scenery.   _____

d. The car breaks down in the middle of their trip.   _____

e. They get a speeding ticket in Vancouver.   _____

f. They don't arrive at their destination.   _____

2. Look at the pictures. Match.

1.

2.

3.

4.

5.

6.

7.

8.

_____ a. They get a speeding ticket.

_____ b. The car breaks down.

_1_ c. They pack their bags.

_____ d. They arrive at their destination.

_____ e. They see beautiful scenery.

_____ f. They run out of gas.

_____ g. They have a flat tire.

_____ h. They get lost.

3. Look in your dictionary. Circle the words to complete the sentences.

a. Their (destination) / starting point is New York City.

b. They put their bags in the trunk / on the back seat.

c. They have a 4-door sedan / sports car.

d. Joe gives the police officer / tow truck driver his auto club card.

e. There is a flat / spare tire in the trunk.

4. Look at the pictures in Exercise 2. Complete the postcard. Use the words in the box.

auto club card	broke down	~~destination~~	got	had	pack	ran out

Well, we finally reached our _destination_ . The trip was
                                    a.
terrible. We got lost four times and we had a lot of
problems with the car. First, we _____ a speeding
                                   b.
ticket for driving over 140 km/h. Then, we _____ a
                                            c.
flat tire. Next, we _____ of gas. Then, the
                    d.
car _____ . I'm glad I had my _____ with me.
    e.   **f.**
We called a tow truck and the driver towed us all the
way to Winnipeg. We arrived at Mia's today—five days
late, and by taxi! Tomorrow our car will be ready, we'll
_____ our bags and start for home. See you soon.
g.
                                              Amy

Shaun Hensher
45 Consumers Road
Toronto, ON
M15 3A7

5. What about you? Did you ever experience the following? Check (✓) the answers.

If *yes*, where?

☐ have a flat tire _____

☐ run out of gas _____

☐ get a speeding ticket _____

☐ see beautiful scenery _____

☐ use an auto club card _____

Challenge Work with a partner. Look in your dictionary. Plan a trip. What's your starting point? How will you travel? What will you pack? What's your destination? Compare your answers with those of your classmates.

1. Look in your dictionary. *True* or *False*?

a. Irina Sarkov is the receptionist.   *false*

b. The receptionist sits across from the entrance.   _____

c. The time clock shows 9:15.   _____

d. The safety regulations are in the office.   _____

e. There are two employees in the office.   _____

f. The employer is writing paycheques now.   _____

g. A customer is at the entrance.   _____

h. The employer is also the owner.   _____

2. Who said these things? Use the words in the box.

employee	~~employer~~	payroll clerk	receptionist	customer	supervisor

a. My company is growing. I need to hire more employees.   *employer*

b. Great. Now, please do this next.   _____

c. Here's your paycheque for this week.   _____

d. Hello, this is R & M, Inc. Can I help you?   _____

e. I don't understand my pay stub.   _____

f. Something is wrong with my computer.   _____

3. **Look in your dictionary. Circle the answers to complete the sentences.**

   a. <u>An employee</u>/ The boss is fixing a computer.

   b. Kate Babic is talking to the <u>payroll clerk / supervisor</u>.

   c. Her <u>deductions / wages</u> are $800.

   d. Irina Sarkov's signature is on the <u>paycheque / pay stub</u>.

   e. The time clock is near the <u>receptionist / entrance</u>.

4. **Look at the pay stub.** *True* or *False*?

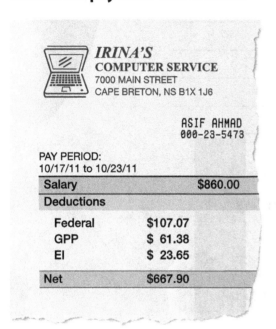

IRINA'S
COMPUTER SERVICE
7000 MAIN STREET
CAPE BRETON, NS B1X 1J6

ASIF AHMAD
000-23-5473

PAY PERIOD:
10/17/11 to 10/23/11

Salary	$860.00
Deductions	
Federal	$107.07
GPP	$ 61.38
EI	$ 23.65
Net	$667.90

   a. Irina is Asif's supervisor.   *false*

   b. Asif is an employee at Irina's Computer Service.   _____

   c. This pay stub is for one month.   _____

   d. His wages are $667.90 after deductions.   _____

   e. Asif pays three different deductions.   _____

   f. The pay stub shows the office phone number.   _____

   g. The EI deduction is $61.38.   _____

Challenge Go to page 254 in this book. Follow the instructions.

1. Look in your dictionary. Who is doing the following things?

    a. putting together computer parts   _assembler_

    b. making bread   _____

    c. repairing a refrigerator   _____

    d. working in a theatre   _____

    e. planning a building   _____

    f. reading stories to children   _____

    g. taking notes at a meeting   _____

    h. using a computer on a plane   _____

    i. standing in front of a store   _____

    j. working at a table with children   _____

2. Match.

    _4_ **a.** baker   **1.**

    ___ **b.** accountant   **2.**

    ___ **c.** mechanic   **3.**

    ___ **d.** butcher   **4.**

    ___ **e.** carpenter   **5.**

    ___ **f.** artist   **6.**

    ___ **g.** cashier   **7.**

Challenge Look in your dictionary. Choose one job. Would you like that job? Why or why not? Write three sentences.

1. Look in your dictionary. Where do they work? Check (✓) the columns.

	Inside	Outside
a. gardener		✓
b. electronics repair person		
c. customer service representative		
d. dockworker		
e. delivery person		
f. home health care aide		
g. graphic designer		
h. dental assistant		
i. hairdresser		

2. Look at the bar graph. Who works more hours? Circle the job.

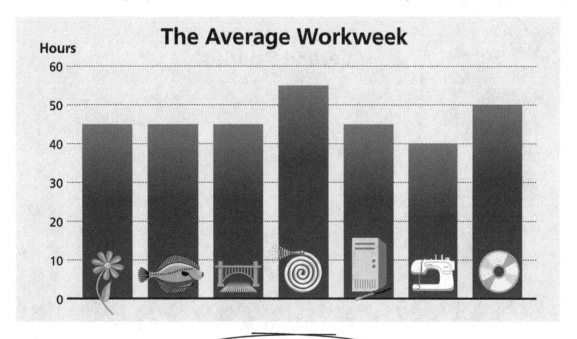

a. a computer technician or a(computer software engineer)

b. a commercial fisher or a firefighter

c. an engineer or a computer software engineer

d. a garment worker or a commercial fisher

e. a florist or a garment worker

Challenge Go to page 255 in this book. Follow the instructions.

1. **Look in your dictionary.** *True* or *False*? **Write a question mark (?) if you don't know.**

   a. The interpreter can speak Spanish.   _____?_____

   b. The manicurist is painting the woman's toenails.   _____

   c. The occupational therapist is helping a woman
      use a microwave.   _____

   d. The homemaker is in the kitchen.   _____

   e. The lawyer is in court.   _____

   f. The movers are carrying a table.   _____

   g. The physician assistant is talking to a patient.   _____

   h. The messenger rides a bicycle.   _____

   i. The medical records technician works in a hospital.   _____

2. **Look at the bar graph. Number the jobs in order of how much money people make.**
   (1 = the most money)

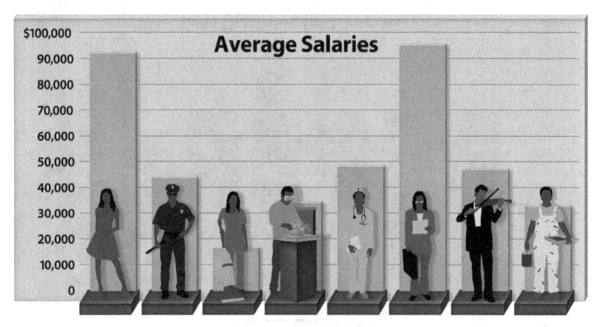

   Average Salaries

   ____ a. house painter   _1_ e. lawyer

   ____ b. police officer   ____ f. housekeeper

   ____ c. musician   ____ g. nurse

   ____ d. model   ____ h. machine operator

Challenge What are the differences between a homemaker and a housekeeper?
Write three sentences.

1. **Look in your dictionary. Circle the words to complete the sentences.**

   a. The (receptionist) / server sits at a desk all day.

   b. The <u>sanitation worker / security guard</u> works outside.

   c. The <u>stock clerk / writer</u> uses a computer.

   d. The <u>postal worker / printer</u> wears a uniform.

   e. The <u>truck driver / veterinarian</u> travels from place to place.

2. **Look at the job preference chart. Choose a job for each person.**

Likes to . . .	Ari	Luisa	Tom	Chris	Mia	Dave
work with people				✓		
speak on the phone	✓					
be inside	✓	✓	✓	✓		✓
be outside		✓	✓		✓	
sell things	✓					✓
be on TV				✓		
travel				✓	✓	
repair things		✓				
help people				✓		
wear a uniform					✓	
do physical work					✓	

   a. telemarketer _____Ari_____   d. welder _____

   b. social worker _____   e. retail clerk _____

   c. soldier _____   f. reporter _____

3. **What about you? Look at pages 166–169 in your dictionary. Write two jobs on each line.**

   Jobs I can do now: _____

   Jobs I can't do now: _____

   Jobs I would like to do: _____

   Jobs I wouldn't like to do: _____

Challenge Look at your answers in Exercise 3. Explain your choices.

Job Skills

1. **Look in your dictionary. Circle the job skills in the job ads below. Then, write the name of the job. Use the words in the box.**

Administrative Assistant	Assembler	Carpenter	Chef	Childcare Worker
Home Health Care Aide	Manager	~~Salesperson~~	Server	Garment Worker

www.jobskills.ca

Job Title and Description	Company
a. _Salesperson_ needed part-time to (sell cars) at our new Highway 29 location. Must have experience and be able to work weekends.	Herb Rupert
b. _____ wanted to take care of small children. Part-time. Must speak English and Spanish. Experience and references required.	ChildCare
c. _____ wanted to assist medical patients. Good income. Experience required.	Medical Homecare
d. _____ needed to assemble telephone components in midtown factory. Immediate full-time employment.	Top Telecom
e. _____ wanted to make tables and chairs in our small shop.	Woodwork Corner
f. _____ wanted to supervise staff full-time at our small, friendly architecture company.	Nicolas Pyle, Inc.
g. _____ needed for busy law office. Must type 50 words per minute.	DeLucca, Smith, & Rotelli
h. _____ wanted to sew clothes in our downtown factory. Experience necessary.	L & H Clothing, Inc.
i. _____ wanted to cook everything from hamburgers to duck à l'orange at our small neighbourhood restaurant.	The Corner Bistro
j. _____ needed to wait on customers at a busy downtown coffee shop. Part-time only. Experience preferred.	Kim's

2. **What about you? Check (✓) the job skills you have. Circle the skills you want to learn.**

- ☐ assemble components
- ☐ drive a truck
- ☐ operate heavy machinery
- ☐ sew clothes
- ☐ supervise people
- ☐ take care of children

- ☐ cook
- ☐ fly a plane
- ☐ program computers
- ☐ solve math problems
- ☐ teach
- ☐ Other: _____

- ☐ do manual labour
- ☐ make furniture
- ☐ repair appliances
- ☐ speak another language
- ☐ use a cash register
- ☐ Other: _____

Challenge Choose two job ads from Exercise 1. Can you do the jobs? Why or why not?

1. **Look in your dictionary. For which skills do the employees need the following? Put the words in the correct columns.**

A Computer	Paper	
type a letter	_type a letter_	_____
_____	_____	_____
_____	_____	_____
_____	_____	_____
_____	_____	_____
	_____	

2. **Match.**

_2_ **a.** | Smith, Cohen, and Soto. Good morning. | **1.** put the caller on hold

____ **b.** | Give me your name and number, and he'll call you back. | **2.** greet the caller

____ **c.** | I'll connect you to Ms. Soto's office. | **3.** transfer the call

____ **d.** | One minute, please. I'll see if she's in her office. | **4.** take a message

3. **What about you? Check (✓) the office skills you have.**

☐ type a letter   ☐ collate papers

☐ enter data   ☐ staple

☐ transcribe notes   ☐ scan a document

☐ take dictation   ☐ fax a document

☐ organize materials   ☐ print a document

☐ make copies   ☐ take a message

Challenge Work with a partner. Role-play a phone call. Student A is a caller. Student B is a receptionist. Leave a message and take a message.

See page 303 for listening practice.

1. Look in your dictionary. Cross out the word that doesn't belong.

a. Forms	interest inventory	~~training~~	skill inventory
b. People	career counsellor	internship	recruiter
c. Job training	online course	vocational training	new job
d. Job information	entry-level job	job fair	recruiter

2. Put the career planning steps in the correct order. Use your dictionary for help.

____ **a.** promotion

_1_ **b.** career counsellor

____ **c.** entry-level job

____ **d.** interest and skill inventories

____ **e.** on-the-job training

3. What about you? Complete the form.

jt TRAINING INSTITUTE

Please check (✓) the job training you have had. For what job?

☐ vocational training _____

☐ internship _____

☐ on-the-job training _____

☐ online course _____

☐ Other: _____

Which type of job training do you prefer? Why? _____

_____

_____

Challenge Look in your dictionary. Write about Ms. Diaz's career path. **Example:** *First, she had an entry-level job. She pushed a clothing rack. Then, . . .*

 See page 304 for listening practice.

1. Look in your dictionary. Fill out Dan King's job application.

EMPLOYMENT APPLICATION   ⊞ *S&K GROCERY, INC.*

NAME: Dan King	JOB APPLYING FOR: _____

1. HOW DID YOU HEAR ABOUT THIS JOB? (PLEASE CHECK (✓) ALL APPROPRIATE BOXES.)

☐ FRIENDS   ☐ INTERNET JOB SITE   ☐ HELP WANTED SIGN

☐ JOB BOARD   ☐ CLASSIFIEDS   ☐ EMPLOYMENT AGENCY

2. HOURS: ☐ PART-TIME   ☐ FULL-TIME

3. HAVE YOU HAD ANY EXPERIENCE?   IF YES, WHAT? WHEN?

☐ YES   ☐ NO   _____

4. REFERENCES: Lily Wong, Manager, Zhou Market

FOR OFFICE USE ONLY

RESUME RECEIVED: 9/17	INTERVIEWED BY: Ron Hill 9/21
HIRED? ☐ YES ☐ NO	WAGES:

2. Look in your dictionary and at Exercise 1. *True* or *False*?

a. Dan filled out an application.   _____true_____

b. Dan wrote a resume.   _____

c. He didn't write a cover letter.   _____

d. He sent in his resume before the interview.   _____

e. He set up an interview for the job.   _____

f. He went on an interview with Lily Wong at Zhou Market.   _____

g. Dan didn't get hired.   _____

3. What about you? What do you think are the best ways to find a job? Number them in order. (1 = the best)

____ look in the classifieds   ____ check Internet job sites

____ look for a help wanted sign   ____ go to an employment agency

____ network   ____ Other: _____

Challenge Survey four classmates. How did they find their jobs?

Interview Skills

1. **Look in your dictionary. When did Mr. Shirazi do the following things? Check (✓) the columns.**

	Before the Interview	During the Interview	After the Interview
a. ask questions		✓	
b. dress appropriately			
c. prepare			
d. talk about his experience			
e. shake hands			
f. greet the interviewer			
g. write a thank-you note			

2. **Look at the picture. Check (✓) Amy's interview skills.**

3. **What about you? Check (✓) the things you do on a job interview.**

Interview Skills Checklist

☐ be on time   ☐ bring resume   ☐ make eye contact

☐ dress appropriately   ☐ bring ID   ☐ listen carefully

☐ be neat   ☐ turn off cellphone   ☐ talk about your experience

Challenge Make a list of questions to ask on a job interview. **Example:** *What are the hours?*

  See page 305 for listening practice.

1. **Look in your dictionary. *True* or *False*?**

    a. The factory manufactures lamps.   _____true_____

    b. The factory owner and the designer are in the warehouse.   _____

    c. A worker is operating a yellow forklift.   _____

    d. The line supervisor is pushing a hand truck.   _____

    e. There are three boxes on the pallet.   _____

2. **Cross out the word that doesn't belong.**

    a. **People**   designer   shipping clerk   ~~forklift~~   packer

    b. **Places**   factory owner   warehouse   factory   loading dock

    c. **Machines**   hand truck   forklift   order picker   conveyor belt

    d. **Jobs**   ship   parts   assemble   design

3. **Complete the Lamplighter, Inc. job descriptions. Use the words in the box.**

    | ~~designer~~   factory worker   line supervisor   order picker   packer   shipping clerk |

    ### ☀ LAMPLIGHTER, Inc.

    a. design the lamp   _____designer_____

    b. watch the assembly line   _____

    c. assemble parts   _____

    d. count boxes on the loading dock   _____

    e. move boxes on a hand truck   _____

    f. put lamps in boxes on the conveyor belt   _____

4. **What about you? Look at the jobs in Exercise 3. Which one would you like? Which one wouldn't you like? Why?**

    Example: *I would like to be a line supervisor. I like to supervise people.*

    Challenge Rewrite the false sentences in Exercise 1. Make them true.

1. Look in your dictionary. *True* or *False*?

a. The gardening crew leader is talking to the landscape designer.   _true_

b. One of the gardening crew has a wheelbarrow.   _____

c. The landscape designer is holding a leaf blower.   _____

d. The shovel is between the lawn mower and the rake.   _____

e. The pruning shears are to the right of the trowel.   _____

f. The hedge clippers are to the left of the weed whacker.   _____

2. Look at the Before and After pictures. Check (✓) the *completed* jobs.

✓ install sprinkler system	☐ water the plants	☐ weed the flower beds
☐ plant trees	☐ mow the lawn	☐ trim the hedges
☐ fertilize the plants	☐ rake the leaves	

Challenge What can people use these tools for: shovel, hedge clippers, trowel, pruning shears?
Example: *shovel—to plant a tree*

1. **Look in your dictionary. Circle the words to complete the sentences.**

   a. A farmer / (rancher) is on a horse.

   b. In Picture C, a farmhand is milking / feeding a cow.

   c. There is hay / alfalfa near the fence of the corral.

   d. There is farm equipment / livestock next to the vegetable garden.

   e. A farmer is in the orchard / vineyard.

   f. In Picture B, two hired hands are harvesting / planting lettuce.

2. **Look at the bar graph. Number the crops in order. (1 = the biggest crop)**

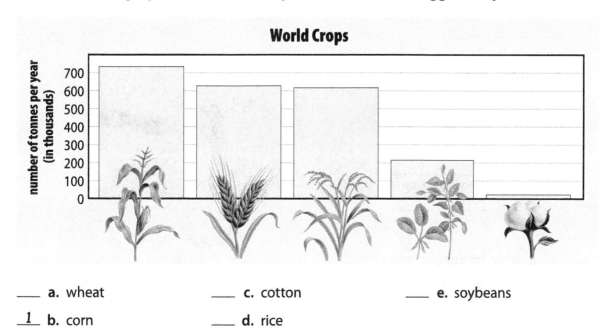

   World Crops

   ____ **a.** wheat   ____ **c.** cotton   ____ **e.** soybeans

   _1_ **b.** corn   ____ **d.** rice

3. **What about you? Have you ever been in the following places? Check (✓) Yes or No.**

	Yes	No	If yes, where?
a. a field	☐	☐	_____
b. an orchard	☐	☐	_____
c. a barn	☐	☐	_____
d. a vineyard	☐	☐	_____
e. a vegetable garden	☐	☐	_____

Challenge Work with a classmate. List products that are made from wheat, soybeans, corn, cotton, and cattle. **Example:** *wheat—bread*

1. Look in your dictionary. Put the words in the correct category.

Heavy Machines	Tools	Building Material	
cherry picker	jackhammer	concrete	_____
_____	_____	_____	_____
_____	_____	_____	_____
_____	_____	_____	_____

Things To Stand On

ladder	_____	_____
_____		_____
_____		

2. Look at the items. Match.

__3__ **a.** Install these tiles in the bathroom.

1.

____ **b.** Lay the bricks for the south wall.

2.

____ **c.** Hammer those nails into the wood.

3.

ADHESIVE

____ **d.** Paint it green.

4.

3. What about you? Check (✓) the materials your school building has.

☐ concrete   ☐ stucco

☐ shingles   ☐ tile

☐ bricks   ☐ wood

Challenge Look in your dictionary. What are the construction workers doing? Write sentences.
Example: *One construction worker is using a jackhammer.*

1. Look in your dictionary. Match.

1.   2.   3.   4.   5.

_3_ **a.** frayed cord

____ **b.** slippery floor

____ **c.** poisonous fumes

____ **d.** flammable liquids

____ **e.** radioactive materials

2. Look at the worker. Check (✓) his safety equipment.

Super Safe Sam

Job Safety
Better safe than sorry!

☑ back support belt	☐ respirator
☐ earmuffs	☐ safety boots
☐ ear plugs	☐ safety glasses
☐ fire extinguisher	☐ safety goggles
☐ hard hat	☐ safety visor
☐ knee pads	☐ two-way radio
☐ particle mask	☐ work gloves

3. What about you? Which safety equipment do you use at work? At home? Write a list for each. Discuss your list with a classmate.

At Work

_____

_____

_____

_____

_____

At Home

_____

_____

_____

_____

_____

Challenge Imagine you work at the place in your dictionary. Which safety equipment will you wear or use?

1. Look in your dictionary. Cross out the word that doesn't belong.

a. **Hardware**   nail   eye hook   ~~outlet cover~~   wood screw

b. **Plumbing**   C-clamp   plunger   pipe   fittings

c. **Power tools**   circular saw   hammer   router   electric drill

d. **Paint**   wood stain   paint roller   spray gun   chisel

e. **Electrical**   wire stripper   plane   wire   extension cord

f. **Hand tools**   hacksaw   work light   pipe wrench   mallet

2. Look at the pictures. What do you need? Choose the correct tool from the box.

drill bit	~~electrical tape~~	level	paintbrush
Phillips screwdriver	sandpaper	scraper	screwdriver

a. _electrical tape_   b. _____   c. _____   d. _____

e. _____   f. _____   g. _____   h. _____

3. Look at the picture. How many of the following things are there?

a. nuts   _6_

b. nails   ___

c. screws ___

d. washers ___

e. bolts   ___

f. hooks   ___

4. Look at the chart. *True* or *False*?

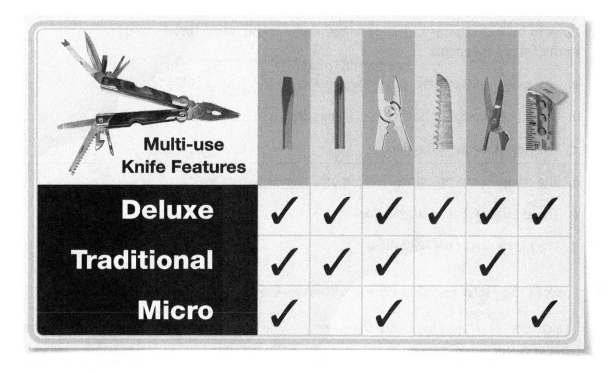

Multi-use Knife Features						
Deluxe	✓	✓	✓	✓	✓	✓
Traditional	✓	✓	✓		✓	
Micro	✓		✓			✓

a. The "Traditional" has a blade. _____*false*_____

b. The "Micro" has a Phillips screwdriver. _____

c. All three models have screwdrivers. _____

d. All three models have a tape measure. _____

e. The "Deluxe" has pliers. _____

f. Only the "Deluxe" has a wire stripper. _____

5. What about you? Check (✓) the tools and supplies you have.

☐ hammer   ☐ plunger

☐ handsaw   ☐ vise

☐ power sander   ☐ axe

☐ electric drill ☐ masking tape

☐ adjustable wrench ☐ duct tape

☐ jigsaw   ☐ plane

☐ metre stick   ☐ chisel

☐ screwdriver   ☐ Other: _____

Challenge Look at the chart in Exercise 4. Which model would you buy? What can you use it for?

See page 306 for listening practice.

1. **Look in your dictionary. *True* or *False*? Correct the underlined words in the false sentences.**

   a. The receptionist is in the ~~conference room~~. *reception area*   _____false_____

   b. The office manager is at his desk in a <u>cubicle</u>.   _____

   c. The <u>clerk</u> is cleaning the floor.   _____

   d. The computer technician is working on a <u>scanner</u>.   _____

   e. The <u>executive</u> is at a presentation.   _____

   f. The <u>file clerk</u> is at the file cabinet.   _____

2. **Look at the pictures. What do the office workers need? Use the words in the box.**

calculator	electric pencil sharpener	file folder	mailing label	~~staples~~
paper cutter	photocopier	fax machine	postal scale	

   a. _____staples_____   b. _____   c. _____

   d. _____   e. _____   f. _____

   g. _____   h. _____   i. _____

3. Look at the supply cabinet. Complete the office inventory.

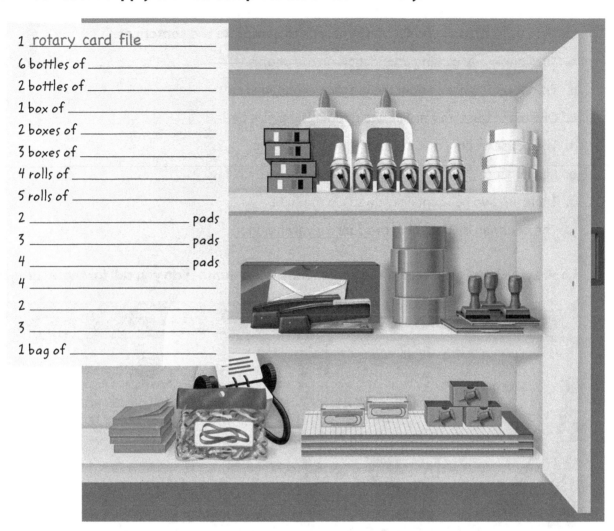

1 <u>rotary card file</u>
6 bottles of _____
2 bottles of _____
1 box of _____
2 boxes of _____
3 boxes of _____
4 rolls of _____
5 rolls of _____
2 _____ pads
3 _____ pads
4 _____ pads
4 _____
2 _____
3 _____
1 bag of _____

4. What about you? How often do you use the following things? Check (✓) the columns.

	Often	Sometimes	Never
a fax machine			
sticky notes			
an inkjet printer			
a laser printer			
an organizer			
an appointment book			
a rotary card file			
a paper shredder			

Challenge Make a shopping list of office supplies you need for your home. What will you use them for? **Example:** *envelopes—to pay bills*. Discuss your list with a classmate.

1. **Look in your dictionary. Circle the words to complete the sentences.**

   a. The (concierge) / parking attendant is on the phone.

   b. The elevator is across from the gift shop / luggage cart.

   c. One of the guest rooms has two double / king-size beds.

   d. The housekeeping cart is in the hallway / ballroom.

   e. Maintenance / The desk clerk is repairing the ice machine.

   f. There are two bell captains / guests in the suite.

   g. The doorman isn't opening the door / revolving door.

2. **Look at the hotel directory in the guest room. What number do you call for these things?**

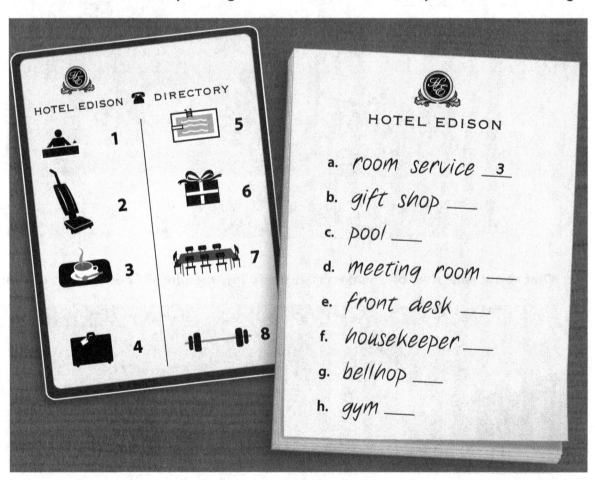

3. **What about you? Would you like to be a guest at the hotel in your dictionary?**

   ☐ Yes   ☐ No   Why? _____

Challenge Look in your dictionary. Write five questions that you can ask the desk clerk about the hotel. **Example:** *What time does the pool open?*

1. Look in your dictionary. Who is doing the following things?

a. leaving the walk-in freezer   _food preparation worker_

b. washing dishes   _____

c. sitting near the buffet   _____

d. talking to the bus person   _____

e. working in the banquet room   _____ and _____

f. carrying food to a diner   _____

g. seating a diner at a table   _____

2. Look in your dictionary. Where are they? Check (✓) all the correct columns.

	Dining Room	Banquet Room	Kitchen
a. servers	✓	✓	
b. diners			
c. short-order cook			
d. sous chef			
e. caterer			
f. bus person			
g. head chef			
h. maitre d'			
i. runner			

3. Look in your dictionary. Who said these things?

a. | Would you like a cup of coffee with that? | _server_

b. | The plates are all clean. | _____

c. | These two hamburgers are ready. | _____

d. | Thanks. The rolls look great. | _____

Challenge Imagine you own a hotel. Make a list of food to have at a breakfast buffet. Compare your list with a classmate's. Do you have any of the same items?

Go to page 250 for Another Look (Unit 9).

1. Look in your dictionary. *True* or *False*?

a. The contractor is holding a floor plan. _____false_____

b. Three bricklayers called in sick. _____

c. One construction worker is going to the clinic. _____

d. The man operating the crane is not being careful. _____

e. The wiring is dangerous. _____

f. The budget is three thousand dollars. _____

g. There's an electrical hazard in the office. _____

2. Look in your dictionary. Check (✓) the things at the construction site.

☐ ladder   ☐ insulation   ☐ bricks

✓ I-beams   ☐ hard hats   ☐ pickaxe

☐ forklift   ☐ shovel   ☐ trowel

☐ scaffolding   ☐ crane   ☐ tiles

☐ tractor   ☐ jackhammer   ☐ sledgehammer

☐ cherry picker   ☐ backhoe   ☐ safety regulations

☐ bulldozer   ☐ wheelbarrow   ☐ wood

3. Look at the list in Exercise 2. Choose two items. What do people use them for?

Example: *You can use a ladder to reach high things.*

_____

_____

4. Look in your dictionary. Circle the words to complete the sentences.

a. There is an electrical hazard in the clinic / (at the construction site).

b. One worker isn't wearing a hard hat / shoes.

c. One worker fell into bricks / concrete.

d. Another worker dropped a hammer / jackhammer.

e. An I-beam / Drywall is going to hit two workers.

f. A piece of tile / wood is going to fall on a worker.

g. The worker with the headphones and red hard hat is very careful / careless.

5. **Look in your dictionary. Answer the questions.**

a. Who is Sam Lopez? _____contractor_____

b. Who are Jack and Tom? _____

c. What is the name of the clinic? _____

d. How much will the wiring cost? _____

e. How many months does the schedule give the
   workers from start to finish? _____

6. **Complete the building owner's report. Use the words in the box.**

bricklayer	budget	careful	clinic	contractor
~~dangerous~~	electrical hazard	floor plan	sick	wiring

7/2

I went to the construction site today. It's a _____dangerous_____ place! I saw some
           a.

_____ coming out of a box. This is a real _____.
      b.   **c.**

Some of the workers are not very _____. One
                              d.

_____ fell in cement and needed to go to the _____!
      e.   **f.**

Other workers didn't have hard hats on. Two workers called in _____
                                        g.

and weren't at work. Sam, the _____, said it was a bad day. Then,
                h.

I showed Sam the new _____ with more offices. He looked very upset.
                      i.

He's worried about the schedule. He's worried about the schedule, and I'm worried about the

_____. Sam doesn't think three million dollars is enough!
      j.

7. **What about you? Would you like a job at the construction site in your dictionary?
Why or why not?**

Challenge Look in your dictionary. What safety equipment do the workers need?
Why do they need it? Make a list. Use page 179 in your dictionary for help.

1. **Look in your dictionary. In which school can you hear people say these things?**

> Today we are going to learn about the provinces of Canada.

a. _____ middle school _____

> I have biology on Tuesday afternoons.

d. _____

> That's the engine.

b. _____

> Today we are going to talk about World War I.

e. _____

> OK, class. How much is three plus three?

c. _____

> OK, children. Let's count the ducks now.

f. _____

2. **Match the student ages with the schools. Use your dictionary for help.**

   _2_ **a.** 20 years old   **1.** high school

   ___ **b.** 3 years old   **2.** university

   ___ **c.** 7 years old   **3.** preschool

   ___ **d.** 16 years old   **4.** adult school

   ___ **e.** 12 years old   **5.** elementary school

   ___ **f.** 30 years old   **6.** middle school

3. **What about you? Complete the chart.**

Check (✓) the schools you have attended:	Name	Location	Dates
☐ elementary school			
☐ junior high school			
☐ high school			
☐ vocational school			
☐ adult school			
☐ college			
☐ university			
☐ Other: _____			

4. Look in your dictionary. In which class can students do the following things?

a. learn about World War II   _____ history _____

b. work with numbers   _____

c. do exercises outside   _____

d. learn French   _____

e. sing   _____

f. talk about books   _____

g. paint   _____

h. use this workbook   _____

5. Label the class notes. Use the words in the box.

math	science	world languages	music	ESL	~~history~~

a. _____ history _____

1914-1918,
   World War I

1941-1945,
   World War II

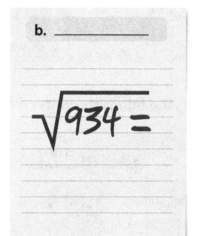

b. _____

$\sqrt{934} =$

c. _____

d. _____

学校
教師

e. _____

come came come
go went gone
write wrote written

f. _____

CO_2

Challenge Go to page 255 in this book. Follow the instructions.

1. **Look at the essay in your dictionary. How many of the following are there? Check (✓) the columns.**

	0	1	2	3	4
a. words in the title					✓
b. paragraphs					
c. sentences in the last paragraph					
d. quotation marks					
e. commas in the first paragraph					
f. exclamation marks					
g. apostrophes					
h. parentheses					
i. colons					
j. hyphens					
k. question marks					
l. footnotes					

2. **Look at the essay. Check (✓) the things the writer did.**

<u>Another Move</u>

My family and I came to this country five years ago. At first I was lonely and missed my own country, but now I feel at home here.

Next september we're moving again—to Charlottetown, Prince Edward Island. I'm worried. Will I like it? Where will we live. My father says, "Don't worry." My mother says that soon Charlottetown will feel like home. "But I'm happy here?" I exclaim. I watch my father's face and listen to my mother's words, and I feel better. My new city will soon be my new home.

a. ✓ The writer gave the essay a title.

b. ☐ He wrote an introduction.

c. ☐ He indented the first sentence in a paragraph.

d. ☐ He capitalized names all the time.

e. ☐ He used correct punctuation all the time.

f. ☐ He wrote a conclusion.

3. Look in your dictionary. *True* or *False*?

a. The writing assignment is due on September 3. <u>false</u>

b. The student has time to think about the assignment. _____

c. He brainstorms ideas with other students. _____

d. He organizes his ideas in his notebook. _____

e. He writes a first draft on his computer. _____

f. He edits his paper in red. _____

g. He revises his paper before he turns it in. _____

h. The student gets feedback from his teacher. _____

i. He turns in his paper late. _____

j. The composition is about his job. _____

4. Put the words in the box into the correct columns.

~~edit~~	brainstorm	get feedback	organize	rewrite

Prewriting	Writing and Revising	Sharing and Responding
_____	*edit*	_____
_____	_____	

5. What about you? Check (✓) the columns.

When I write a composition, I	Always	Sometimes	Never, but I would like to try this!
think about the assignment			
brainstorm ideas			
organize my ideas			
write a first draft			
edit my draft			
revise my draft			
get feedback			
write a final draft on a computer			

Challenge Write a three-paragraph essay about your life in this country. Write a first draft, edit your paper, get feedback, rewrite your essay, and turn it in to your teacher.

1. Look in your dictionary. Cross out the word that doesn't belong.

a. Shapes   ~~endpoint~~   rectangle   circle   square

b. Parts of a circle   radius   right angle   diameter   circumference

c. Types of math   geometry   algebra   calculus   parallelogram

d. Geometric solids   triangle   cone   sphere   cylinder

e. Lines   straight   perpendicular   pyramid   curved

f. Math operations   add   subtract   variable   divide

g. Answers to math operations   base   difference   sum   product

h. Types of integers   even   odd   positive   quotient

i. Types of angles   acute   obtuse   rectangle   right

2. Complete the test. Use the words in the box.

denominator	equation	negative	numerator
~~odd~~	product	sum	variable

MATH 103   TEST

Complete the sentences.

1. 121 is an _____*odd*_____ number.

2. –7 is a _____ number.

3. The _____ in 1/2 is 2.

4. The _____ in 1/2 is 1.

5. The _____ of 10 + 3 is 13.

6. The _____ of 10 x 3 is 30.

7. An _____ has an equal (=) sign.

8. In an equation, *x* is a _____.

3. Look in your dictionary. Circle the words to complete the sentences.

  a. A triangle has three curved / (straight) lines.

  b. A graph / parallelogram has a horizontal and vertical axis.

  c. Perpendicular lines make acute / right angles.

  d. For $18 \div 2 = x$, $x = 9$ is the product / solution.

  e. A word problem / An equation ends with a question.

4. Label the pictures. Use the words in the box.

~~circle~~	cube	curved line	cylinder	triangle
cone	pyramid	sphere	square	

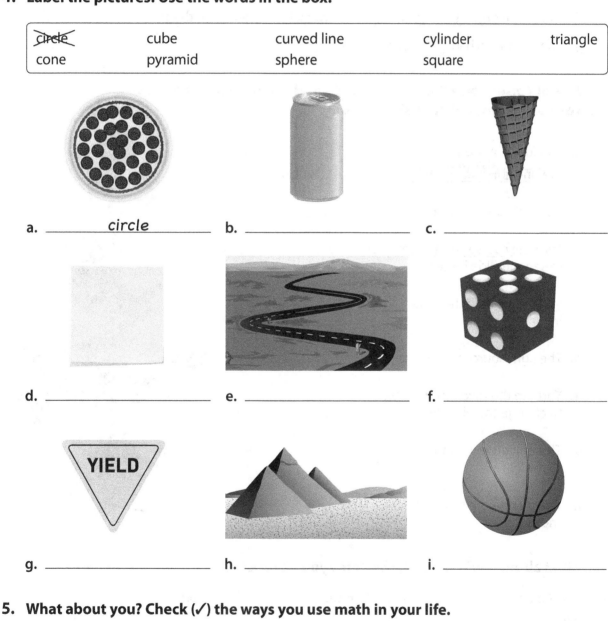

  a. _____circle_____   **b.** _____   **c.** _____

  d. _____   **e.** _____   **f.** _____

  g. _____   **h.** _____   **i.** _____

5. What about you? Check (✓) the ways you use math in your life.

☐ add   ☐ divide   ☐ multiply   ☐ read graphs

Challenge Look at Exercise 4. Think of objects you see every day. Write more examples of lines, shapes, solids, parts of a circle, and parts of a square. **Example:** *A mattress is a rectangle.*

1. Look in your dictionary. Circle the words to complete the sentences.

a. The (biologist) / chemist is observing something through a microscope.

b. The <u>chemist / physicist</u> has a formula on the board.

c. The chemist is using <u>the periodic table / a prism</u>.

d. An atom has <u>chromosomes / protons.</u>

e. Birds are <u>vertebrates / invertebrates</u>.

f. Plants use <u>organisms / photosynthesis</u> to make oxygen from the sun.

g. The ocean is a <u>habitat / stage</u> for fish.

2. *True* or *False*? Correct the <u>underlined</u> words in the false sentences. You can use your dictionary for help.

a. You look through
   the ~~fine adjustment knob~~. *eyepiece*   ___false___

b. The slide goes on the <u>base</u>.   _____

c. Turn the <u>coarse adjustment knob</u>
   to see the slide better.   _____

d. <u>Stage clips</u> hold the slide
   in place.   _____

e. The light source is on the <u>stage</u>.   _____

f. You use the <u>revolving nosepiece</u>
   to change the objective.   _____

g. The <u>objective</u> is connected
   to the base.   _____

h. The <u>diaphragm</u> is under
   the stage.   _____

3. What about you? Check (✓) the items you have used.

☐ balance   ☐ dropper   ☐ magnet

☐ beaker   ☐ forceps   ☐ microscope

☐ crucible tongs   ☐ funnel   ☐ prism

4. Complete the inventory. Write the number of items in the science lab.

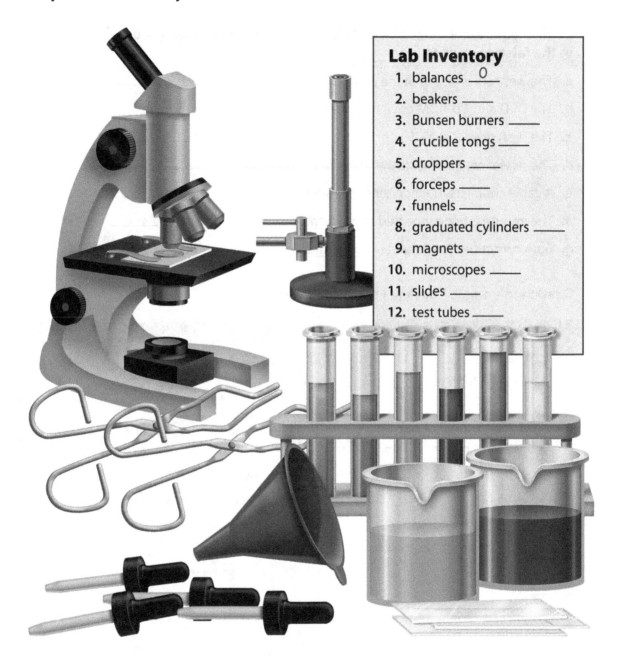

Lab Inventory
1. balances ___0___
2. beakers _____
3. Bunsen burners _____
4. crucible tongs _____
5. droppers _____
6. forceps _____
7. funnels _____
8. graduated cylinders _____
9. magnets _____
10. microscopes _____
11. slides _____
12. test tubes _____

5. Number the steps of an experiment in the correct order. (1 = the first step)

___ **a.** Observe.

_1_ **b.** State a hypothesis.

___ **c.** Draw a conclusion.

___ **d.** Do an experiment.

___ **e.** Record the results.

Challenge Find out about three items in Exercise 4. What are they used for? Make a list.
       Example: *crucible tongs—to hold hot items*

1. **Look in your dictionary. *True* or *False*? Correct the <u>underlined</u> words in the false sentences.**

   a. The webcam is on top of the ~~printer~~. *monitor*　　　　　　___false___

   b. The DVD and CD-ROM drive is in the <u>tower</u>.　　　　　_____

   c. The flash drive is in a <u>USB port</u>.　　　　　　　　　_____

   d. The power cord connects the tower to the <u>monitor</u>.　_____

   e. A <u>cable</u> connects the monitor to the keyboard.　　　_____

   f. The mouse is not connected to the <u>printer</u>.　　　　　_____

   g. Both computers have the same <u>software</u>.　　　　　_____

2. **Read Sara's email. Check (✓) the things Sara did.**

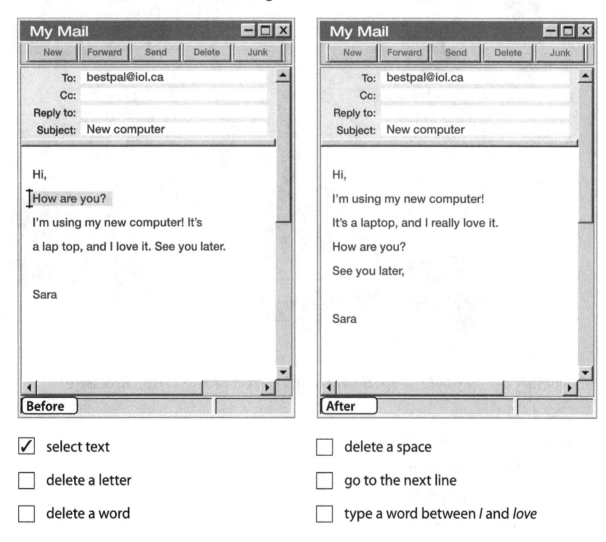

My Mail				▭ ☐ ✕
New	Forward	Send	Delete	Junk

To: bestpal@iol.ca
Cc:
Reply to:
Subject: New computer

Hi,

How are you?

I'm using my new computer! It's
a lap top, and I love it. See you later.

Sara

Before

My Mail				▭ ☐ ✕
New	Forward	Send	Delete	Junk

To: bestpal@iol.ca
Cc:
Reply to:
Subject: New computer

Hi,

I'm using my new computer!

It's a laptop, and I really love it.

How are you?

See you later,

Sara

After

✓ select text　　　　　☐ delete a space

☐ delete a letter　　　　☐ go to the next line

☐ delete a word　　　　☐ type a word between *I* and *love*

Challenge Which do you think is better: a desktop computer or a laptop? Why?
Tell a classmate.

1. Look in your dictionary. Match.

1. **2.** I **3.** **4.**

__4__ **a.** back button ____ **b.** pointer ____ **c.** forward button ____ **d.** cursor

2. What do you need to do the following? Use the words in the box.

scroll bar	~~search box~~	search engine	text box	video player

a. look for information on the Web ____search box____ and _____

b. move up and down the screen _____

c. type your password _____

d. watch a movie on your computer _____

3. Look at Todd's email. *True* or *False*?

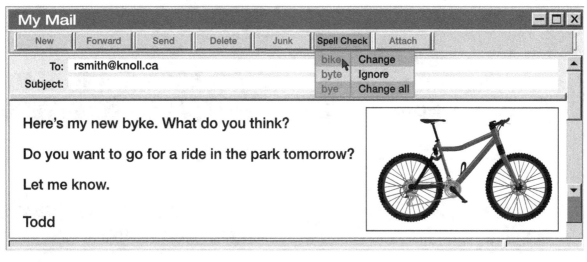

My Mail	⊟ ☐ ☒

New	Forward	Send	Delete	Junk	Spell Check	Attach

To: rsmith@knoll.ca
Subject:

bike → Change
byte — Ignore
bye — Change all

Here's my new byke. What do you think?

Do you want to go for a ride in the park tomorrow?

Let me know.

Todd

a. Todd addressed the email. ____true____ **d.** He attached a picture. _____

b. He typed the subject. _____ **e.** He attached a file. _____

c. He typed the message in blue. _____ **f.** He checked the spelling. _____

4. What about you? Check (✓) the ways you use the Internet.

☐ send email ☐ shop ☐ pay bills ☐ play online games

Challenge List other ways to use the Internet. Compare your list with a classmate's.

See page 308 for listening practice.

Canadian History

1. Look in your dictionary. Cross out the word that doesn't belong.

a. **People** — Fathers of Confederation — settlers — ~~British North America Act~~

b. **Leaders** — John Cabot — Sir John A. Macdonald — first prime minister

c. **Ethnic Groups** — First Nations — provinces — Inuit

d. **Conflicts** — Battle of the Plains of Abraham — War of 1812 — Halifax explosion

2. Look at the headlines. Label the events. Use the words in the box.

> Canadian Pacific Railway is completed   Vancouver hosts Winter Olympics
>
> Great Depression   Official Languages Act signed
>
> Free Trade Agreement signed   Halifax Explosion

Brown Town Metro
Thousands Feared Dead or Injured

a. _Halifax Explosion_

Canada, Mexico, and the United States to Expand Trade

b. _____

City BULLETIN
Canadian Athletes Go for the Gold

c. _____

NEWS from Space
ALL ABOARD AND READY TO TRAVEL

d. _____

COMMUNITY BULLETIN
Would You Like That in English or en Français?

e. _____

Millions of People without Jobs

f. _____

3. What about you? Check (✓) the events you know about. Circle the events you want to learn more about.

☐ Vimy Ridge   ☐ Stock Market Crash   ☐ World War II

☐ Terry Fox Run   ☐ Banting and Best develop insulin   ☐ Other: _____

Challenge Choose a time period from Exercise 3. Look online, or in an encyclopedia or history book. Write a short paragraph about that time period. When was it? What are two interesting events from that period?

See page 309 for listening practice.

1. Look in your dictionary. Match.

_4_ **a.** president

___ **b.** prime minister

___ **c.** emperor

___ **d.** dictator

1. Churchill

2. Mussolini

3. Qin Shi Huang

4. Juarez

2. What are these photos of? Use the words in the box.

ancient civilization	composition	exploration	monarch
war	modern civilization	~~invention~~	immigration

a. ___invention___

b. _____

c. _____

d. _____

e. _____

f. _____

g. _____

h. _____

Challenge Write the name of a famous explorer, an inventor, and an immigrant. Where did they come from? What are they famous for? **Example:** *Sammy Sosa is a famous baseball player from the Dominican Republic.*

1. **Look in your dictionary. Answer the questions.**

   a. Which states in the United States are on the Gulf of Mexico?

   ___Texas___   _____   _____   _____   _____

   b. Which parts of Canada border Hudson Bay?

   _____   _____   _____   _____

   c. Which states in Mexico touch the United States?

   _____   _____   _____   _____   _____

   d. Which countries in Central America are on the Pacific Ocean?

   _____   _____   _____   _____   _____

   _____

   e. Name four islands in the Caribbean Sea.

   _____   _____   _____   _____

2. **Label the parts of Canada and the United States. Use your dictionary for help.**

   In Canada

         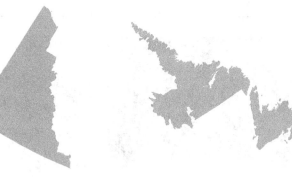

   a. _Prince Edward Island_   b. _____   c. _____

   In the United States

   d. _____   e. _____   f. _____

3. **Look in your dictionary. Circle the words to complete the sentences.**

   In Canada

   a. Alberta is (east) / west of British Columbia.

   b. Yukon is east / west of the Northwest Territories.

   c. Nova Scotia is east / west of New Brunswick.

   In the United States

   d. California is north / south of Oregon.

   e. Idaho is north / south of Utah.

   f. Wisconsin is east / west of Minnesota.

   In Central America

   g. Nicaragua is north / south of Costa Rica.

   h. Honduras is northeast / northwest of El Salvador.

   i. Guatemala is southeast / southwest of Belize.

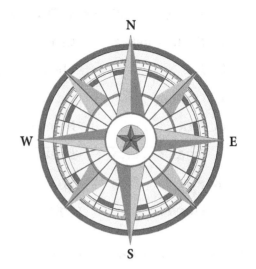

4. **Match the state or province with the region and country. Write the number and a letter for each item. Use your dictionary for help.**

	State or Province	Region	Country
_5, A_	**a.** Alberta	**1.** The Maritime Provinces	**A.** Canada
_____	**b.** Campeche	**2.** The Midwest	**B.** Mexico
_____	**c.** Illinois	**3.** New England	**C.** United States
_____	**d.** Massachusetts	**4.** The Southern Uplands	
_____	**e.** Nova Scotia	**5.** The Prairie Provinces	
_____	**f.** Jalisco	**6.** The Yucatan Peninsula	

5. **What about you? Look at the map in your dictionary. Where have you visited? When were you there? Write sentences.**

   Example: *I drove to Nova Scotia in 2007.*

   _____

   _____

   _____

   _____

Challenge Imagine you are driving from Manitoba, Canada, to Durango, Mexico. List, in order, the states you drive through. Use your dictionary for help.

1. Look in your dictionary. Cross out the word that doesn't belong.

a. North America	Canada	United States	~~Chile~~	Mexico
b. Asia	China	Poland	India	Philippines
c. Europe	Latvia	Ukraine	Belarus	Kazakhstan
d. Africa	Namibia	Peru	Botswana	Sudan
e. South America	Brazil	Paraguay	Guatemala	Colombia
f. Asia	Syria	Iran	Saudi Arabia	Romania
g. Europe	Egypt	France	Germany	Sweden

2. List the countries in the box in order of population size. (1 = the most people) Use your dictionary for help.

Argentina	Belarus	Italy	Kenya
Mexico	~~Pakistan~~	Saudi Arabia	South Korea

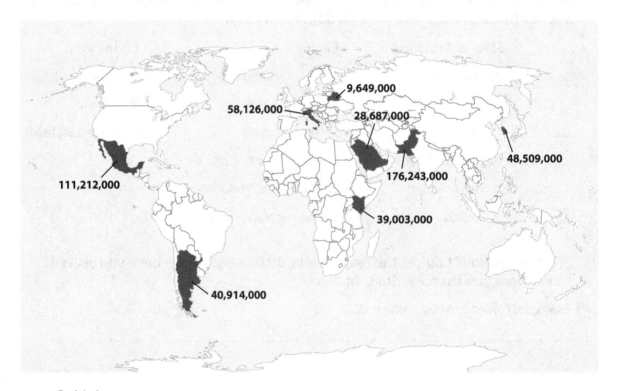

1. _Pakistan_   5. _____

2. _____   6. _____

3. _____   7. _____

4. _____   8. _____

3. **Look in your dictionary. How many neighbours does each country have? Write the number. Then write the names of the countries.**

   a. **In Europe**

      Romania   <u>5</u>   <u>Moldova, Bulgaria, Ukraine, Serbia, Hungary</u>

   b. **In South America**

      Paraguay   ____   _____

   c. **In Africa**

      Chad   ____   _____

   d. **In Asia**

      Thailand   ____   _____

   e. **In North America**

      Mexico   ____   _____

4. **Label the oceans. Use the words in the box.**

   | Atlantic Ocean | ~~Arctic Ocean~~ | Indian Ocean | Pacific Ocean |

   a. *Arctic Ocean*

   b. _____

   c. _____

   d. _____

5. **What about you? Complete the information.**

   My native country   Continent   Population

   _____   _____   _____

   Number of neighbours   The names of your country's neighbours

   _____   _____

   Challenge Choose one country. Find out information about it. Use Exercise 5 as an example.

Geography and Habitats

1. Look in your dictionary. Put the words in the correct columns.

	Land		Water
rainforest	_____	_____	_____
_____	_____	_____	_____
_____	_____	_____	_____
_____	_____	_____	_____
_____	_____	_____	_____
			_____

2. Complete the chart. Use words from Exercise 1.

a. largest	_lake_ _____		Caspian Sea (Asia/Europe)	371, 000 km²
b. highest	_____		Everest (Asia)	8,848 m
c. largest	_____		Sahara (N. Africa)	9,000,000 km²
d. largest	_____		Greenland (Denmark)	2,166,086 km²
e. longest	_____		Nile (Africa)	6,650 km
f. deepest	_____		Pacific	10,911 m
g. largest	_____		Bengal (S. Asia)	2,173,000 km²

3. What about you? Check (✓) the places you've visited.

☐ waterfall   ☐ desert   ☐ ocean

☐ canyon   ☐ bay   ☐ mountain range

Challenge Look at pages 202 and 203 in your dictionary. Write the names of two islands and two oceans. Do not use the ones from Exercise 2.

1. Look in your dictionary. *True* **or** *False*?

a. There are nine planets in our solar system. _____false_____

b. The sun looks dark during a solar eclipse. _____

c. The astronaut is looking through a telescope at the space station. _____

d. The astronomer is at an observatory. _____

e. There are six stars in the constellation. _____

2. Complete the chart with the names of the planets. Then answer the questions.

Which planet . . .

a. is closest to the sun? _____Mercury_____

b. is farthest from the sun? _____

c. is the largest? _____

d. is between Mercury and Earth? _____

e. has many rings around it? _____

f. is between Saturn and Neptune? _____

g. is our home? _____

3. What about you? Check (✓) the things you see in the sky tonight.

☐ planets   Which one(s)? _____

☐ the moon   Which phase?   ☐ new   ☐ full   ☐ quarter   ☐ crescent

☐ stars   ☐ constellations   ☐ comets   ☐ satellites

Challenge Find out the names of three different constellations. What do they look like? Talk about your answers with a classmate.

1. Look in your dictionary. *True* or *False*?

a. Adelia is wearing a red cap and gown. _____false_____

b. The photographer is upset with the students. _____

c. Adelia is crying in the serious photo. _____

d. The guest speaker is taking a picture. _____

e. The mayor is standing at the podium. _____

f. The ceremony is funny. _____

g. The students celebrate after the ceremony. _____

2. Look at the pictures and the captions. Match.

__5_ **a.** Here's my Dad taking pictures.

____ **b.** Nice cap and gown!

____ **c.** My Mom cries when she's happy!

____ **d.** Hey! Where's the guest speaker?

____ **e.** A serious ceremony.

____ **f.** It's time to celebrate!

3. Look at the photos in Exercise 2. Circle the words to complete the email.

```
┌─────────────────────────────────────────────────────────────────────┐
│ My Mail                                                    ─ □ X      │
├─────────────────────────────────────────────────────────────────────┤
│   Send To:   Paljo@eol.ca                                        ▲   │
│                                                                      │
│   Subject:   Graduation                                              │
├─────────────────────────────────────────────────────────────────────┤
│                                                                      │
│      I'm attaching some photos from my graduation day.               │
│                                                                      │
│      Do you remember my father? There he is with his camera. He's    │
│      the family                                                      │
│                                                                      │
│      guest speaker / (photographer.)                                 │
│                     a.                                               │
│      That's a picture of the cap / podium before the mayor spoke.    │
│                               b.                                     │
│      She was the                                                     │
│      guest speaker this year.                                        │
│                                                                      │
│      The woman is my mother. She always celebrates / cries at        │
│      ceremonies.                              c.                     │
│      The funny / serious photo of me is at the ceremony. I'm getting │
│            d.                                                        │
│      my diploma / gown.                                              │
│            e.                                                        │
│      Finally, it was time to celebrate / take a picture! That's me   │
│                                      f.                              │
│      with Adelia and                                                 │
│      another classmate. Don't we look happy?                         │
│                                                                      │
│      I wish you had been there, too!                                 │
│                                                                      │
│                                                                      │
│      M                                                           ▼   │
└─────────────────────────────────────────────────────────────────────┘
```

4. What about you? Answer the questions.

a. Were you ever at a graduation? ☐ Yes ☐ No

b. Who was there? ☐ a photographer ☐ a guest speaker

   ☐ Other: _____

c. Did you cry? ☐ Yes ☐ No   If *yes*, why? _____

d. Did you celebrate after the graduation? ☐ Yes ☐ No   If *yes*, how? _____

Challenge Look in your dictionary. Read the comments on page 207. Write five more comments about the photos on Adelia's webpage.

1. Look in your dictionary. *True* or *False*?

a. You can buy flowers at the nature centre. _____false_____

b. There's a bird on the roof. _____

c. Some of the plants are red. _____

d. There's a shovel near the soil. _____

e. Some children are playing on the path. _____

f. A man is painting a picture of the trees. _____

2. Look in your dictionary. How many types of the following things can you see?

a. trees ___4___   c. birds ___   e. fish ___

b. insects ___   d. mammals ___   f. flowers ___

3. Complete the signs. Use the words in the box.

birds	sun	flowers	paths	rocks	~~trees~~

a.

PLEASE DON'T CLIMB THE ___trees___.

b.

Look and smell, but please DON'T pick the _____!

c.

Please DON'T feed the _____!

d.

Keep off the grass. Stay on the _____.

e.

Don't throw the _____!

f. The _____ is strong. Wear a hat and drink water!

4. Look in your dictionary. Circle the words to complete the sentences.

   a. A man with a magnifying glass is looking at fish / (insects.)

   b. There's a sign with pictures of fish / mammals.

   c. The sky / sun is blue.

   d. There are no birds in the nest / water.

5. Look at the sign. Label the pictures. Use the words in the box.

birds	fish	flowers	insects	mammals
paths	water	sun	~~trees~~	

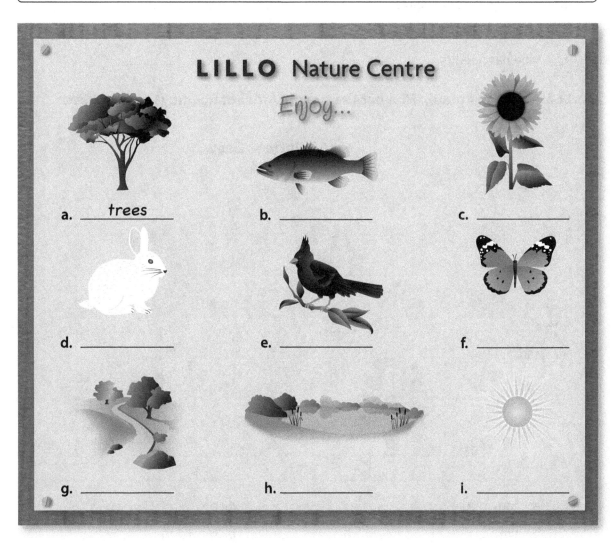

LILLO Nature Centre

Enjoy...

a. ___trees___   b. _____   c. _____

d. _____   e. _____   f. _____

g. _____   h. _____   i. _____

6. What about you? Check (✓) the things you can find near your school.

☐ trees   ☐ paths   ☐ plants

☐ birds   ☐ rocks   ☐ flowers

Challenge Look at page 255 in this book. Follow the instructions.

1. Look in your dictionary. *True* or *False*?

a. A tree has roots, limbs, branches, and twigs. _____true_____

b. Holly is a plant. _____

c. The birch tree has yellow leaves. _____

d. The magnolia and dogwood trees have flowers. _____

e. The cactus has berries. _____

f. Poison sumac has a trunk. _____

g. Poison ivy has three leaves. _____

h. The willow has pine cones. _____

i. A vine has needles. _____

2. Look at the bar graph. Number the trees in order of height. (1 = the tallest)

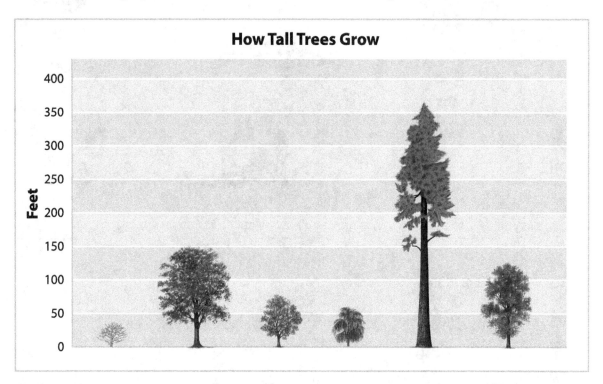

How Tall Trees Grow

_____ a. dogwood   _____ d. oak

_____ b. elm   _1_ e. redwood

_____ c. maple   _____ f. willow

Challenge Which trees grow near your home? Make a list.

1. **Look in your dictionary. Circle the words to complete the sentences.**

    a. The <u>bouquet</u> / (<u>marigold</u>) is orange.

    b. The <u>tulip / crocus</u> and the <u>gardenia / poinsettia</u> are red.

    c. The <u>chrysanthemum / daffodil</u> and the <u>houseplant / lily</u> are yellow.

    d. The <u>carnation / jasmine</u> and the <u>daisy / orchid</u> are white.

2. **What goes below the ground? What goes above the ground? Put the words in the box in the correct part of the diagram.**

    | ~~bud~~ | ~~bulb~~ | leaves | petals | roots | seed | stems | thorn | shoot |

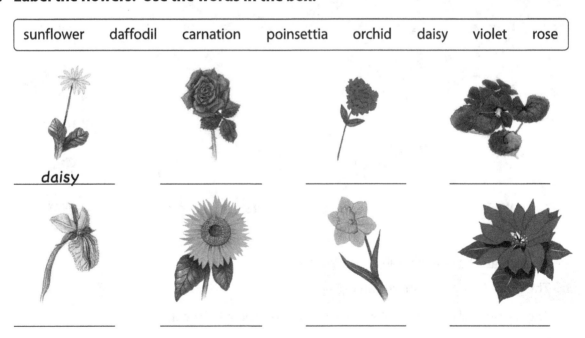

    above the ground   bud

    below the ground   bulb

3. **Label the flowers. Use the words in the box.**

    | sunflower | daffodil | carnation | poinsettia | orchid | daisy | violet | rose |

    _____daisy_____   _____   _____   _____

    _____   _____   _____   _____

4. **What about you? What flowers grow in your . . .**

    home? _____   neighbourhood? _____   country? _____

Challenge Find out the names of three provincial flowers. Make a list.

1. Look in your dictionary. Cross out the word that doesn't belong. Write the category.

a. _____Reptiles_____ turtle alligator ~~seal~~ crocodile

b. _____ fin gills scales scallop

c. _____ sea horse frog toad newt

d. _____ sea lion dolphin lizard sea otter

e. _____ tuna whale bass swordfish

2. Look at the chart. Circle the words to complete the sentences. Use your dictionary for help.

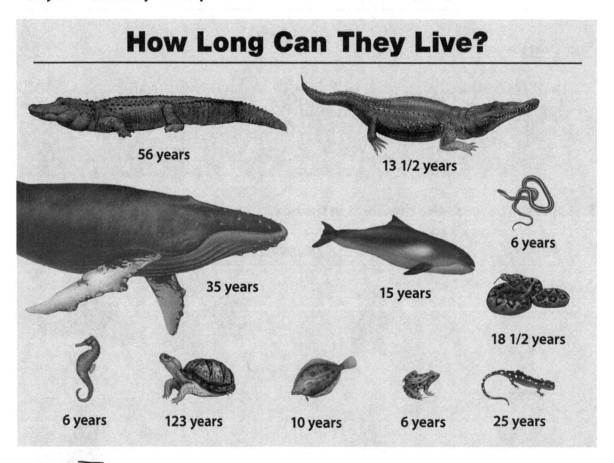

How Long Can They Live?

56 years

13 1/2 years

6 years

35 years

15 years

18 1/2 years

6 years   123 years   10 years   6 years   25 years

a. The (alligator) / crocodile can live fifty-six years.

b. The flounder / garter snake can live ten years.

c. The garter snake / rattlesnake can live eighteen and a half years.

d. The porpoise / sea horse can live fifteen years.

e. The frog / salamander can live twenty-five years.

f. The turtle / whale can live 123 years!

3. **Find and circle 14 more sea animal words. The words go across (→) and down (↓).**

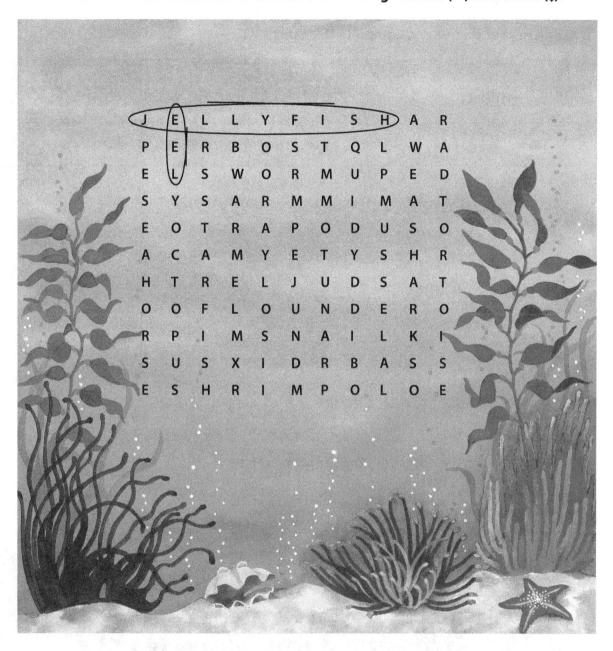

4. **What about you? Make two lists using the words from Exercise 3.**

Things I Eat	Things I Don't Eat

Challenge Add to your lists in Exercise 4. Use your dictionary for help.

Birds, Insects, and Arachnids

1. Look in your dictionary. Complete the chart.

	Name of Bird	Habitat*	Physical Appearance
a.	robin	1, 4, 5, 6	brown with orange breast
b.		1, 5	blue with white on wings, head, and breast
c.		3, 6	large; brown with white head and tail; big yellow beak and claws
d.		1	large head, flat face with big eyes; brown and white feathers
e.		4, 6	blue-black feathers with purple throat
f.		1, 5	green with red throat; long, thin bill
g.		2	large; long black neck and head; white "chin" and breast
h.		1	black and white with small red spot on head; small bill
i.		2	green head and neck; white neck "ring"; brown chest and tail
j.		4, 6	small; brown, white, and grey feathers

*where the bird lives: 1 = forests   2 = water   3 = mountains   4 = farms   5 = suburban gardens   6 = cities

2. Look at the picture. Check (✓) the things you see.

✓ honeybee	☐ scorpion	☐ grasshopper	☐ ladybug	☐ mosquito
☐ fly	☐ moth	☐ spider	☐ wasp	☐ tick
☐ beetle	☐ butterfly	☐ caterpillar		

Challenge Make a list of the birds and insects you can see near your home.

214

1. Look in your dictionary. Cross out the word that doesn't belong.

a. Pets	dog	goldfish	guinea pig	~~prairie dog~~
b. Farm animals	horse	cow	gopher	pig
c. Rodents	rat	mouse	squirrel	goat
d. Birds	parakeet	donkey	rooster	hen

2. Look at the ad. Check (✓) the animals you see.

PETE'S PET STORE

We have...
The Most Popular Pets in North America

Visit us at 232 Parkside Avenue.

✓ goldfish	☐ gopher	☐ dog	☐ parakeet
☐ mouse	☐ donkey	☐ cat	☐ guinea pig
☐ pig	☐ sheep	☐ rabbit	☐ chipmunk

Challenge Survey your classmates. Find out if they had pets in their native countries. Which pets are popular?

1. Look in your dictionary. *True* or *False*?

    a. The beaver lives in North America.   <u>   true   </u>

    b. The lion lives in South America.   <u>   </u>

    c. The chimpanzee lives in Africa.   <u>   </u>

    d. The orangutan lives in Asia.   <u>   </u>

    e. The llama lives in Australia.   <u>   </u>

2. Look at the pictures. Circle the words to complete the sentences.

a. The <u>antelope /</u>(<u>deer</u>) has <u>antlers / horns</u>.

b. The <u>platypus / porcupine</u> has long, sharp <u>quills / whiskers</u>.

c. The <u>camel / llama</u> has a <u>hump / trunk</u>.

d. The <u>lion / mountain lion</u> has four <u>hooves / paws</u>.

e. The <u>bear / monkey</u> has a long <u>tail / neck</u>.

f. The <u>hyena / kangaroo</u> has a <u>pouch / trunk</u>.

g. The <u>elephant / rhinoceros</u> has <u>horns / tusks</u>.

h. The <u>raccoon / skunk</u> has a black and white <u>coat / mane</u>.

3. Look at the chart. Check (✓) the mammals that are endangered.*

SOME ENDANGERED* MAMMALS

*endangered = very few are still living; they may not continue to live.

Based on information from: World Wildlife Fund (2006) and WildFinder: Online database of species distributions, ver. Jan-06. http://www.worldwildlife.org/WildFinder

☐ anteater	✓ hippopotamus	☐ baboon	☐ black rhinoceros
☐ brown bear	☐ buffalo	☐ camel	☐ coyote
☐ elephant	☐ giraffe	☐ gorilla	☐ grey bat
☐ raccoon	☐ kangaroo	☐ koala	☐ leopard
☐ moose	☐ mountain lion	☐ opossum	☐ panda
☐ panther	☐ red wolf	☐ tiger	☐ zebra

Challenge Look online or in an encyclopedia for information about one of the mammals in your dictionary. Where does it live? What does it eat? How long does it live? Is it endangered? Write a paragraph.

217

1. **Look in your dictionary. Which energy sources come from the following?**

Atoms	The Earth	Water
nuclear energy	_____	_____
_____	_____	**The Sun**
Air	_____	_____
_____	_____	
	_____	

2. **Look at the newspaper headlines. Match them with the types of pollution.**

1. **Beaches Safe for Swimming This Summer** *AS IT HAPPENS*

2. *COMMUNITY BULLETIN* **CARS GET NEW ANTI-SMOG DEVICE**

3. **Media** *WATCH* **Farmers Stop Using Dangerous Chemicals on Grapes**

4. WORLD NEWS **Countries Agree to Stop Making Atomic Bombs**

5. **DAILY** *OBSERVER* **Petroco Cleans up Water after Boating Accident**

6. MOUNTAIN POST **Hospitals More Careful with Medical Garbage**

____ **a.** oil spill   _1_ **c.** water pollution   ____ **e.** hazardous waste

____ **b.** pesticide poisoning   ____ **d.** radiation   ____ **f.** air pollution

3. **Look at the bar graph. Number the energy sources in order. (1 = used the most)**

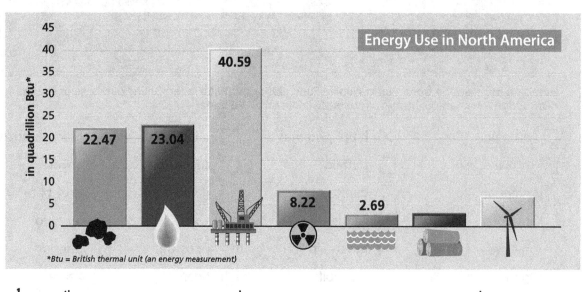

Energy Use in North America

in quadrillion Btu*

22.47   23.04   40.59   8.22   2.69

*Btu = British thermal unit (an energy measurement)

_1_ **a.** oil   ____ **c.** coal   ____ **e.** natural gas

____ **b.** biomass   ____ **d.** hydroelectric power   ____ **f.** nuclear energy

4. Look in your dictionary. What do these people do to conserve energy and resources?

> I never leave lights on
> when I leave a room.

a. ___*turn off lights*___

> I really don't need to use hot or
> warm water to get my shirts clean.

b. _____

> I don't use paper cups
> for my coffee.

c. _____

> I turn off the faucet when
> I brush my teeth.

d. _____

> I *never* throw things out
> the car window!

e. _____

> I always keep it at 20°
> in the winter.

f. _____

> I drive to work with three
> people from my office.

g. _____

> This plastic bottle goes in
> one of the blue containers.

h. _____

> I always bring
> my own bag.

i. _____

> I repair our faucets
> so they use less water.

j. _____

5. What about you? How often do you do the following? Check (✓) the columns.

	Always	Sometimes	Never
buy recycled products			
save water			
turn off lights			
use energy-efficient bulbs			
adjust the thermostat			
carpool			
compost food scraps			
plant trees			
Other: _____			

Challenge List three other ways to conserve water or electricity. **Example:** *I don't water my lawn.*

Go to page 252 for Another Look (Unit 11). | See page 311 for listening practice.

Canadian National Parks

1. **Look in your dictionary. In which pictures can you see these things? Check (✓) the columns.**

	Glacier	Gros Morne	Wapusk
a. landmarks	✓	✓	
b. a ferry			
c. caves			
d. park rangers			
e. wildlife			
f. people taking a tour			

2. **Look at the map symbols. Match.**

1.
2.
3.
4.
5.
6.

_2_ **a.** park ranger

___ **b.** ferry

___ **c.** landmark

___ **d.** path

___ **e.** tour

___ **f.** wildlife

3. Look at the map. *True* or *False*? Use the symbols in Exercise 2 for help.

a. There are two landmarks in this park. _____true_____

b. You can get a ferry near one of the landmarks. _____

c. There's a path to the wildlife area. _____

d. There are park rangers near the landmarks. _____

e. You can take a tour of this park. _____

4. Complete the postcard. Use the words in the box.

| caves |
| landscape |
| park ranger |
| ~~tour~~ |
| paths |
| wildlife |

Glacier National Park is great! Today we took
a ___tour___ of the _____. They are DARK!
    a.   b.
A _____ held a big flashlight so we could see.
   c.
Tania was afraid of the bats. I prefer bats to
other _____. (Last year we saw bears at
       d.
Gros Morne!) She also says she likes to hike on
_____ above ground—not deep underground.
  e.
And, of course, she loved the pretty _____
                      f.
we saw in Jasper two years ago. But for me,
Glacier is the best park in the world!
            Vlad

BRITISH COLUMBIA

ADDRESS

5. What about you? Look in your dictionary. Which national park would you like to visit? Why? Tell a classmate.

Challenge Imagine you visited Gros Morne National Park or Wapsuk National Park. What did you do there? What did you see? Write a postcard about the experience.

Places to Go

1. **Look at page 222 in your dictionary. Put the words in the correct columns.**

   Inside Events   Outside Events

   _____   _____ zoo _____

   _____   _____

   _____   _____

   _____

2. **Look at the events in Exercise 1. Where can you go to do the following things?**

   a. listen to music   _____ rock concert _____

   b. see animals   _____

   c. see fish   _____

   d. buy clothes   _____

   e. watch a film   _____

   f. see flowers and plants   _____

   g. play a game   _____

3. **Circle the words to complete the sentences.**

   a. It's nice to walk through the (botanical gardens) / movies.

   b. Elissa bought a used T-shirt at the bowling alley / swap meet.

   c. There's a new baby elephant at the aquarium / zoo.

   d. The music was very loud at the botanical gardens / rock concert.

4. **What about you? How often do you go to the following places? Complete the chart.**

	Often	Sometimes	Never	Never, but I'd like to go
a zoo				
the movies				
a botanical garden				
a bowling alley				
a swap meet				
a rock concert				
an aquarium				

222

5. Look at page 223 in your dictionary. Complete the event listings below.

WHAT'S HAPPENING

ART

NORTH RIDGE ___Art Gallery___
a.
Special exhibit of sculpture and paintings by local artists. Through August 25, **Tickets $5.00**.

MUSIC

CITY CENTRE

Adriana Domingo sings the leading role in Antonio Rivera's new _____,
b.
Starry Night. 8:00 P.M., **August 14 and 15**.

Tickets $10–$30.

PLUM HALL

Oakland Chamber Orchestra, with Lily Marksen at the piano, performs a _____
c.
featuring works by Beethoven, Bach, and Brahms. 8:00 P.M., **August 15**.

Tickets $20–$30.

THEATRE

CURTAINS UP

The Downtown Players perform *The Argument*, a new _____ by J.L. Mason, starring
d.
Vanessa Thompson and Tyrone Williams as a married couple. Through August 20. **Tickets $20**.

CHILDREN

CROWN_____
e.
Roller coaster, merry-go-round, and other rides provide fun for kids and adults. Great popcorn, too! Open daily.

10:00 A.M. TO 5:00 P.M. **Free admission**.

GENERAL INTEREST

NORTH RIDGE _____
f.
Food, exhibitions, and prizes for best cow, best quilt, and more.

August 14–15, 10:00 A.M. TO SUNSET. **Free**.

Sal's_____
g.
Dance to the music of the rock band, Jumpin' Lizzards. 8:00 P.M. TO MIDNIGHT. Must be 18 or older (ID required). **$10.00** (includes 1 beverage).

6. Look at the events in Exercise 5. *True* or *False*?

a. The play is free. _____false_____

b. You can see an opera at City Centre. _____

c. The county fair is open nights. _____

d. A seventeen-year-old can go to Sal's. _____

e. There's an afternoon concert at Plum Hall on August 15. _____

f. Tickets to the amusement park are expensive. _____

g. You can see the special art exhibit for $5.00. _____

Challenge Look at the listings in Exercise 5. Talk to two classmates and agree on a place to go. Write your decision and give a reason.

The Park and Playground

1. Look in your dictionary. Where can you do the following?

    a. have a picnic   *picnic table*   **d.** get a drink   _____

    b. play baseball   _____   **e.** push a swing   _____

    c. see a cyclist   _____   **f.** sit and read   _____

2. Look at the map. Complete the legend. Use the words in the box.

> ball field   bike path   fountain   picnic table   playground   ~~tennis court~~   water fountain

    a. *tennis court*

    b. _____

    c. _____

    d. _____

    e. _____

    f. _____

    g. _____

3. Look at the map in Exercise 2. *True* or *False*?

    a. There's a water fountain in the playground.   _____*true*_____

    b. The tennis court is to the left of the ball field.   _____

    c. There's a see-saw in the playground.   _____

    d. There are benches near the swings.   _____

    e. The bike path goes around the fountain.   _____

4. What about you? Check (✓) the activities you did as a child.

    ☐ ride a tricycle   ☐ go down a slide   ☐ use a jump rope

    ☐ climb the bars   ☐ pull a wagon   ☐ picnic in the park

    ☐ play in the sandbox   ☐ ride a skateboard   ☐ Other: _____

Challenge Look at the park in your dictionary. What are people doing? Write eight sentences.
                Example: *A little boy is riding a tricycle.*

1. **Look in your dictionary. What are people using to do these things?**

   a. play in the sand   _____*pail*_____

   b. sit on the sand   _____ and _____

   c. keep drinks and food cold   _____

   d. protect their skin from the sun   _____ and _____

   e. stay warm in the ocean   _____

   f. breathe underwater   _____

   g. see underwater   _____

2. **Look at the chart. *True* or *False*?**

	umbrella	lifeguard	surf	sailboat	swim	scuba	pier
Charles Beach	•		•		•	•	•
Moonstone Beach				•	•		•
Town Beach	•	•	•			•	

   a. You can swim at Charles Beach.   ____*true*____

   b. Surfers can use their surfboards only at Moonstone Beach.   _____

   c. You can go out in your sailboat at Town Beach.   _____

   d. You can use a scuba tank at Charles Beach.   _____

   e. You can rent a beach umbrella at Moonstone Beach.   _____

   f. There's a lifeguard at all three beaches.   _____

   g. There's a pier at Town Beach.   _____

3. **What about you? How important are these things to you? Circle the number.**

	Very Important				Not Important
clean sand	4	3	2	1	0
big waves	4	3	2	1	0
seashells	4	3	2	1	0
lifeguard station	4	3	2	1	0

Challenge Look at the chart in Exercise 2. Which beach would you like to go to? Why?

1. **Look in your dictionary. How many people are doing the following things?**

    a. backpacking _1_ **b.** rafting ___   **c.** camping ___   **d.** canoeing ___

2. **Look at the bar graph. *True* or *False*?**

    Favourite Outdoor Recreation Activities

    a. Only one percent of people said boating is their favourite activity. ___*true*___

    b. Nine percent said fishing is their favourite. _____

    c. Three percent said camping is their favourite. _____

    d. Three percent said hiking is their favourite. _____

    e. Two percent said horseback riding is their favourite. _____

3. **Read the sentences. What do the people need? Match.**

    _5_ **a.** It's too dark in this tent. I can't read.   **1.** camping stove

    ___ **b.** It's cold. Let's build a campfire.   **2.** canteen

    ___ **c.** Where's my backpack? I'm thirsty.   **3.** fishing pole

    ___ **d.** Ouch! These mosquitoes keep biting me!   **4.** insect repellent

    ___ **e.** Brian's afraid of the water. He can't swim.   **5.** lantern

    ___ **f.** Everyone's hungry. I'll start the hamburgers.   **6.** life vest

    ___ **g.** I'm tired. Good night.   **7.** matches

    ___ **h.** I'd like to catch some of those trout in the lake. **8.** sleeping bag

4. **What about you? Check (✓) the activities you like.**

    ☐ camping   ☐ mountain biking   ☐ fishing   ☐ canoeing

Challenge Choose your favourite outdoor activity. What do you need to do it? Make a list.

1. Look in your dictionary. Circle the words to complete the sentences.

  a. The man in the red vest is cross-country skiing /(downhill skiing.)

  b. Two people are snowboarding / sledding.

  c. The skater with the white skates is figure skating / ice skating.

  d. A woman and man are scuba diving / snorkelling.

2. Look at the hotel information. Where should people stay? Write the letter(s).

www.holidaypackagesvacations.ca

Holiday Packages

1. Caribe Plaza

2. Mirror Lake Inn

3. Hillside Lodge

4. Wicker Inn

  a. Ana likes water sports.   1, 2

  b. Mei-yuan likes winter sports.   _____

  c. Jason loves downhill skiing.   _____

  d. Crystal wants to go snorkelling.   _____

  e. Paulo wants to take his children sledding. _____

  f. Kyle wants to go water skiing and sailing. _____

  g. Olga wants to go surfing.   _____

  h. Taro loves sailing and windsurfing.   _____

3. What about you? Look at Exercise 2. Where would you like to stay? Why?

  Example: *I want to stay at the Wicker Inn or Hillside Lodge. I like ice skating.*

Challenge Interview two people. Which winter or water sports do they like? Recommend a hotel
           from Exercise 2.

1. Look in your dictionary. Put the words in the correct columns.

Outdoor Sports	Indoor Sports	
archery		

2. Look at the chart. List the sports in order of popularity. (1 = the most popular)

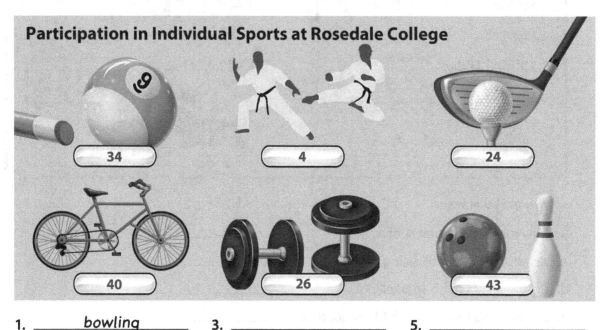

Participation in Individual Sports at Rosedale College

34	4	24
40	26	43

1. ____bowling____   3. _____   5. _____

2. _____   4. _____   6. _____

3. What about you? Check (✓) the sports you like.

☐ boxing   ☐ wrestling   ☐ horse racing   ☐ Other: _____

Challenge Interview four people in your class. Which individual sports do they like? Make a list.
Example: *Two students like weightlifting.*

1. **Look at the basketball court at the top of your dictionary page. Write the numbers.**

   a. How many teams are there? <u>2</u>

   b. How many fans are holding a sign? ___

   c. How many players can you see? ___

   d. How many coaches can you see? ___

   e. How many referees can you see? ___

   f. What's the score for the home team? ___

2. **Look at the bar graph.** *True* or *False*? **Correct the <u>underlined</u> words in the false sentences.**

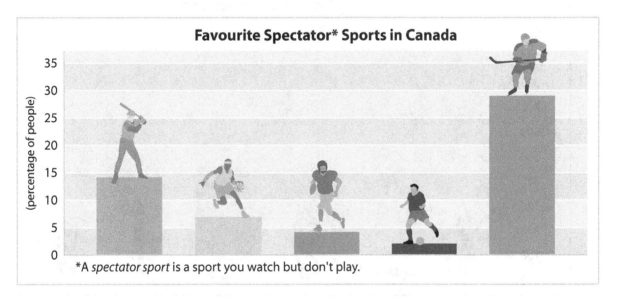

Favourite Spectator* Sports in Canada

*A *spectator sport* is a sport you watch but don't play.

   a. Almost 15% said ~~hockey~~ *baseball* is their favourite sport. <u>false</u>

   b. Only 2% said <u>hockey</u> is their favourite. _____

   c. Almost 5% said <u>baseball</u> is their favourite. _____

   d. About 7% said <u>basketball</u> is their favourite. _____

   e. For almost 30%, <u>football</u> is their favourite sport. _____

3. **What about you? Circle the sports you play. <u>Underline</u> the sports you watch.**

softball	football	basketball	baseball
volleyball	hockey	water polo	soccer

Challenge Go to page 256 in this book. Follow the instructions.

1. Look in your dictionary. Circle the words to complete the sentences.

  a. One man is ⟨kicking⟩/ passing / throwing a football.

  b. A woman is bending / swimming / racing at the gym.

  c. The woman at the gym is jumping / tackling / exercising.

  d. The man on the tennis court is pitching / serving / swinging.

  e. A man in orange shorts at the track is finishing / starting / stretching.

  f. A man on the baseball field is catching / hitting / swinging with his glove.

2. Look at the bar graph. Complete the sentences.

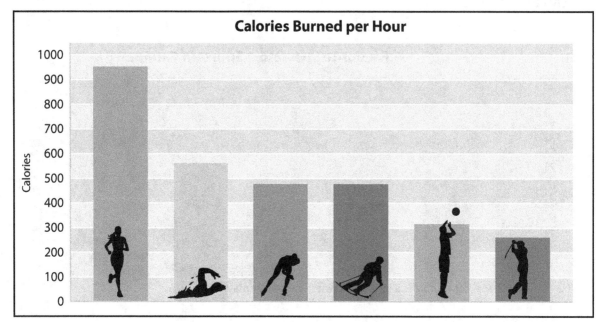

Calories Burned per Hour

Based on information from: NutriStrategy, http://www.nutristrategy.com/activitylist4.htm 2007.

  a. When you _____*swim*_____ , you burn 563 calories per hour.

  b. When you _____ a golf club, you burn 281 calories per hour.

  c. When you _____ baskets, you burn 317 calories per hour.

  d. When you _____ in track and field, you burn 950 calories per hour.

  e. When you _____ or _____ , you burn 493 calories per hour.

3. What about you? Check (✓) the activities you do.

  ☐ work out   ☐ swim   ☐ race   ☐ skate   ☐ dive   ☐ ski

Challenge Look in your dictionary. Which activities need more than one person? **Example:** *tackle*

1. Look in your dictionary. What do you see? Put the words in the correct categories.

arrow	bat	boots	bow	catcher's mask
club	glove	helmet	poles	racket
inline skates	~~uniform~~	shoulder pads	target	shin guards

Baseball   **Skiing**   **Golf**   **Skating**

uniform _____   _____   _____

_____   _____   **Tennis**   **Archery**

_____   **Football**   _____   _____

_____   _____   **Soccer**

_____   _____   _____

2. Look at the chart. Number the items in order of size. (1 = the biggest)

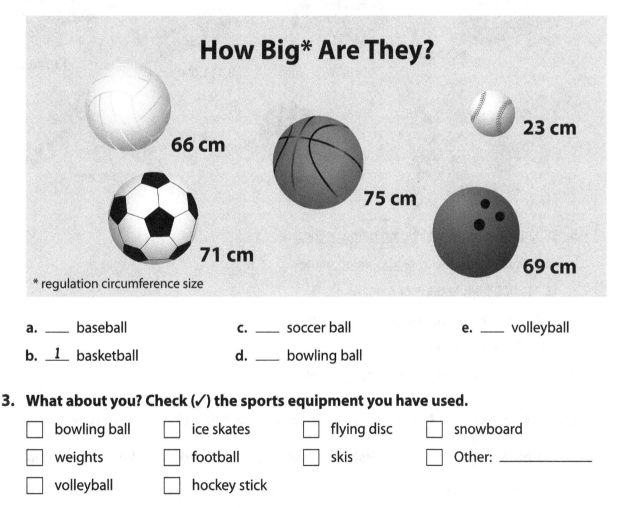

How Big* Are They?

66 cm

75 cm

23 cm

71 cm

69 cm

* regulation circumference size

a. ___ baseball   **c.** ___ soccer ball   **e.** ___ volleyball

b. _1_ basketball   **d.** ___ bowling ball

3. What about you? Check (✓) the sports equipment you have used.

☐ bowling ball   ☐ ice skates   ☐ flying disc   ☐ snowboard

☐ weights   ☐ football   ☐ skis   ☐ Other: _____

☐ volleyball   ☐ hockey stick

Challenge Look at pages 228 and 229 in your dictionary. What kinds of sports equipment do you see? Make a list. You have only three minutes!

1. Look in your dictionary. Cross out the word that doesn't belong.

a. Types of paint   acrylic   ~~glue stick~~   oil   watercolour

b. Things to collect   action figures   baseball cards   clubs   figurines

c. Games   cards   checkers   chess   crochetting

d. Cards   hearts   diamonds   paper dolls   spades

e. Painting   canvas   easel   paintbrush   dice

2. Look at the chart. Circle the words to complete the sentences.

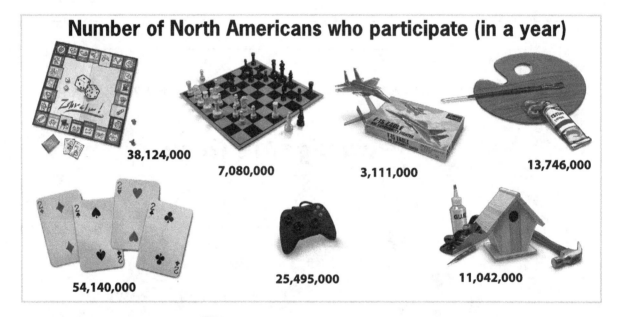

Number of North Americans who participate (in a year)

38,124,000

7,080,000

3,111,000

13,746,000

54,140,000

25,495,000

11,042,000

a. 38,124,000 people play (board games)/ chess.

b. 25,495,000 people play cards / video games.

c. 13,746,000 people draw or paint /quilt.

d. 11,042,000 people use model / woodworking kits.

e. 7,080,000 play checkers / chess.

f. 3,111,000 people use doll-making / model kits.

3. What about you? Look at the hobbies in Exercise 2. Write them in the correct column.

Hobbies I Do	Hobbies I Don't Do	Hobbies I Would Like to Do
_____	_____	_____
_____	_____	_____
_____	_____	_____

4. **Unscramble these hobby and game words. You can use your dictionary for help.**

a. DEMLO STIRAN   M   O   D   (E)   L   T   R   A   I   N   S

b. DIVOE MAGE   __ __ ◯ __ __ __ __ ◯ __

c. RANY   ◯ __ __ __

d. TUILQ CLOBK   __ __ ◯ __ __ ◯ __ __ __

e. TROARY TRUTEC   __ ◯ __ __ __ __ __ __ __ __ ◯

f. TREASH   __ ◯ __ ◯ __ __

Put the letters into the circles.

◯ ◯ ◯ ◯ ◯ ◯ ◯ ◯ ◯ ◯

Unscramble the letters in the circles.

A hobby: __ __ __ __ __ __ __ __ __ __

5. **What is it? Use unscrambled words from Exercise 4 to write what people are talking about.**

I'm going to play *it* for hours.

a. _____ *video game* _____

It's one of the red cards.

b. _____

I love to put *them* on the track.

c. _____

I'm using *it* to knit a sweater.

d. _____

6. **What about you? How much do you like to do the following? Check (✓) the columns.**

	I love it.	I like it.	It's OK.	I don't like it.	I don't know.
paint					
do crafts					
play cards					
collect things					
play games					
pretend					

Challenge What can you do with construction paper? **Example:** *You can make posters.*

Electronics and Photography

1. Look in your dictionary. Cross out the word that doesn't belong.

a. **Things you carry**	CD boom box	~~DVD player~~	portable cassette player
b. **Things you watch**	flat screen TV	portable DVD player	microphone
c. **Things that are small**	MP3 player	portable TV	tuner
d. **Things for music**	adapter	speakers	turntable
e. **Things that take pictures**	digital camera	LCD projector	film camera
f. **Things for a camera**	dock	tripod	zoom lens

2. Look at the ad. How much money can you save?

a. speakers __$25.00__   e. CD boom box _____

b. portable cassette player _____   f. MP3 player _____

c. personal CD player _____   g. film camera _____

d. camcorder _____   h. digital camera _____

234

3. Look at the universal remote buttons. Write the function. Use the words in the box.

fast forward	pause	play	~~rewind~~

a. _____rewind_____   b. _____   c. _____   d. _____

4. Look at the pictures. Which one matches each description? Write the number.

1.

2.

3.

4.

a. overexposed   _3_   **c.** out of focus   ___

b. good for a photo album   ___   **d.** underexposed   ___

5. What about you? Check (✓) the items you have. Circle the items you want.

☐ CD boom box   ☐ portable DVD palyer   ☐ tripod

☐ MP3 player   ☐ digital camera   ☐ camera case

☐ personal CD player   ☐ film camera   ☐ LCD projector

☐ flat screen TV   ☐ camcorder   ☐ photo album

Challenge Look in the newspaper or online. Find out today's prices for three of the items in Exercise 2. Compare the prices with the prices in the ad.

1. Look in your dictionary. Circle all the dictionary words in the TV schedule.

Saturday Evening ◀▶ ▼▲

	8:00	8:30	9:00	9:30	10:00	10:30	11:00
2	It's Family!! Eddie goes to the office in the last show of this popular sitcom.	Lisa! Talk show host interviews a soap opera star.	Movie: There He Goes! (2001 comedy) Karl Chaps looks for a job in the big city, but finds many problems along the way–including a banana peel! Lots of laughs. **				News
4	Italy v. France Final game of the World Cup				Movie: Jersey Jim (2006 action-adventure) Snakes, rocks, waterfalls, and much more. With Johnny Diamond.****		
5	Wild World Nature program looks at the endangered panda.	Mystery! Holmes investigates a murder in a small town. Filled with suspense.			The Truth is Out There Visitors from Mars.		News
6	Movie: Marta (2008) Two lonely people find romance in this sweet movie by director Emanuel Soto.****				Home The camera follows 16 real people as they do their daily activities, such as brushing their teeth. But do they floss, too?		
7	Time's Up! New game show	Max and Minnie Cartoon	Movie: The Shadow (2008) A mysterious stranger terrorizes a town. Directed by Hideaki Tanaka.**				

2. Look at Exercise 1. Write the time and channel to watch these types of shows. You can use your dictionary for help.

a. watch a funny program _____8:00, Channel 2_____

b. watch a sports program _____

c. see a program about animals _____

d. watch a funny movie _____

e. see a reality show _____

f. watch a science fiction story _____

g. see a love story _____

h. learn what's happening in the world _____ or _____

i. be scared by a movie _____

3. What about you? Work with a partner. Look at the TV schedule in Exercise 1. Try to find a program you both want to watch.

4. What kind of entertainment is it? Match.

_4_ **a.** "Romeo and Juliet are dead!"

____ **b.** "And the score is: Alicia 25, Todd 12."

____ **c.** "You can buy this for just $29.99 plus shipping."

____ **d.** "Goodbye boys and girls. See you tomorrow."

____ **e.** "Get off your horses, cowboys!"

1. children's program
2. shopping program
3. game show
4. tragedy
5. western

5. Look at the chart. Circle the words to complete the sentences. Use your dictionary for help.

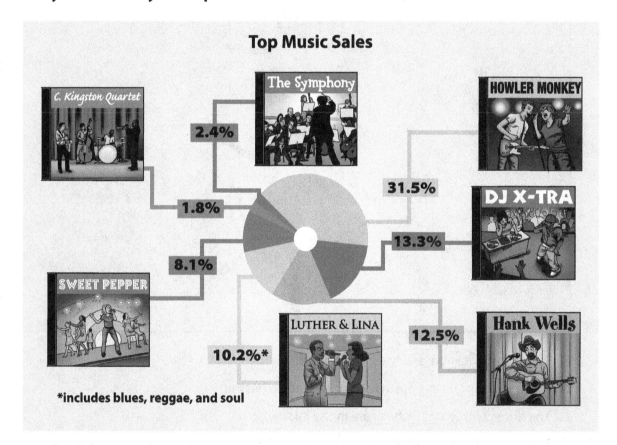

Top Music Sales

2.4%

1.8%

8.1%

31.5%

13.3%

10.2%*

12.5%

*includes blues, reggae, and soul

Based on information from: *The World Almanac and Book of Facts 2007.* (NY: World Almanac Education Group, Inc, 2007)

a. (Rock) / Hip hop was 31.5% of the total sales.

b. Classical / Country was 12.5%.

c. Pop / Jazz was 1.8%.

d. The most popular music was rock / pop.

e. Blues / Hip hop was 13.3% of total sales.

6. What about you? What kind of music do you listen to? When do you listen to it?

Challenge Take a survey. Find out your classmates' favourite kind of music.
Example: *Five students prefer reggae.*

1. Look in your dictionary. Which instruments have the following?

a. strings   __violin__ _____ _____ _____ _____

b. a keyboard   __piano__ _____ _____ _____

2. Look at the orchestra seating plan. Circle the words to complete the sentences. Use your dictionary for help.

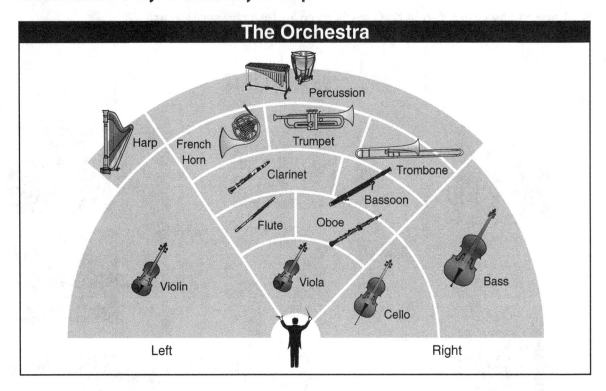

The Orchestra

a. The cellos / (violins) are to the left of the conductor.

b. The bassoons / drums are in the back of the orchestra.

c. The flutes and basses / oboes are in the middle.

d. The trumpets / trombones are also in the middle.

e. The trumpets are between the French horns and the tambourines / trombones.

f. The cellos / clarinets are to the right of the conductor.

g. There are no harmonicas / xylophones in this orchestra.

3. What about you? What would you like to do? Check (✓) the items.

☐ sing a song   ☐ conduct an orchestra

☐ be in a rock band   ☐ play an instrument (Which one?) _____

Challenge Find out about these instruments: viola, harmonica, harp, and bugle. What kinds of instruments are they? Look at the categories in your dictionary for help.

1. **Look in your dictionary.** *True* or *False*?

   a. There's a parade on New Year's Day.   _____true_____

   b. Children get candy canes on Halloween.   _____

   c. Couples use string lights on Valentine's Day.   _____

2. **Write the names of the holidays on the cards. Then circle the words to complete the sentences.**

Happy _____New Year's Day_____ !

SEND

Happy _____ !

SEND

a. The card shows (confetti) / fireworks.

b. There's a float / jack-o'-lantern on the card.

Happy _____ !

SEND

Happy _____ !

SEND

c. There's candy / turkey on the plate. It's part of a holiday costume / feast.

d. There's a red heart / mask on the card.

Merry _____ !

SEND

Happy _____ !

SEND

e. There's a flag / tree with confetti / ornaments on the card.

f. The card shows fireworks / string lights.

Challenge Make a holiday card.

Go to page 253 for Another Look (Unit 12).

1. Look in your dictionary. Who is doing the following things? Match.

1. Lou

2.  Amaka

3.  Lou's mother

4.  Todd

5. Gani

_4_ **a.** hiding   ___ **c.** videotaping   ___ **e.** blowing out candles

___ **b.** wrapping a present   ___ **d.** making a wish

2. Melissa is planning a party. Look at her list and the picture. Check (✓) the things Melissa did.

For The Party

- ☑ buy decorations
- ☐ hang decorations
- ☐ buy a present
- ☐ wrap the present
- ☐ buy candles
- ☐ sweep the deck
- ☐ bake a cake

3. Look in your dictionary. Where are they? Check (✓) the columns.

	Backyard	Deck
a. decorations	✓	✓
b. presents		
c. cakes		
d. lemonade		
e. tables		
f. candles		
g. the woman videotaping		
h. the boy hiding		
i. the girl wrapping		

4. Complete Lou's sister's diary entry. Use the words in the box.

blow out	brought	~~deck~~	hid
make	presents	videotaped	wrapped

March 3

Today was Lou and Grandpa Gani's birthday party! It was great. Mom made hamburgers

on the _____deck_____, and we all ate at a big table in the backyard. Lou got a lot of cool
　　　　　a.

_____. One man _____ two boxes—one for Lou and one for
　b.　　　　　　　　　**c.**

Grandpa. He _____ them with pretty blue paper. Best of all, there were two
　　　　　d.

cakes! I wanted Lou and Grandpa to hurry up and _____ a wish and
　　　　　　　　　　　　　　　　　　　　e.

_____ the candles so we could eat them! Mom _____ the whole
　f.　　　　　　　　　　　　　　　　　**g.**

party. Poor Todd. He _____ because he doesn't like to sing. This year Lou is 18
　　　　　　　　h.

and Grandpa is 80. Next year, I'll be 14! I hope I get two cakes, too.

5. What about you? Think about a party you went to. Check (✓) the things that happened. Did people . . .

☐ bring presents?　☐ videotape the party?　☐ blow out candles?　☐ make a wish?

Challenge Look in your dictionary. Imagine you were at Lou and Gani's birthday party. Write a paragraph about it. Who was there? What did they do?

"C" Search

Look at the picture. There are more than 20 items that begin with the letter **c.** Find and circle them. Make a list of the items that you circled.

Example: *coins*

Picture Crossword Puzzle

Complete the puzzle.

		¹					
²S	C	I	S	S	O	R	³S
			⁴				
	⁵						
				⁶		⁷	
⁸							
⁹							

Across →

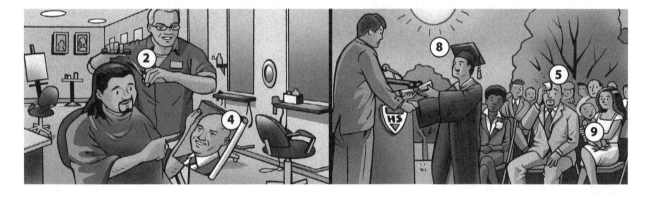

Down ↓

Another Look (Unit 3)

Picture Word Search

There are 15 housing words in the word search. They go across (→) and down (↓). Find and circle 13 more.

"C" Search

Look at the picture. There are more than 25 items that begin with the letter *c*. Find and circle them. Make a list of the items that you circled.

Example: *coconut*

Picture Word Search

There are 17 clothing words in the word search. They go across (→) and down (↓). Find and circle 15 more.

S	W	E	A	T	S	H	I	R	T
O	A	T	S	I	O	A	B	I	U
C	L	A	V	E	S	T	E	N	R
K	L	O	A	F	E	R	S	G	T
S	E	T	E	N	N	O	R	O	L
S	T	H	R	E	A	D	O	B	E
B	R	A	O	E	N	I	R	O	N
E	L	M	E	D	I	U	M	O	E
L	O	R	A	L	R	P	A	T	C
T	E	N	J	E	A	N	S	S	K

Picture Crossword Puzzle

Complete the puzzle.

¹T	A	²B	L	E	³T		⁴		
					⁵			⁶	
⁷									
⁸		⁹		¹⁰					
						¹¹			
	¹²		¹³						
				¹⁴			¹⁵		
	¹⁶								

Down ↓

1.   2.

3.   4.

6.   9.

10.   12.   13.   14.   15.

Across →

1.   5.   7.   8.   11.

14.   16.

"C" Search

Look at the picture. There are more than 10 items that begin with the letter **c.** Find and circle them. Make a list of the items that you circled.

Example: *coffee shop*

Where Have All the Flowers Gone?

Look at the picture. Circle all the flowers. Write the locations of the flowers.

Example: *on the bus*

Another Look (Unit 9)

Picture Word Search

There are 18 work words in the word search. Find and circle 16 more.

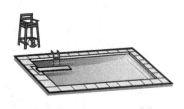

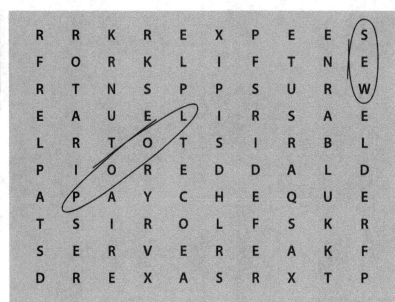

```
R   R   K   R   E   X   P   E   E   S
F   O   R   K   L   I   F   T   N   E
R   T   N   S   P   P   S   U   R   W
E   A   U   E   L   I   R   S   A   E
L   R   T   O   T   S   I   R   B   L
P   I   O   R   E   D   D   A   L   D
A   P   A   Y   C   H   E   Q   U   E
T   S   I   R   O   L   F   S   K   R
S   E   R   V   E   R   E   A   K   F
D   R   E   X   A   S   R   X   T   P
```

Scrambled Notes

Unscramble the words for these school subjects.

English Composition

gEnshil poCmsooniti

rapagrhap _____

nestneec _____

locno _____

deti _____

greyohGap _____

aslind _____

eacon _____

verir _____

palsin _____

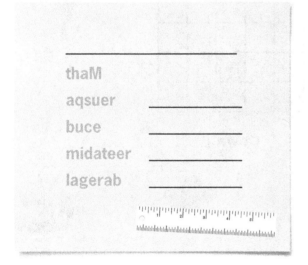

_____

thaM

aqsuer _____

buce _____

midateer _____

lagerab _____

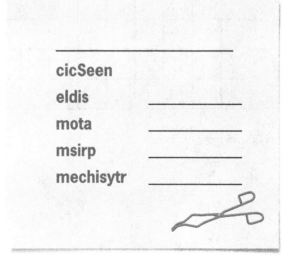

_____

cicSeen

eldis _____

mota _____

msirp _____

mechisytr _____

_____

tuCrompse

trinper _____

somue _____

wreto _____

tofsrwae _____

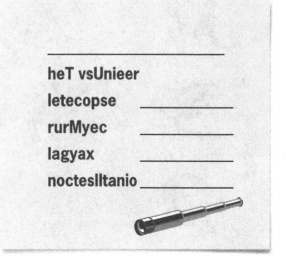

_____

heT vsUnieer

letecopse _____

rurMyec _____

lagyax _____

nocteslltanio _____

Picture Crossword Puzzle

Complete the puzzle.

			¹S								³		
²			T										
			A		⁴				⁵				
	⁶		R										
			F				⁷	⁸					
⁹			I			¹⁰							
			S										
			H			¹¹				¹²			
			¹³										
								¹⁴					
			¹⁵										

Across →

2.

4.

5.

7.

9.

11.

14.

15.

Down ↓

1.

3.

4.

6.

8.

10.

12.

13.

"C" Search

Look at the picture. There are more than 25 items and activities that begin with the letter **c.** Find and circle them. Make a list of the items and activities that you circled.

Example: *cooler*

Challenge Exercises

Challenge for page 27

Complete the receipt.

CHEAP EDDIE'S
Every Day is a Sale Day

6/11

1 ___cellphone___   _____

Tax @ 15% $10.49

Total   _____

Cash $90.00

Change   _____

THANK YOU

$79.95
$69.95

Challenge for page 75

Look at Exercise 2 on page 75 in this book. Convert the metric measurements to imperial (U.S.) measurements. Use the charts in your dictionary for help.

a. _____680 grams_____ = ___about 1 1/2 pounds___

b. _____ = _____

c. _____ = _____

e. _____ = _____

Challenge for page 165

Complete Asif Ahmad paycheque from page 165. Use the information in Exercise 4 and your dictionary for help.

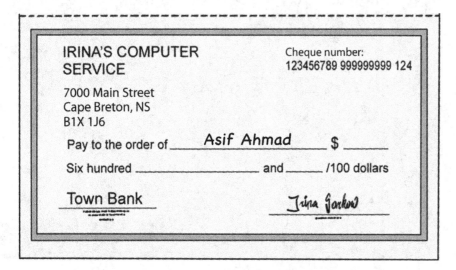

IRINA'S COMPUTER SERVICE

Cheque number:
123456789 999999999 124

7000 Main Street
Cape Breton, NS
B1X 1J6

Pay to the order of _____Asif Ahmad_____ $ _____

Six hundred _____ and _____ /100 dollars

Town Bank   Irina Gorkov

Challenge for page 167

Ask four people about their jobs. What do they do? How many hours a week do they work? Fill in the chart below. Then, write sentences about them. Follow the example below.

What is your name?	What do you do?	How many hours a week do you work?
Meng	cashier	25
1.		
2.		
3.		
4.		

Example: *Meng is a cashier. She works twenty-five hours a week.*

Challenge for page 189

Think of different types of schools in another country. List in order the schools and students' ages. Follow the example below.

Country	School	Ages
Peru	preschool	2 to 5 years old
	primary school	6 to 11 years old
	secondary school	12 to 17 years old

Country	School	Ages

Challenge for page 209

Work with a partner. Look at pages 208 and 209 in your dictionary. Write at least two examples for each category. Use pages 211, 212, 214, and 216 in your dictionary for help.

In the Lillo Nature Centre	
Trees	oak,
Flowers	
Insects	
Mammals	

Challenge for page 229

How many players are there on the following teams? If you don't know, try to find out.

basketball   _____

soccer   _____

baseball   _____

hockey   _____

football   _____

volleyball   _____

HIGH BEGINNING
Workbook

LISTENING
EXERCISES

Audio clips at
http://www.oupcanada.com/OPDWorkbook

Username: **opdworkbook**
Password: **moose**

🎧 **1.** Listen to the entire conversation. Answer the questions with your class.

    a. Where is Carlos?

    b. What is he doing?

🎧 **2.** Listen to each part of the conversation. Match the sentences below to the parts of the conversation in which you hear them.

> 1. _____   **a.** And what's your date of birth?
>
> 2. _____   **b.** Is there an apartment number with that?
>
> 3. _____   **c.** Put your signature right there.
>
> 4. _____   **d.** What city do you live in?
>
> 5. _____   **e.** Can you spell that for me, please?
>
> 6. _____   **f.** Now I need your phone number.

🎧 **3.** Listen again. Complete the form.

School Registration Form

_____   _____
first name   last name

_____   _____   _____
address   apartment number   city

_____   _____   _____   (___) ___-____
province   postal code   phone number   cell phone number

                                                     M   F
_____   _____   _____   _____
birthplace   DOB   SIN   sex

4. Where have you completed forms like this? Make a list of places.

_____   _____

_____   _____

Oxford Picture Dictionary pp. 6–7

🎧 1. Look at the picture at the top of pages 6 and 7 in the OPD. Listen to the entire conversation. Answer the questions with your class.

    a. What is Tom looking for?

    b. How many people does he ask for help?

    c. Does he find it?

🎧 2. Close your dictionary. Listen to each part of the conversation. Match the sentences below to the parts of the conversation in which you hear them.

1. _____	**a.** Well, look in the bookcase.
2. _____	**b.** It's near her notebook.
3. _____	**c.** We'll return at one o'clock.
4. _____	**d.** The teacher is at the projector.
5. _____	**e.** I think it's over there by the computer.
6. _____	**f.** He's over there, in front of the map.

🎧 3. Complete the paragraph. Use the words in the box. Then listen again and check your answers.

open	dictionary	textbooks	headphones
workbooks	listening	sit down	talking

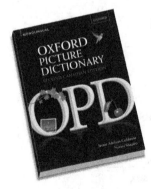

Mrs. Olsen says the _____ is by the computer, but it's not there. Tom looks in the bookcase. He sees a lot of _____, but no dictionaries. He looks under some _____ too. Albert's dictionary is on Linda's desk. Linda is _____ to the _____. Tom asks Linda for the dictionary, but she says, "Shhh! The teacher is _____." Mrs. Olsen says, "Please _____ and _____ your books to page 18." Tom never gets to look in the dictionary.

4. Write five sentences describing the things in your classroom.

There is a large whiteboard. _____

_____

_____

_____

🎧 1. Look at the weather map on page 13 in the OPD. Listen to the entire forecast. Answer the questions with your class.

    a. What five places are in the forecast?

    b. Which place is hot?

    c. Which place is cold?

🎧 2. Close your dictionary. Listen to each part of the forecast. Underline *True* or *False*.

a. It's sunny and clear in Toronto.	True	False
b. It's sunny and warm in Regina.	True	False
c. It's raining and cold in Vancouver.	True	False
d. There's a thunderstorm in Montreal.	True	False

🎧 3. Complete the sentences. Use the words in the box. Then listen again and check your answers.

thunderstorm	foggy	heat wave	snowing
raining	clear	snowstorm	cool

In Toronto, it's a _____ day. They're having a _____.

In Regina and Calgary, it's _____ and cloudy. It isn't _____.

In Vancouver, it's _____ in many places. There could be a _____ later this afternoon.

It's _____ in Montreal. The _____ should end this afternoon.

4. Write five sentences about the weather in your area.

Today it's sunny and hot. _____

_____

_____

_____

_____

Oxford Picture Dictionary p. 16

🎧 **1.** Listen to the commentators on the recording. Answer the questions with your class.

    a. What event is taking place?

    b. When is it taking place?

🎧 **2.** Listen to each part of the conversation. Match the sentences below to the parts of the conversation in which you hear them.

1. _____	**a.** This morning, he placed first in both the 100-metre and 200-metre races.
2. _____	**b.** What a beautiful day here — nineteen degrees and sunny — just perfect weather for running.
3. _____	**c.** We'll return at one o'clock.

🎧 **3.** Complete the paragraph. Use the words in the box. Then listen again and check your answers.

first	fifty-four	eight	twelfth
two hundred	four hundred	eighth	three

The commentators are at the _____ annual Provincial Track and Field
Championship. They are waiting for the _____-metre race to begin.
Before the race starts, _____ runners line up. The commentators think
that Stanley Cheng, who is in lane _____, will win the race because he
placed _____ in the one hundred-metre and _____-metre
races earlier in the day. Stanley actually finishes in _____ place
because he trips over his shoelace. Oscar Anderson wins the race with a time of
_____ seconds.

4. Look at the picture at the top of pages 6 and 7 in the OPD. Make a list of the things you see.

    7 chairs

    _____   _____

    _____   _____

    _____   _____

    _____   _____

🎧 1. Listen to the entire conversation. Answer the questions with your class.

    a. What is the couple talking about?

    b. What does the couple decide to do?

🎧 2. Listen to each part of the conversation. Match the sentences below to the parts of the conversation in which you hear them.

1. _____	**a.** You mean we wouldn't be home for Thanksgiving or my birthday?
2. _____	**b.** We can spend Christmas there.
3. _____	**c.** We can't miss the wedding!
4. _____	**d.** We should start planning our next vacation soon, dear.

🎧 3. Complete the paragraph. Use the words in the box. Then listen again and check your answers.

wedding	Boxing Day	birthday	Canada Day
Thanksgiving	vacation	anniversary	New Year's Day

The man and woman are trying to plan a _____. The woman suggests spending

_____ in Ottawa. The man wants to visit British Columbia in October, but the

woman doesn't want to be away from her family for _____ or her _____.

The couple cannot travel in November because it is a busy month — they have to attend a

_____ and a 60th-_____ party. They finally decide to fly to

Cuba on _____ and return on _____.

4. Which Canadian holidays do you enjoy? What do you do to celebrate these days?

_____

_____

_____

_____

_____

Oxford Picture Dictionary p. 26

🎧 1. Listen to the conversations. Answer the questions with your class.

a. Where are the conversations taking place?

b. How many customers does the vendor have?

🎧 2. Listen to each part of the conversation. Match the sentences below to the parts of the conversation in which you hear them.

1. _____	a. I've got...a toonie, two loonies, six quarters, three nickels, and seven pennies.
2. _____	b. Here's your change: a five, a toonie, and a quarter.
3. _____	c. Three dollars and ten cents, please.
4. _____	d. Here you go — three dollars.

🎧 3. Complete the paragraph. Use the words in the box. Then listen again and check your answers.

fifty	pennies	ten	nickels
toonie	cents	dime	dollars

The first customer pays for her hot dog with a _____-dollar bill and receives a

five-dollar bill, a _____, and a quarter in change. The second customer wants

to give the vendor a _____-dollar bill, but pays with three loonies and a

_____ instead. The third customer shows the vendor all the money he has. It

includes three _____ and seven _____. The fourth customer

gives the vendor three _____ and lets him keep the change, which is five

_____.

4. Look in your purse or wallet. Make a list of the bills and coins that you have.

_____   _____

_____   _____

_____   _____

_____   _____

🎧 1. Listen to all four conversations between the clerk and her customers. Answer the questions with your class.

    a. What does this store sell?

    b. What do the customers want to do?

🎧 2. Listen to each conversation. Match the sentence with the conversation.

> 1. _____
>
> 2. _____
>
> 3. _____
>
> 4. _____
>
> **a.** I want to pay with a personal cheque.
>
> **b.** I want to return this lamp.
>
> **c.** I want to exchange this lamp.
>
> **d.** The sale price for this lamp is $12.50.

🎧 3. Complete the paragraph. Use the words in the box. Then listen again and check your answers.

receipt	exchange	pay	buy
total	return	sales tax	credit card

```
----------------------------
       LAMP SHOP
     221 QUEEN STREET
----------------------------

ITEM                PRICE
1 DESK LAMP @       $12.50
1 DESK LAMP @       $12.50

SUBTOTAL            $25.00
SALES TAX           $ 2.06
TOTAL               $27.06

PAYMENT METHOD:      CASH
```

Darla works at the returns desk at the Lamp Shop. Her first customer can't _____ his lamp because he didn't _____ it at the Lamp Shop. Darla's second customer isn't happy because he doesn't want to _____ cash or use a _____. Her third customer doesn't understand why his _____ is $27.06. He forgot about the _____ of $2.06. Darla's last customer can _____ her lamp with no problem because she has her _____.

    4. Write five sentences that describe your shopping habits.

    I usually pay with cash. _____

    _____

    _____

    _____

    _____

Oxford Picture Dictionary p. 32

🎧 1. Listen to the entire conversation. Answer the questions with your class.

    a. What does the woman ask Nishad to do?

    b. How does she try to help him?

🎧 2. Listen to each part of the conversation. Match the sentences below to the parts of the conversation in which you hear them.

> **1.** _____   **a.** Just look for three attractive young women.
>
> **2.** _____   **b.** Wow, that is tall.
>
> **3.** _____   **c.** Oh, she's an average height, like me.
>
> **4.** _____   **d.** Well, Meghan is short and thin.

🎧 3. Complete the paragraph. Use the words in the box. Then listen again and check your answers.

thin	blind	tattoo	taller
attractive	young	mole	pregnant

    The woman asks Nishad to pick up her friends from the airport. She describes them as

_____ and _____. Meghan is short and _____.

She has a _____ and a butterfly _____. Barbara is _____

than Nishad and she is seven months _____. Malia is heavier than the other two

friends and she is _____.

    4. Imagine that someone you have never met will be picking you up from the airport. Write a clear description of yourself so that he or she can find you.

_____

_____

_____

_____

_____

Oxford Picture Dictionary pp. 34–35

🎧 **1.** Look at pages 34 and 35 in the OPD. Listen to the entire conversation. Answer the questions with your class.

    a. Who is talking to Sue?

    b. What is happening tonight?

🎧 **2.** Close your dictionary. Listen to each part of the conversation. Match the sentences below to the parts of the conversation in which you hear them.

1. _____	**a.** My daughter is 12.
2. _____	**b.** My wife is cleaning the house.
3. _____	**c.** My wife's family is coming over tonight.
4. _____	**d.** My brother-in-law and sister-in-law are coming.
5. _____	**e.** My mother-in-law and father-in-law are coming.
6. _____	**f.** My niece is six.

🎧 **3.** Complete the paragraph. Use the words in the box. Then listen again and check your answers.

grandparents	daughter	son	children
niece	cousins	mother-in-law	nephew

Carlos's _____ and father-in-law are coming. Alice and Eddie are looking forward to

seeing their _____. Carlos has two _____. His _____

is starting middle school next year. His _____ is 14 years old. Carlos's brother- and

sister-in-law are also coming. Carlos's _____ is 2 years old. His nephew and

_____ are very active. Alice and Eddie call them "our crazy _____."

4. Draw a family tree. Name the people and write a few sentences describing how they are related to each other.

Oxford Picture Dictionary pp. 36–37

🎧 **1.** Listen to the entire conversation between a husband and a wife. Answer the questions with your class.

    a. Why is the woman leaving?

    b. Who is staying with the baby?

    c. How does the mother feel? How does the father feel?

🎧 **2.** Listen to each part of the conversation. Match the sentences below to the parts of the conversation in which you hear them.

1. _____	**a.** Take the car safety seat.
2. _____	**b.** Don't feed him until 3:00, though.
3. _____	**c.** Don't forget to bathe Joey tonight.
4. _____	**d.** Rock him before bed.
5. _____	**e.** Be sure you have wipes if you take him out.
6. _____	**f.** There are diapers on the table.

🎧 **3.** Complete the paragraph. Use the words in the box. Then listen again and check your answers.

baby food	bib	buckle up	sing
baby bag	diapers	rock	bathe

Don's wife is going away overnight. She tells Don to _____ Joey that night. She says

the extra _____ are in the cabinet. There's _____ on the shelf, and

she reminds him to use the _____. Don helps take care of Joey every day, so he isn't

worried. He knows there are wipes in the _____. He'll _____ in the car.

He won't forget to _____ Joey before bed. But he won't _____.

Don is a good father, but he's a terrible singer.

4. Imagine you are leaving your baby with a friend. Write instructions.

🎧 1. Look at pages 38 and 39 in the OPD. Listen to the story. Point to the times you hear. Answer the question with your class.

Who is telling the story?

🎧 2. Close your dictionary. Listen to each part of the story. Write the times you hear.

> **a.** At my house, we eat breakfast together at _____.
>
> **b.** My parents take us to school at _____.
>
> **c.** My mom picks us up from school at _____.
>
> **d.** After dinner, usually around _____, my sister and I do homework.
>
> **e.** At _____, I'm still working hard on my homework.
>
> **f.** About _____, my sister and I go to bed.

🎧 3. Complete the paragraph. Use the words in the box. Then listen again and check your answers.

clean the house	takes the bus	reads the paper	drives
do homework	watches TV	checks email	relax

Jimmy's parents take him to school in the morning. Then his mother _____ to adult school and his father _____ to work. After school Jimmy, his mother and his sister _____. In the evening, he and his sister _____. His parents _____, and his mom _____. When Jimmy and his sister go to bed, his dad _____ and his mom _____.

4. Make a schedule for yourself for tomorrow.

> *9:00 am go to school*
>
> _____
>
> _____
>
> _____
>
> _____
>
> _____

Oxford Picture Dictionary pp. 40–41

🎧 1. Look at pages 40 and 41 in the OPD. Listen to two people talk about family photos. Listen to the entire conversation. Answer the questions with your class.

   a. Who is the woman that is speaking?

   b. Who is the man that is speaking?

   c. Where was Grandfather born?

🎧 2. Close your dictionary. Listen to each part of the conversation. Write the years you hear.

> **a.** We went to Egypt in _____.
>
> **b.** He was born in _____, two years before me.
>
> **c.** He immigrated with his parents in _____.
>
> **d.** He graduated in _____.
>
> **e.** He got his degree in _____.
>
> **f.** We bought this house in _____.

🎧 3. Complete the paragraph. Use the words in the box. Then listen again and check your answers.

> | fell in love | get married | graduated | immigrated |
> |---|---|---|---|
> | retired | was born | bought a home | travelled |

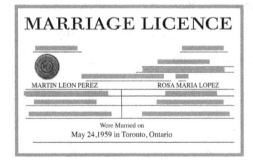

MARRIAGE LICENCE

MARTIN LEON PEREZ   ROSA MARIA LOPEZ

Were Married on
May 24, 1959 in Toronto, Ontario

Martin _____ in Nicaragua. He _____ when he was 15 years old, and he _____ from high school three years later. Martin and Rosa met in 1955. They _____, but they didn't _____ until 1959. Six years later, they _____. Martin _____ in 2000, and he and Rosa _____ for a few years.

4. Write five sentences about your life.

I was born in 19____. _____

_____

_____

_____

_____

Oxford Picture Dictionary pp. 42–43

🎧 **1.** Listen to the entire conversation. Answer the questions with your class.

    a. Why hasn't Riyaad been studying for his exam?

    b. What advice does Danny give Riyaad?

🎧 **2.** Listen to each part of the conversation. Match the sentences below to the parts of the conversation in which you hear them.

    1. _____   **a.** I met someone last week and I think I'm in love!

    2. _____   **b.** You didn't have to be afraid to ask her out.

    3. _____   **c.** I can concentrate better when I'm full.

    4. _____   **d.** You always help me out when I'm confused by the professor.

    5. _____   **e.** You're upset over nothing.

🎧 **3.** Complete the paragraph. Use the words in the box. Then listen again and check your answers.

hungry	worried	surprises	relieved
in love	thirsty	crazy	frustrated

Riyaad started studying for his exam last night, but stopped because he was

_____. This _____ Danny, because Riyaad is usually a good

student. Riyaad explains that he could not concentrate on studying because he is

_____ with someone, but he is _____ that she doesn't know

he exists. Danny tells Riyaad that this is _____ and convinces Riyaad to call the

woman. Riyaad is _____ when she asks him out for coffee. With Riyaad's

problem solved, the two friends order some pizza and pop, because they are

_____ and _____.

4. Answer the questions.

    a. How did you feel the first time you had to use English to communicate with someone?

    _____

    b. How did you feel the first time you travelled by plane?

    _____

Oxford Picture Dictionary pp. 48–49

🎧 **1.** Listen to the entire conversation. Answer the questions with your class.

    a. What is Mrs. Denunzio doing?

    b. Does she mention anything that she doesn't like?

🎧 **2.** Listen to each part of the conversation. Match the sentences below to the parts of the conversation in which you hear them.

1. _____	**a.** Hmm, I would have to paint this room.
2. _____	**b.** Your classified ad said that the apartment is 800 dollars a month.
3. _____	**c.** First, I'll need you to submit an application.
4. _____	**d.** I'll start packing today.
5. _____	**e.** Are utilities included?

🎧 **3.** Complete the paragraph. Use the words in the box. Then listen again and check your answers.

unfurnished apartment	pay the first and last month's rent	paint
packing	sign the rental agreement	utilities
classified ad	submit an application	

708 Apartments for rent

Westside Apartments

3 bdrm 2 ba furn apt New kit
$1000/mo Util incl Call mgr

555-1002 eves

Mrs. Denunzio is looking at an _____ that she saw listed in a _____. She is happy when she finds out that some of the _____, water and electricity, are included. She does not like the colour of one of the rooms, though, and would have to _____. The manager asks Mrs. Denunzio to _____, and tells her that once she has been approved, she can _____. When she returns, she should bring a cheque for 1,600 dollars, then she can _____. Mrs. Denunzio is so excited that she plans to start _____ that day.

4. Have you ever rented an apartment? What steps did you have to take?

_____

_____

_____

_____

Oxford Picture Dictionary pp. 50–51

🎧 **1.** Listen to the entire conversation between a manager and a woman looking for an apartment. Answer the questions with your class.

    a. What kind of apartment is the woman looking for?

    b. Is she going to move in?

🎧 **2.** Listen to each part of the conversation. Underline *True* or *False*.

a. The woman saw a vacancy sign and wants to look around.	True	False
b. The woman is happy about the playground because she has children.	True	False
c. All of the second-floor apartments have balconies.	True	False
d. There are six storage lockers on the first floor.	True	False
e. Every apartment has an intercom and a deadbolt lock.	True	False
f. The apartment is really nice, but it's expensive.	True	False

🎧 **3.** Complete the paragraph. Use the words in the box. Then listen again and check your answers.

apartment complex	peepholes	laundry room	washers
recreation room	second floor	dryers	swimming pool

Sara visits an _____. She's looking for an apartment on the _____. She likes the _____ in the courtyard. There's also a _____ with a big-screen TV. There's a _____ on the first floor of every building. It has six _____ and four _____. She also likes the security features. All of the doors have dead bolt locks and _____.

4. Imagine a perfect apartment. Write five sentences that describe it.

It has a large balcony.

_____

_____

_____

_____

_____

Oxford Picture Dictionary p. 56

🎧 **1.** Listen to the entire conversation. Answer the questions with your class.

    a. What are the son and daughter doing?

    b. Why aren't they happy about the carpet?

🎧 **B.** Listen to each part of the conversation. Match the sentences below to the parts of the conversation in which you hear them.

1. _____	**a.** Put the houseplant on the coffee table.
2. _____	**b.** When I get my new carpet, it will be perfect.
3. _____	**c.** Should I put the end tables by the sofa?
4. _____	**d.** Put it here across from the window.
5. _____	**e.** I'll put the throw pillows on it later.
6. _____	**f.** I'll bring in the TV.

🎧 **3.** Complete the paragraph. Use the words in the box. Then listen again and check your answers.

loveseat	coffee table	sofa	end tables
houseplant	entertainment centre	lamp	TV

Amanda and Tom are helping their mother move. They put the _____ across from the window and the _____ near the fireplace. They set up the _____ to the right of the fireplace. Amanda brought in the _____. They put the _____ in front of the sofa and put a _____ on it. There are two _____. The mother wants her _____ on the one next to the sofa. When Amanda and Tom are finished, they're tired, but their mother is happy.

4. Write five sentences that describe your living room.

There is a picture above the sofa. _____

_____

_____

_____

_____

🎧 **1.** Listen to the entire conversation. Answer the questions with your class.

    a. What does the couple have to do?

    b. What does the man tell the woman not to do? Why?

🎧 **2.** Listen to each part of the conversation. Match the sentences below to the parts of the conversation in which you hear them.

1. _____	**a.** I'll just take out these bags of garbage.
2. _____	**b.** I'll tell them to put away their toys.
3. _____	**c.** Don't forget to sweep the floor first.
4. _____	**d.** I'll wash the dishes and you can dry them.

🎧 **3.** Complete the paragraph. Use the words in the box. Then listen again and check your answers.

taking out	clean	vacuums	putting away
making	recycling	mopping	wash

The couple is cleaning the house. The man starts by _____ the kitchen floor while the woman _____ the living room carpet. In the kitchen, they _____ and dry the dishes, and then _____ the oven. The kids have to clean their own bedrooms by _____ their toys and _____ their beds. As the man's parents arrive, the couple finishes cleaning by _____ the garbage and _____ the old newspapers.

4. Complete this chart with the types of housework you enjoy doing and the types you do not enjoy doing.

Housework I Enjoy	Housework I Do Not Enjoy

Oxford Picture Dictionary pp. 62–63

1. Listen to the entire conversation between a husband and a wife. Answer the questions with your class.

   a. What did the man find?

   b. How does the woman feel at first? How does she feel at the end of the conversation?

2. Listen to each part of the conversation. Match the sentences below to the parts of the conversation in which you hear them.

1. _____	a. And the kitchen faucet is dripping a little bit.
2. _____	b. Are there cockroaches?
3. _____	c. I think we'll need to call a roofer.
4. _____	d. Well, one of the bedroom windows is broken.

3. Complete the paragraph. Use the words in the box. Then listen again and check your answers.

overflowing	broken	roofer	plumber
exterminator	rats	dripping	leaking

   The house is cheap, but it needs a lot of repairs. One of the bedroom windows is _____,
   but that's a small problem. There are also problems with the kitchen sink. The faucet is
   _____, and the sink is _____. Joel and Anna might need to call a
   _____. Unfortunately, they might also have to call a _____ because the
   roof is _____. Finally, they probably need an _____ because there
   are _____ in the basement.

4. Answer the questions.

   a. Which problem do you think will be the most expensive to fix? Why?

   _____

   b. Which problem should Joel and Anna fix first? Why?

   _____

   c. Should they move into this house? Why or why not?

   _____

Oxford Picture Dictionary p. 69

1. Listen to the entire conversation about two different salads. Answer the questions with your class.

   a. What is the difference between the two salads?

   b. Which salad would you like better?

2. Listen to each part of the conversation. Match the ingredients below to the parts of the conversation in which you hear them.

1. _____		**a.**	onions
2. _____		**b.**	bell peppers
3. _____		**c.**	a bag of lettuce
4. _____		**d.**	cabbage
5. _____		**e.**	a head of lettuce
6. _____		**f.**	cucumber

3. Complete the paragraph. Use the words in the box. Then listen again and check your answers.

cucumber	head of lettuce	bell peppers	radishes
tomato	carrots	mushrooms	onion

The man and the woman both made salads for a party. The man used a _____. He likes colours, so he put in yellow _____ and red _____. He also put in half a _____, a few _____, a little bit of green _____ and a few white _____. The woman used a bag of lettuce and a _____ for her salad.

4. Write five sentences explaining which vegetables you like and don't like in salads.

   I like to put celery in my salad. I don't like... _____

   _____

   _____

   _____

   _____

Oxford Picture Dictionary pp. 72–73

🎧 1. Listen to the entire conversation between the customer and the clerk. Answer the questions with your class.

    a. Why does the woman need a cake?

    b. Why is the customer confused?

🎧 2. Listen to each part of the conversation. Match the sentences below to the parts of the conversation in which you hear them.

1. _____	**a.** Do you like ice cream?
2. _____	**b.** And I need eggs.
3. _____	**c.** Oh, I also need flour and oil.
4. _____	**d.** Where are the checkouts?
5. _____	**e.** I'm looking for the sugar.
6. _____	**f.** Maybe I should buy a cake.

🎧 3. Complete the paragraph. Use the words in the box. Then listen again and check your answers.

bakery	cashiers	baking products	frozen foods
aisle	cake	checkouts	dairy

Mrs. Mills wants to bake a _____, so the grocery clerk takes her to the

_____ aisle. Then he tells her that the _____ section is at the back

of the store. If Mrs. Mills wants to buy a cake, the store has lots of them in the _____

section, and she can find ice cream in _____ 2B in the _____

section. Fortunately, they didn't move the _____. The _____

are still working at the front of the store.

4. Imagine you are shopping for a party. Make a shopping list.

_____	_____
_____	_____
_____	_____
_____	_____

1. Listen to the entire conversation between a husband and a wife. Answer the questions with your class.

   a. Where is the man going? Why?

   b. How does he remember everything?

2. Listen to each part of the conversation. Underline *True* or *False*.

a. He wants a six-pack of pop.	True	False
b. She wants strawberry juice.	True	False
c. She wants two jars of peanut butter.	True	False
d. They need two boxes of cereal.	True	False
e. They need two cartons of eggs.	True	False
f. She wants a carton of milk.	True	False

3. Complete the man's shopping list. Then listen again and check your answers.

   _____ bread _____

   _____ cereal

   _____ jam

   _____ eggs

   _____ orange juice

   _____ milk

   _____ cookies

4. Write five sentences describing the foods and other items in your kitchen.

   I have two boxes of cereal. _____

   _____

   _____

Oxford Picture Dictionary pp. 76–77

🎧 **1.** Listen to the entire conversation. Answer the questions with your class.

    a. Why is Chef Zamora on the show?

    b. Is the show's host happy with what Chef Zamora makes?

🎧 **2.** Listen to each part of the conversation. Match the sentences below to the parts of the conversation in which you hear them.

1. _____	**a.** Would you like me to preheat the oven?
2. _____	**b.** I'll probably just microwave them; that's much faster.
3. _____	**c.** Now add in that cheese that I grated earlier.
4. _____	**d.** We're going to sauté the onions and garlic.

🎧 **3.** Complete the recipe. Use the words in the box. Then listen again and check your answers.

grated	mix	dice	spoon
sauté	chop	slice	stir

CHILES RELLENO

Step 1: Broil the peppers.

Step 2: _____ the onions and _____ the garlic.

Step 3: _____ the onions and garlic. Add the ground beef.

Step 4: Add spices and tomato paste and _____ everything together.

Step 5: _____ in the raisins, almonds, and olives. Add some _____ cheese.

Step 6: _____ the peppers open and stuff them with the beef mixture.

Step 7: Batter and fry the stuffed peppers.

Step 8: _____ some sauce over top and serve.

4. Name something that you enjoy cooking. How is it prepared? Write the recipe.

🎧 **1.** Look at the menu on pages 80 and 81 in the OPD. Listen to the entire conversation between the server and the customer. Answer the questions with your class.

    a. Does the man have the spaghetti dinner? Why?

    b. What is the customer's final order?

🎧 **2.** Close your dictionary. Listen to each part of the conversation. Underline *True* or *False*.

a. The customer orders a cup of regular coffee.	True False
b. The customer is going to eat dinner.	True False
c. He wants tea instead of coffee.	True False
d. He eats a club sandwich.	True False

🎧 **3.** Complete the paragraph. Use the words in the box. Then listen again and check your answers.

grilled cheese sandwich	tea	cheesecake	chef's salad
ranch dressing	milk	club sandwich	soup

Menu **

The customer can't decide what he wants. At first, he orders a slice of

_____. Then he asks for a _____. He also

orders a _____ with _____. Then he orders

a cup of _____ with _____. In the end, he changes his

order again. He gets a _____ with _____ instead.

4. Create a new conversation between a server and a customer. Write at least six lines. Read the conversation with a partner.

Server: How can I help you?

Customer: I'd like... _____

Server: _____

Customer: _____

Server: _____

Customer: _____

Server: _____

Customer: _____

Oxford Picture Dictionary pp. 88–89

🎧 1. Look at pages 88 and 89 in the OPD. Listen to the entire conversation. Point to the people who are described. Answer the questions with your class.

    a. What are the women doing in the hotel lobby?

    b. Does the woman prefer the evening gown or cocktail dress?

    c. How do they know the two people are working?

🎧 2. Close your dictionary. Listen to each part of the conversation. Underline *True* or *False*.

a. They see a cute little girl wearing overalls.	True	False
b. Both women think the evening gown is pretty.	True	False
c. They think the bellhop is probably hot in his uniform.	True	False
d. They both think the man's tie is nice.	True	False

🎧 3. Complete the paragraph. Use the words in the box. Then listen again and check your answers.

evening gown	tie	capris	clutch bag
overalls	cocktail dress	business suits	maternity dress

Michelle and Amy are sitting in a hotel lobby. There's a cute little girl wearing _____.
They see a woman on a sofa. She's wearing a _____. There are two women
who are probably going to the prom. One of them is wearing an _____.
The other one is wearing a _____ and carrying a _____.
There's another woman talking to a bellhop. She's wearing _____ and sandals.
There are two people wearing _____. Amy doesn't like the man's
_____, but Michelle does.

4. Write five sentences describing the people in your classroom. What are they wearing?

There's a woman wearing a red blouse. _____

_____

_____

_____

_____

1. Listen to the entire conversation between Tom and his friend at the store. Answer the questions with your class.

   a. What is Tom looking for?

   b. What will he get his wife?

2. Listen to each part of the conversation. Match the sentences below to the parts of the conversation in which you hear them.

   1. _____   a. Well, how about those plastic beads?

   2. _____   b. I'm going to look at the purses.

   3. _____   c. Maybe I'll get her some earrings.

   4. _____   d. I'm just looking at the jewellery.

   5. _____   e. These wallets are nice.

   6. _____   f. I don't like hats.

3. Complete the paragraph. Use the words in the box. Then listen again and check your answers.

pierced earrings	string of pearls	necklace	scarves
backpack	display case	clip-on earrings	wallets

Tom thinks about buying a _____, but the _____ is too

expensive. The store has _____, but it doesn't have any _____.

He thinks about the _____, but he doesn't know what colours she likes.

Tom wants to get her a _____, but Joe says that's not a good idea. Finally,

Tom sees some _____ in a _____. He decides to buy one

for himself and a gift card for his wife.

4. What shoes and accessories do you wear? Make a chart on your paper.

Shoes	Jewellery	Other Accessories

Oxford Picture Dictionary p. 101

🎧 1. Listen to the entire conversation between a mother and her son. Answer the questions with your class.

   a. Who is doing the laundry?

   b. What does Billy need to do first?

   c. Why must Billy take out the red T-shirt?

🎧 2. Listen to each part of the conversation. Match the sentences below to the parts of the conversation in which you hear them.

1. _____	**a.** First, you need to sort the clothes.	
2. _____	**b.** The ironing board is right there.	
3. _____	**c.** You need to unload the clothes.	
4. _____	**d.** Do you want to wear dirty clothes?	
5. _____	**e.** Now you have to put the clothes in the dryer.	
6. _____	**f.** Now load the washer.	

🎧 3. Complete the paragraph. Use the words in the box. Then listen again and check your answers.

load	dryer	laundry	laundry detergent
iron	wrinkled	dryer sheet	fold

 Billy's mom wants him to help with the _____. He has to set the washer to use hot water and add _____. Then he has to

_____ the washer with white clothes. When the clothes are clean,

Billy puts them in the _____ and puts in a _____. When the

dryer stops, he needs to _____ the clothes. One of his shirts is _____,

but he doesn't want to _____ it.

4. Write the steps you follow when you do the laundry.

   a. Sort the laundry.

   b.

🎧 **1.** Listen to the woman and her daughter in the store. Answer the questions with your class.

    a. What does the girl want?

    b. Which items won't the mother buy for her daughter?

🎧 **2.** Listen to each part of the conversation. Match the sentences below to the parts of the conversation in which you hear them.

1. _____	**a.** Look at this blow dryer.
2. _____	**b.** We don't need conditioner.
3. _____	**c.** Let's get some razors.
4. _____	**d.** We need shampoo.
5. _____	**e.** Look, there's the makeup.
6. _____	**f.** Let's get some toothpaste.

🎧 **3.** Complete the paragraph. Use the words in the box. Then listen again and check your answers.

shaving cream	makeup	blow dryer	shampoo
wash	razors	toothpaste	lipstick

Amanda and her mother are in a store. Amanda needs _____.
She says, "I _____ my hair every day." Amanda wants to
buy a five-speed _____. She also wants _____
that tastes like cotton candy. Her mother thinks that's a terrible idea. They get some
blue _____ and some _____ for Amanda's dad.
Then they go to the _____ section. Amanda wants _____ and
mascara. Her mother says no, but she might buy some mascara for herself.

4. How often do you buy the items in exercises 2 and 3? Make a chart on your paper.

Often	Not Often	Never

Symptoms and Injuries
LISTENING EXERCISES

Oxford Picture Dictionary p. 110

🎧 1. Mandy is a receptionist at a doctor's office. Listen to her telephone conversations. Answer the questions with your class.

    a. Which caller is coming in first?

    b. Which caller is not coming in?

🎧 2. Listen to each conversation. Underline *True* or *False*.

a. Mr. Han gets an afternoon appointment.	True	False
b. Annie Jackson can't get there right away.	True	False
c. Mandy doesn't get the man's name.	True	False
d. Brian is calling because he needs to see the doctor.	True	False

🎧 3. Complete the paragraph. Use the words in the box. Then listen again and check your answers.

cough	headache	sore throat	rash
swollen	temperature	insect bite	chills

Mandy works in Dr. Shin's office. Her first call today is from Mr. Han. He has a bad _____.

Her second call is from Annie Jackson. Annie's baby has a _____ of 39 and a

_____. She's very worried. Another caller has had a _____

for a week. Yesterday he started to _____, and now he has the

_____. Then Brian calls. He says he has an _____, but his

finger isn't red or _____. He just wants to talk to Mandy.

4. Think about the last time you were sick. List your symptoms.

    _____   _____

    _____   _____

    _____   _____

    _____   _____

🎧 **1.** Listen to the conversations at the pharmacy. Answer the questions with your class.

    a. What will the customer take for back pain?

    b. What things does the pharmacist tell customers to not do??

🎧 **2.** Listen to each conversation. Underline *True* or *False*.

a. Mr. Randall is dropping off a prescription.	True	False
b. He has terrible back pain.	True	False
c. The dosage is two pills every four hours.	True	False
d. This customer is picking up a prescription.	True	False

🎧 **3.** Close your book. Complete the paragraphs. Use the words in the box. Then listen again and check your answers.

take	over-the-counter medication	pain reliever	dosage
syrups	prescription label	pills	capsules

The pharmacist talks to Mr. Randall about his _____. The medication is a _____. Mr. Randall should _____ two tablets every four hours. He can't drive.

The pharmacist explains the correct _____ for Mr. Tam's medication. He is getting _____. He can't drink alcohol.

The last customer has a cold. He wants an _____. He doesn't want _____ because they're too big. He can buy tablets or _____.

4. Why do some medicines need a prescription, while others are sold over the counter?

_____

_____

_____

_____

_____

Oxford Picture Dictionary pp. 114–115

🎧 1. Listen to the conversations. Answer the questions with your class.

    a. What does Dr. Ohja tell the second patient to do?

    b. Which patient does Dr. Ohja send to the hospital?

🎧 2. Listen to each part of the conversation. Match the sentences below to the parts of the conversation in which you hear them.

> 1. _____   **a.** Didn't you get immunized before you left?
>
> 2. _____   **b.** If you stay fit and eat a healthy diet, you should have more energy.
>
> 3. _____   **c.** I can recommend a support group for you.
>
> 4. _____   **d.** Have you been having any vision problems?

🎧 3. Complete the paragraph. Use the words in the box. Then listen again and check your answers.

immunized	vision problems	stress	seek medical attention
bed rest	optometrist	pains	eating a healthy diet

Dr. Ohja's first patient says she always feels tired. The doctor thinks this is due to

_____. He recommends staying fit and _____. The second

patient complains of headaches. Dr. Ohja thinks these might be due to _____,

and he recommends an _____. The third patient is sick because she didn't get

_____ before her vacation. Dr. Ohja gives her some medicine and advises her to

get some _____. The fourth patient says he has chest _____.

Dr. Ohja believes that this is due to the fact that the patient smokes; he advises the patient to

_____ at the hospital right away.

4. Look at page 114 in the OPD. What things do you do to get well when you are sick? What things do you do to stay well when you are healthy? Complete the chart.

Ways I Get Well	Ways I Stay Well

🎧 **1.** Listen to the entire conversation. Answer the questions with your class.

    a. Why does the patient visit Dr. Willis?

    b. Why does Dr. Willis decide to do more tests?

🎧 **2.** Listen to each part of the conversation. Match the sentences below to the parts of the conversation in which you hear them.

1. _____	**a.**	Check with my receptionist.
2. _____	**b.**	I see you've filled out your health history form.
3. _____	**c.**	Please have a seat on the examination table.
4. _____	**d.**	I'm going to use this syringe to draw some of your blood.
5. _____	**e.**	I'm going to examine your eyes, ears, and throat.

🎧 **3.** Complete the paragraph. Use the words in the box. Then listen again and check your answers.

draw	temperature	appointment	health history form
examines	examination table	blood pressure	syringe

The patient visits Dr. Willis for a checkup. The doctor is pleased with the information on the patient's _____. The patient sits on the _____ while the nurse takes his _____ and checks his _____. Dr. Willis _____ his eyes, ears, and throat, and notices that his throat looks red. She wants to do some tests, so she uses a _____ to _____ some blood. On the way out, the patient makes an _____ to see Dr. Willis when the test results are in.

4. What is your favourite part of visiting the doctor? What is your least favourite part?

Favourite	**Least Favourite**
_____	_____
_____	_____
_____	_____
_____	_____

Oxford Picture Dictionary pp. 120–121

🎧 1. Listen to the conversations at the hospital. Answer the questions with your class.

    a. Why is Mrs. Morales at the hospital?

    b. When can Mrs. Morales eat?

🎧 2. Listen to each part of the conversation. When does Mrs. Morales see each hospital employee? Match the employees below with the parts of the conversation in which you hear them.

1. _____	**a.** nurse
2. _____	**b.** anesthesiologist
3. _____	**c.** phlebotomist
4. _____	**d.** admissions clerk and orderly
5. _____	**e.** nursing assistant

🎧 3. Complete the paragraph. Use the words in the box. Then listen again and check your answers.

hospital gown	phlebotomist	nursing assistant	call button
anesthesiologist	patient	blood test	bed control

Rosa Morales is a _____ at a hospital. First, a _____ comes

into her room and gives her a _____. The nurse tells Mrs. Morales how to use

the _____ and to push the _____ if she needs help.

A _____ comes in because Mrs. Morales needs a _____.

The last person to come in is the _____.

4. Complete the sentence. Use your own ideas.

I think the best job in the hospital would be _____ because

_____.

1. Listen to the entire conversation. Answer the questions with your class.

    a. Why is the man asking for directions?

    b. Which places does he ask for directions to?

2. Listen to each part of the conversation. Match the sentences below to the parts of the conversation in which you hear them.

1. _____	**a.** Do you know how to get to the furniture store?
2. _____	**b.** It's on Maple Street, between the bakery and the church.
3. _____	**c.** Here's the coffee shop.
4. _____	**d.** Is that on the same street as the mosque?
5. _____	**e.** It's across the street from the college.

3. Complete the paragraph. Use the words in the box. Then listen again and check your answers.

mosque	convention centre	stadium	college
gym	coffee shop	furniture store	grocery store

The man asks the woman where the _____ is located, and she informs him

that it is across the street from the _____. He then asks for directions to the

_____. He needs to go to the _____ tomorrow, so the

woman tells him that it is beside the _____, near the _____.

Finally, he asks her for directions to someplace to eat and she suggests a _____.

They walk there together, and pass a _____ along the way.

4. Choose a location in your town or city. Write a description explaining how to get there from your home. Use the buildings along the way to help describe where to turn, how far to walk, etc.

_____

_____

_____

_____

_____

Oxford Picture Dictionary pp. 128–129

🎧 1. Look at pages 128 and 129 in the OPD. Listen to the phone call between two friends. Answer the question with your class.

Where are they going to meet?

🎧 2. Close your dictionary. Listen to each part of the conversation. Match the sentences below to the parts of the conversation in which you hear them.

1. _____	a. The video store opens at 9:00.
2. _____	b. What time does the laundromat open?
3. _____	c. The childcare centre opens at 8:00.
4. _____	d. It's across from the pharmacy.
5. _____	e. There's a newsstand across from Burger Queen.
6. _____	f. It's near the laundromat.

🎧 3. Complete the paragraph. Use the words in the box. Then listen again and check your answers.

laundromat	childcare centre	convenience store	mailbox
doughnut shop	corner	traffic light	dry cleaners

Sue and May are going downtown this morning. May is going to drop off her daughter at the

_____. After that, she's going to pick up her jacket at the _____.

Sue is going to the _____ first. She's also going to buy some soap at the

_____. May needs to buy some magazines and mail a letter. There's a newsstand

next to the _____ and a _____ next to the newsstand. At 10:00,

the women are going to meet at the _____ on the _____.

4. Write five sentences about places you go and what you do at those places.

I buy coffee at the doughnut shop. _____

_____

_____

_____

_____

Oxford Picture Dictionary p. 132

🎧 **1.** Listen to the entire conversation. Answer the questions with your class.

    a. Why is the woman at the bank?

    b. What does the account manager give to the woman right away?

    c. What is he going to send to her in a few weeks?

🎧 **2.** Listen to each part of the conversation. Match the sentences below to the parts of the conversation in which you hear them.

> 1. _____   **a.** I'm the account manager here, so I can help you open your account.
>
> 2. _____   **b.** Finally, would you like to rent a safety deposit box?
>
> 3. _____   **c.** No, you'll just have to carry your ATM card and remember your PIN.
>
> 4. _____   **d.** If you'd like, you can bank online instead.
>
> 5. _____   **e.** You'll just need to fill out a deposit slip.

🎧 **3.** Complete the paragraph. Use the words in the box. Then listen again and check your answers.

tellers	customer	bank online	account manager
deposit	ATM card	chequebook	deposit slip

The woman is a new _____ at the bank. She
meets with the _____ to open her bank accounts.
He tells her that she doesn't need to memorize her account numbers,
as long as she carries her _____ and remembers her PIN.
She doesn't receive her _____ right away — the bank will send it to her in a few weeks.
She does, however, want to make a _____ that day. The manager tells the woman
that one of the _____ can help her do this if she fills out a _____.
The lineups are too long, though, so the woman decides to _____ instead.

4. What things do you do at the bank? What things do you prefer to do online?

Bank	**Online**
_____	_____
_____	_____
_____	_____

Oxford Picture Dictionary p. 133

1. Listen to the library information line. Listen to all the messages. Answer the questions with your class.

   a. What is the name of the library?

   b. When is the library open?

2. Listen to each message. Underline *True* or *False*.

a. For a library card, you need a photo ID and a utility bill.	True	False
b. You can find non-fiction and biographies on the first floor.	True	False
c. The late fine for books is 35 cents each day.	True	False
d. You can return DVDs to the circulation desk or put them in the box.	True	False

3. Complete the paragraph. Use the words in the box. Then listen again and check your answers.

check out	novels	look for	self-checkout
get	DVDs	return	picture books

   Tom takes his daughter to the Sun City library. Suzie is five years old. Next year, she can

   _____ a library card. First, they _____ books in the online

   catalogue. On the first floor, they get _____ for Suzie. They go upstairs to get

   _____ for Suzie's mom. They go downstairs to get _____.

   Suzie likes to _____ books, but not at the circulation desk. She likes to go to

   the _____. She also likes to _____ books because she can

   put them in the box.

4. Create a conversation between a reference librarian and a library patron. Write at least four lines.
   Read the conversation with a partner.

   Library Patron: Excuse me. How can I...?

   Librarian: _____

   Library Patron: _____

   Librarian: _____

   Library Patron: _____

   Librarian: _____

🎧 **1.** Look at pages 136 and 137 in the OPD. Listen to the conversations between the licensing clerk and the customers. Answer the questions with your class.

    a. How many customers are there?

    b. What is the second customer's problem?

🎧 **2.** Close your book. Listen to each conversation. Match the sentences below to the parts of the conversation in which you hear them.

1. _____	**a.** What kind of identification do you need?
2. _____	**b.** I'd like to get a beginner's permit.
3. _____	**c.** I'm ready to take my written test.
4. _____	**d.** I want to get my driver's licence.

🎧 **3.** Complete the paragraphs. Use the words in the box. Then listen again and check your answers.

driving test	beginner's permit	show	written test
pay	vision exam	window	signature

The licensing clerk at _____ 3 helps two

people. Her first customer passes her _____.

She has to go to window 6 for a _____ and

window 5 so the clerk can get her _____.

Then she can make an appointment for her _____.

The second customer wants to get a _____.

He has to _____ his passport, and he's ready to _____

the application fee, but the clerk says no. She'll see him next year.

4. Write five sentences describing how to get a driver's licence.

You have to take a written test. _____

_____

_____

_____

_____

Oxford Picture Dictionary pp. 138–139

🎧 1. Listen to the entire conversation. Answer the questions with your class.

    a. What job does the woman have?

    b. What other jobs has she had in the past?

🎧 2. Listen to each part of the conversation. Match the sentences below to the parts of the conversation in which you hear them.

1. _____	**a.** My opponents in the riding were very experienced and were excellent speakers.
2. _____	**b.** I worked in the House of Commons for almost ten years.
3. _____	**c.** I don't know, maybe I'll become a senator!
4. _____	**d.** Earlier today, our new prime minister was sworn in.
5. _____	**e.** And what did you do before becoming a member of parliament?

🎧 3. Complete the paragraph. Use the words in the box. Then listen again and check your answers.

opponents	city council	serve	member of parliament
prime minister	debate	senator	House of Commons

The reporter is talking to the new _____, who has just been sworn in. He asks about her experience in government. She explains that she used to be a _____, working in the _____ for almost 10 years. At the beginning of her political career she was on _____. After this, she ran for office in the provincial government, where she had to _____ some very experienced _____. Now she wants to _____ as prime minister as well as she can. She jokes that her next job might be as a _____.

4. Would you ever consider running for a government office? Why or why not?

_____

_____

_____

_____

Oxford Picture Dictionary p. 140

🎧 **1.** Listen to the entire conversation. Answer the questions with your class.

   a. What is Mustafa doing today?

   b. Why does he want to do this?

🎧 **2.** Listen to each part of the conversation. Match the sentences below to the parts of the conversation in which you hear them.

1. _____	**a.** We were able to do that because of our right to peaceful assembly.
2. _____	**b.** For example, they should obey the country's laws and help others in their communities.
3. _____	**c.** I'm on my way to take my citizenship test.
4. _____	**d.** Once I'm a citizen, it will also be my responsibility to vote in elections.
5. _____	**e.** In Canada, I can use my writing to express my opinions because I have the freedom of thought, belief, opinion, and expression.
6. _____	**f.** You must be at least 18 years old.

🎧 **3.** Complete the paragraph. Use the words in the box. Then listen again and check your answers.

thought, belief, opinion, and expression peaceful assembly	obeying citizenship test	vote in elections 18 or older	lived helping

Mustafa is on his way to take his _____. He was not able to take it before now

because he hadn't _____ in Canada for three of the last four years —

this is one of the requirements for citizenship. There is also an age requirement: he must be

_____. Mustafa wants to become a citizen because he enjoys the freedoms

that Canadians have, such as the freedom of _____ and the right to

_____. Mustafa is also aware of his responsibilities as a Canadian citizen, which

include _____ the country's laws and _____ others in his

community. It will also be his responsibility to _____ once he becomes a citizen.

4. Look at page 140 in the OPD. Which responsibility of Canadian citizens do you think is the most important?

_____

_____

Oxford Picture Dictionary p. 143

🎧 **1.** Listen to the entire conversation. Answer the questions with your class.

    a. Why does Sabrina take Paula's purse?

    b. What advice does Paula give to Sabrina?

🎧 **2.** Listen to each part of the conversation. Match the sentences below to the parts of the conversation in which you hear them.

> 1. _____   **a.** You didn't lock your apartment door, Paula.
>
> 2. _____   **b.** We should stay on this street — it's well lit.
>
> 3. _____   **c.** You should always walk with a friend in the evening so you're not alone.
>
> 4. _____   **d.** You should protect your purse by keeping it close to your body.
>
> 5. _____   **e.** Always conceal your PIN when you're at the ATM.

🎧 **3.** Complete the paragraph. Use the words in the box. Then listen again and check your answers.

walk with a friend	locking	aware of her surroundings
stay on well-lit streets	conceal her PIN	protect her purse

Sabrina and Paula are going to a movie. Paula leaves her apartment without _____

her door. Sabrina decides to test Paula on her safety knowledge — she asks whether Paula is always

_____, and advises her to _____ by keeping it close to her

body. She also tells Paula that she should _____ so that she's not alone. She

won't let Paula take a shortcut through the alley because they should _____.

Sabrina finally gets a lesson from Paula, who tells her to _____ at the ATM.

4. Look at page 143 in the OPD. Which public safety advice do you follow? Which advice do you think is the most important?

_____

_____

_____

_____

_____

🎧 **1.** Listen to the guest speaker talk to the class. Listen to the entire talk. Answer the questions with your class.

a. What committee is Ms Thomas from?

b. What is she talking about?

🎧 **2.** Listen to each part of the talk. Match the sentences below to the parts of the conversation in which you hear them.

1. _____	**a.** Don't forget the extra batteries.
2. _____	**b.** You should have blankets.
3. _____	**c.** Include cash and coins.
4. _____	**d.** We need to plan for an emergency.
5. _____	**e.** What about a first aid kit?
6. _____	**f.** You need canned food.

🎧 **3.** Complete the paragraph. Use the words in the box. Then listen again and check your answers.

bottled water	flashlight	plan	copies of important papers
seek	make	first aid kit	can opener

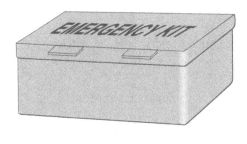

People need to _____ for an emergency. One way is to _____ a disaster kit. You should put in _____ and canned food because stores may be closed. Don't forget a _____ for your food. You need warm things because you may have to _____ shelter. Put in a _____ and extra batteries. It's a good idea to include a _____ in case someone is injured. You should also have _____. You don't want them to get lost.

4. List other items to put in a disaster kit.

_____   _____

_____   _____

_____   _____

_____   _____

Oxford Picture Dictionary p. 152

🎧 **1.** Look at page 152 in the OPD. Listen to the conversations. Point to the locations as you listen.

🎧 **2.** Close your dictionary. Listen to each conversation. Match the location with the conversation.

1. _____	**a.** subway station
2. _____	**b.** bus
3. _____	**c.** bus stop
4. _____	**d.** train station
5. _____	**e.** taxi

🎧 **3.** Complete the sentences. Use the words in the box. Then listen again and check your answers.

fare card	meter	tokens	rider
schedule	ticket	shuttle	vending machine

a. The man is buying a round trip _____ to Churchill.

b. The girl doesn't have any _____. She doesn't have to go to the _____ because the boy will let her have his extra token. He'll use his _____. He just bought one.

c. The man is looking at the wrong _____.

d. The passenger thinks the _____ isn't working because the ride is so expensive. Next time she's going to take the _____.

e. The passenger doesn't know how much the fare is, and he doesn't have the exact change. He's not usually a bus _____.

4. Why do you think public transportation is important?

_____

_____

_____

_____

_____

1. Look at the map at the bottom left of page 155 in the OPD. Listen to the conversations. Point to the streets as you listen.

2. Close your dictionary. Listen to each conversation. Underline True or *False*.

a. Tara is at 19th Street East and Broadway Ave.		True	False
b. Sal is near Friendship Park.		True	False
c. Mary is at 3rd Ave. North and 25th Street East.		True	False
d. Edgar is on 22nd Street West in the Central Business District.		True	False
e. Jin is on Avenue H South near Victoria Park.		True	False

3. Listen again. Complete the sentences. Use the words in the box.

turn left	east	Internet map	go
street	north	turn right	river

    a. Tara: _____ north through the Central Business District,

        then turn right at the next big _____.

    b. Ted: Keep going _____ until you cross the _____. Turn right at

        the next street.

    c. Donna: _____ on 22nd Street West.

    d. Diego: _____ on 3rd Ave. South, make a right at the next street, and then

        make another right. You need to go _____, and then _____.

    e. Jin: Get an _____.

4. Look at the map at the bottom left of page 155. Choose a starting place and an ending place. Write directions. Then ask a partner to follow the directions.

Start at.... _____

Go... _____

_____

_____

_____

_____

Oxford Picture Dictionary pp. 160–161

🎧 **1.** Listen to the entire conversation. Answer the questions with your class.

    a. How does Scott know that the flight will be on time?

    b. Why does Scott's father put Scott's bag in the overhead compartment?

🎧 **2.** Listen to each part of the conversation. Match the sentences below to the parts of the conversation in which you hear them.

1. _____	**a.** There's the boarding area for our gate.
2. _____	**b.** It'll be faster if we check in electronically.
3. _____	**c.** Do you want me to stow your bag in the overhead compartment?
4. _____	**d.** Be sure to fasten your seatbelt.
5. _____	**e.** Do you see any porters?
6. _____	**f.** Do you have your boarding pass?

🎧 **3.** Complete the paragraph. Use the words in the box. Then listen again and check your answers.

boarding area	take off	board the plane	turns off
ticket agent	porter	checking in electronically	stows

Scott and his dad arrive at the airport, and Scott's dad looks for a _____ to take his luggage. Scott's dad wants to go to a _____, but Scott suggests _____ to save time. They wait in the _____ for a short time before they are called to _____. Once on the plane, Scott's dad _____ Scott's bag in the overhead compartment, _____ his cellphone, and they get ready to _____.

4. What do you think is the best part about taking a plane trip? What is the worst part?

Best Part	Worst Part
_____	_____
_____	_____
_____	_____
_____	_____

1. Listen to the entire conversation. Answer the question with your class.

   What tasks does Ms Chang ask Donald to do?

2. Listen to each part of the conversation. Match the sentences below to the parts of the conversation in which you hear them.

   1. _____   **a.** Did Mr. Goldstein leave a message for me?

   2. _____   **b.** Please make twenty copies of these sales reports and staple them.

   3. _____   **c.** First, I'll need you to transcribe these notes.

   4. _____   **d.** Should I transfer the call to you?

   5. _____   **e.** Can you schedule a meeting with Mr. Goldstein so I can discuss my notes with him?

3. Complete the paragraph. Use the words in the box. Then listen again and check your answers.

copies	take a message	prints	transcribe
schedule a meeting	staple	faxes	transferring

   Ms Chang needs help preparing for a meeting, so she asks Donald to _____ some notes for her. Then she asks him to _____ with Mr. Goldstein. Donald's next task is to make 20 _____ of the sales reports and _____ them. Donald receives a call from Mr. Goldstein. Instead of _____ the call to her, Ms Chang asks Donald to _____. Donald finds out that Mr. Goldstein is missing a report, so he _____ a copy of it and _____ it to Mr. Goldstein.

4. Look at page 171 in the OPD. Which of the office skills do you have experience with?

   _____   _____

   _____   _____

   _____   _____

   _____   _____

Oxford Picture Dictionary p. 172

🎧 **1.** Look at page 172 in the OPD. Listen to the conversations at the Job Resource Centre. Answer the questions with your class.

    a. What does the man want?

    b. How does Mrs. Alvarez feel at the end?

🎧 **2.** Listen to each conversation. Match the sentence with the conversation.

1. _____	**a.** I'm interested in finding a new job.
2. _____	**b.** Do you offer training here?
3. _____	**c.** Welcome to the Resource Centre.
4. _____	**d.** Yes, we have a resource centre.
5. _____	**e.** After that, you can complete the skill inventory

🎧 **3.** Complete the paragraph. Use the words in the box. Then listen again and check your answers.

internships	vocational training	interest inventory	job fairs
job board	career counsellor	skill inventory	recruiters

Albert is talking to a _____, Mrs. Alvarez. She's going to give him

an _____ to help him get ideas for jobs. Then she'll give him a

_____ so he can see which skills he has and which skills he'll need.

Mrs. Alvarez knows which schools offer _____ and which companies have

_____. The Resource Centre also has a _____,

and Mrs. Alvarez knows about several _____ where Albert can meet

_____ from local companies. Albert is glad he came to the Resource Centre.

4. What are your interests? What are your skills? Make two lists.

Interests	Skills

🎧 **1.** Look at page 174 in the OPD. Listen to the radio show. Answer the questions with your class.

    a. What is Jill Thurman giving advice about?

    _____

    _____

    b. What should you not do in an interview?

    _____

    _____

🎧 **2.** Close your dictionary. Listen to each part of the show. Complete the suggestions.

    a. First, be _____.

    b. Second, dress _____.

    c. Third, make _____.

    d. And fourth, ask _____.

🎧 **3.** Underline *True* or *False*. Listen to the radio show again and check your answers.

    a. If you are late for the interview, the employer will think you'll be late for work.   True   False

    b. It's OK to dress casually for some job interviews. It's better not to be too formal.   True   False

    c. If you don't look an interviewer in the eye, he or she will think you are respectful.   True   False

    d. "Do you offer training?" is a good question to ask an interviewer.   True   False

4. Write two more suggestions for a good job interview.

    1. _____

    2. _____

Oxford Picture Dictionary pp. 180–181

🎧 1. Look at page 180 and 181 in the OPD. Listen to the entire conversation. Answer the questions with your class.

    a. What is the woman going to paint? _____

    b. What colour does she like? _____

🎧 2. Close your dictionary. Listen to each part of the conversation. Match the sentences below to the parts of the conversation in which you hear them.

1. _____	**a.** The drop cloths are on that wall.
2. _____	**b.** The wood stain is right here.
3. _____	**c.** You'll need a paint roller.
4. _____	**d.** This is a good scraper.

🎧 3. Complete the paragraph. Use the words in the box. Then listen again and check your answers.

paint tray	masking tape	paint roller	scraper
drop cloths	outlet covers	wood stain	sandpaper

The customer needs a lot of supplies for painting. She needs to buy a _____ and a _____ to use with it. She also needs _____ to protect her furniture and some _____ to hold them in place. The sales clerk reminds her to take off the _____. Her windowsills have old, chipped paint. She needs to buy a _____ and _____ to get the old paint off. She's going to put a _____ on the windowsills.

4. Answer the questions.

    a. What is the best colour for a living room?

    _____

    b. Which home repairs have you done yourself?

    _____

    c. Which ones would you phone a repair person to do?

    _____

🎧 **1.** Look at the office on page 182 in the OPD. Listen to the conversations. Answer the questions with your class.

    a. How many phone calls does the receptionist get?

    b. Where is Mrs. Tam?

    c. What is the office manager's problem?

🎧 **2.** Close your dictionary. Listen to each conversation. Match the sentence with the conversation.

1. _____	**a.** Do you mean Roland, the file clerk?
2. _____	**b.** I'd like to speak to the office manager.
3. _____	**c.** Well, how about her administrative assistant?
4. _____	**d.** And please find the computer technician for me.

🎧 **3.** Complete the paragraph. Use the words in the box. Then listen again and check your answers.

desk	conference room	receptionist	office manager
computer	executives	presentation	clerk

Melissa is the _____ at Green Energy Corporation. A caller asks for Mrs. Tam, but she's in the _____ watching a _____. Then Lucinda Majors calls. She wants to talk to the _____. He is at his _____, but he can't talk to Ms Majors because he's busy. His _____ isn't working. He wants to talk to Mark, the new _____, but Mark is making copies. The office manager is not happy. The _____ are at the presentation while he's doing all the work.

4. Write a phone conversation between Melissa and another caller.

Melissa: Green Energy Corporation. How can I help you?

Caller: _____

Melissa: _____

Caller: _____

Melissa: _____

Caller: _____

Oxford Picture Dictionary p. 197

🎧 **1.** Look at page 197 in the OPD. Listen to the entire conversation between the mother and the daughter. Answer the questions with your class.

    a. What is the woman trying to find?

    b. What was the girl using the computer for?

🎧 **2.** Close your dictionary. Listen to each part of the conversation. Match the sentences below to the parts of the conversation in which you hear them.

1. _____	**a.** Just click the back button.
2. _____	**b.** Don't forget to type a subject.
3. _____	**c.** I think the URL is www.TV101.ca.
4. _____	**d.** You have to put your pointer over the box.
5. _____	**e.** Type your user name and your password.

🎧 **3.** Complete the paragraph. Use the words in the box. Then listen again and check your answers.

type	back button	pop-up ad	menu bar
send	video	scroll bar	search box

Hana wants to look at a _____ on the Internet, but she's having some problems. She tries to _____ "cat video" in the _____, but nothing happens. Then an ugly _____ appears on her screen. After Hana sees the video, she wants to _____ it to Guillermo, but she can't find the button. She has to use the _____ to scroll down. Then she wants to watch the video again, but she can't find the _____. So she clicks History in the _____.

4. What do you use the Internet for? Make a list.

_____   _____

_____   _____

_____   _____

_____   _____

Oxford Picture Dictionary p. 198

🎧 1. Look at page 198 in the OPD. Listen to the teacher and the students. Answer the questions with your class.

    a.   What kind of class is this?

    b.   Do the students know the answers?

🎧 2. Close your dictionary. Listen to each part of the conversation. Match the sentences below to the parts of the conversation in which you hear them.

1. _____	**a.** Is it the British North America Act?
2. _____	**b.** There were 36 original Fathers of Confederation.
3. _____	**c.** There were four provinces.
4. _____	**d.** Sir John A. Macdonald was the first prime minister of Canada.
5. _____	**e.** Those people are called the Inuit.

🎧 3. Complete the paragraphs. Use the words in the box. Then listen again and check your answers.

Fathers of Confederation	War of 1812	Confederation	First Nations
British North America Act	settlers	Inuit	

For thousands of years, Canada was inhabited by _____ peoples and _____. In the last several hundred years, _____ began arriving and living here.

Canada has been the site of a number of historical events such as the Battle of the Plains of Abraham, the _____, and, in 1867, _____. This last event took place when the _____ signed the _____ and established the basis of what would become the constitution of Canada.

4. How many Canadian prime ministers can you name? Make a list.

_____

_____

_____

_____

Oxford Picture Dictionary pp. 200–201

🎧 **1.** Look at pages 200 and 201 in the OPD. Listen to Gina talk about her trip. As you listen, point to the provinces you hear.

🎧 **2.** Close your book. Listen to each part of the conversation. Match the sentences below to the parts of the conversation in which you hear them.

1. _____   **a.** Then we drove west to Vancouver.

2. _____   **b.** We drove to Prince Edward Island and saw the Anne of Green Gables farmhouse.

3. _____   **c.** Maybe we'll go to the United States.

4. _____   **d.** After that we went through Quebec again, and we stayed in Quebec City.

🎧 **3.** Complete the paragraph. Use the words in the box. Then listen again and check your answers.

Manitoba	home	east	the north
Nova Scotia	the Prairie Provinces	southeast	the Atlantic provinces

Gina went on a long road trip last summer. She drove through _____.

She kept going _____, passing through Alberta, Saskatchewan, and

_____. Gina didn't go to _____. She drove

_____ through Toronto and Ottawa. Then she went east all the way to

_____. After she left, Gina drove through _____.

She's happy to be back _____. She's tired of driving.

4. How many Canadian provinces can you name without looking in your dictionary? Make a list.

_____   _____

_____   _____

_____   _____

_____   _____

Oxford Picture Dictionary pp. 218–219

🎧 **1.** Look at pages 218 and 219 in the OPD. Listen to the teacher and the students. Answer the questions with your class.

    a. What's the problem with oil?

    b. What's another big problem?

🎧 **2.** Close your dictionary. Listen to each part of the conversation. Match the sentences below to the parts of the conversation in which you hear them.

1. _____	**a.** We can recycle bottles, cans, paper, and plastic.
2. _____	**b.** We use oil for most of our energy needs.
3. _____	**c.** Don't litter.
4. _____	**d.** We can save energy by turning off lights.

🎧 **3.** Complete the paragraphs. Use the words in the box. Then listen again and check your answers.

use	litter	reuse	save
buy	energy	reduce	pollution

The class is talking about ways to _____ _____ and help the environment. We can turn off lights and _____ energy-efficient bulbs in lamps. We can _____ trash, too.

The class also talks about ways to help with _____. We can recycle and _____ recycled products. Another good idea is to _____ shopping bags. And of course we should never _____.

4. How do you save energy? Make a list.

I reuse glass jars. _____   _____

_____   _____

_____   _____

_____   _____

Oxford Picture Dictionary p. 224

1. Look at page 224 in the OPD. Listen to the little girl and her father. Answer the questions with your class.

   a. How does the girl feel at the park?

   b. What does she want to do?

   c. How does the father feel?

2. Close your dictionary. Listen to each part of the conversation. Match the sentences below to the parts of the conversation in which you hear them.

   1. _____   **a.** Did you bring the jump rope?

   2. _____   **b.** I want to go on the swings.

   3. _____   **c.** Can I get a skateboard?

   4. _____   **d.** I want to go in the sandbox.

   5. _____   **e.** I want to climb the bars.

3. Complete the paragraph. Use the words in the box. Then listen again and check your answers.

   | tricycle | see-saw | climb | have a picnic |
   | water fountain | playground | jump rope | push |

   Beto's daughter rides around on her _____. Then she does a lot of things at the

   _____. She asks Beto to _____ her on the swings. She can

   _____ to the top of the bars, but Beto tells her not to go too high. Then she

   wants to _____. She wants Beto to go on the _____, but

   Beto wants to go to the _____ and look at the ducks. Beto is happy when his

   wife arrives and they can _____.

4. What did you like to do when you were a child? Write five sentences describing these things.

   When I was a child, I liked to jump rope.

   _____

   _____

   _____

   _____